TOWARDS SELF-IMPROVING
SCHOOL SYSTEMS

'This is one of the most extraordinarily powerful books on school improvement and positive systemic change I have ever read. And it bears a message that the world needs to acknowledge.'
Andy Hargreaves

'Mel Ainscow does a masterful job in capturing with great clarity how to lead change in complex whole systems. He led the Greater Manchester Challenge and was clearly immersed in it, but as an author he has the uncanny ability to write as if he were an observer. A great book.'
Michael Fullan

This important new book draws lessons from a large-scale initiative to bring about the improvement of an urban education system. Written from an insider perspective by an internationally recognized researcher, it presents a new way of thinking about system change. This builds on the idea that there are untapped resources within schools and the communities they serve that can be mobilized in order to transform schools from places that do well for some children so that they can do well for many more.

Towards Self-improving School Systems presents a strategic framework that can help to foster new, more fruitful working relationships: between national and local government; within and between schools; and between schools and their local communities. What is distinctive in the approach is that this is mainly led from within schools, with senior staff having a central role as system leaders.

The book will be relevant to a wide range of readers throughout the world who are concerned with the strengthening of their national educational systems, including teachers, school leaders, policy makers and researchers. The argument it presents is particularly important for the growing number of countries where increased emphasis on school autonomy, competition and choice is leading to fragmentation within education provision.

Foreword by Andy Hargreaves, Thomas More Brennan Chair in Education, Boston College, USA

Mel Ainscow is Professor of Education and Co-director of the Centre for Equity in Education at the University of Manchester, UK. In the Queen's 2012 New Year honours list he was made a CBE for his services to education.

TOWARDS SELF-IMPROVING SCHOOL SYSTEMS

Lessons from a city challenge

Mel Ainscow

Routledge
Taylor & Francis Group

LONDON AND NEW YORK

First published 2015
by Routledge
2 Park Square, Milton Park, Abingdon, Oxon OX14 4RN

and by Routledge
711 Third Avenue, New York, NY 10017

Routledge is an imprint of the Taylor & Francis Group, an informa business

British Library Cataloguing in Publication Data
A catalogue record for this book is available from the British Library

Library of Congress Cataloging-in-Publication Data
Ainscow, Mel.
Towards self-improving school systems : lessons from a city challenge /
Mel Ainscow.
pages cm
Includes bibliographical references and index.
1. School improvement programs. 2. School improvement programs–
England–Manchester. 3. Inter-school cooperation. 4. Inter-school
cooperation–England–Manchester. 5. Community and school.
6. Community and school–England–Manchester. I. Title.
LB2822.8.A56 2015
371.2'07–dc23
2014041270

ISBN: 978-0-415-73659-6 (hbk)
ISBN: 978-0-415-73660-2 (pbk)
ISBN: 978-1-315-81840-5 (ebk)

Typeset in Bembo
by Deer Park Productions

MIX
Paper from
responsible sources
FSC
www.fsc.org   FSC® C013056

Printed and bound in Great Britain by
TJ International Ltd, Padstow, Cornwall

What is the city but the people?

Coriolanus

CONTENTS

FOREWORD

Andy Hargreaves

In today's world of educational change, education professionals, especially those who work in poor communities, are being compressed and constrained by top-down hierarchies of punitive intervention. At the same time, their schools are being compartmentalized from each other by market forces that set out to establish free schools, charter schools and academies for private profit. Our schools are subject to intense pressure from above and isolation from their peers around them. If we did this to individuals rather than institutions, it would be regarded as a form of abuse.

The last decade has seen orchestrated attempts by the national governments of England, Sweden and the United States, by global consulting organizations, and by billion dollar publishing and technology empires, to diminish and ultimately destroy the role of local communities, local democracies and local control in public educational provision and reform. Despite the overwhelming evidence that many of the highest performing educational systems in the world are either small city states like Hong Kong and Singapore, or invest great authority in local communities and municipalities as in Finland and Canada, international policy organizations like the OECD do little to draw attention to the undeniable importance of local democracy and community as a driving force of successful educational change.

In this scorched earth reform strategy, the advocates and architects of large-scale educational reform concentrate control of curriculum and assessment in the hands of central authorities while granting autonomy over budgets and staffing to individual school owners in a market-based system of competition for talent. In what passes for a transformative philosophy of school autonomy, autonomy has simply been inverted. The areas where schools once had great autonomy in curriculum and assessment have been taken into central control; while the areas over which they had little or no or no autonomy have now become almost entirely their own individual responsibility.

Having denuded local authorities and also teacher unions of their power to interfere with corporate efforts to sell curriculum, testing and technology products to national governments and individual schools, corporate and political change reformers have subsequently come to realize that their destruction of local support systems has also contributed to a loss of system coherence and community that, in turn, threatens their own educational success.

A middle-tier of peer-to-peer learning and school-to-school support has therefore started to emerge, especially in England, to fill the vacuum that the decimated local authorities and municipalities have left. The resulting networks, alliances and federations have had variable results. Some consist of connections between schools across far-flung corners of the country that may stimulate improvement through circulating ideas and offering support but the helping schools usually have no loyalty or connection to the local authority. Some middle-tier initiatives create networks and communities among schools within the same 'chain' operated by a single owner where there is loyalty to the chain and the brand, but not to the local communities in which the schools are located.

Mel Ainscow and the region of Greater Manchester in the north-west of England have come up with a different answer to reconstituting an effective middle-tier. It is uniquely grounded in the region's history, culture and politics, yet also transferable in many respects to other industrial conurbations elsewhere.

Manchester, and the towns and cities around it, is the cradle of the industrial revolution. It was once famously referred to as 'the workshop of the world'. It is a city and a region with a history of invention, enterprise and philanthropy. It hosts a magnificent cathedral, a world-class orchestra, great and less-than-great football and rugby clubs, redbrick civic universities, a state-of-the-art public transportation system, stately national health hospitals, and world-renowned art galleries and museums. Greater Manchester has been home to Gracie Fields and the Gallagher brothers, to Les Dawson and L.S. Lowry. It gave birth to the Cooperative Society and has one of most vibrant gay communities in the world. It is a polyglot metropolis of many languages, ethnicities and faiths.

The Manchester region is *Bend it like Beckham* and *Whistle Down the Wind*. It's built on brash men and brassy women whose families once worked in the ear-splitting atmospheres of engineering factories and textile mills. Like my mother, my grandmother and my brothers who worked there, their voices are loud. Their style is direct. They have 'no side' on them. They 'speak as they find'. They are bold as brass and matter of fact. They know how to bear up when things are hard and laugh raucously at themselves and each other when they 'screw up'. Grit, determination, courage in the face of adversity and scant respect for the repressed emotionality and southern affectations of elite English authority are core characteristics of north-west cultural life. North-westerners are collectively proud of their efforts and industry but also feel that, like anyone else, they are really 'nothing special'. Modesty is about not getting 'too big for your boots' rather than a quiet expression of pious humility.

Economic depressions have dealt cruel blows to the people of this region throughout history. The 1930s depression, the 1970s oil crisis, the economic austerity of Thatcherism, and the global economic collapse, all exacted their toll. So too have ensuing epidemics of poverty, drugs, crime and binge drinking. The immigrants and their families who are now raising the city's achievement were, especially in times of economic hardship, sources, at first, of suspicion, discrimination and prejudice. And some of these prejudices still remain in what are in practice segregated neighborhoods and schools. The Manchester City Challenge is well named.

I was born just outside the region that encompasses the area of Ainscow's work. From my small mill town to the west, it was an hour on the bus, a big day out, to take a girlfriend dancing, or spend a night at the city's Free Trade Hall watching the Beach Boys or the Supremes. Within the past few years, I have travelled the distance again to study unusually high performance in some of the region's most challenging schools.

Our study recognizes many of the characteristics that Ainscow's book describes: the belief that poverty should not inevitably accompany failure; that long term improvements in learning and teaching must be pursued alongside more effective monitoring and tracking in the short term; that collaboration even among competitors is a way to lift a whole community; that people have to be pulled inspirationally into change and sometimes also pushed through and out of it; and that the driving goal is not illusory short-term gains but sustainable success (Hargreaves and Shirley 2012; also Hargreaves, Braun and Harris, 2014).

Manchester is the area of Ainscow's own birth and it is not hard to understand how it has undergirded his lifelong professional values and virtues of the right to a good education, to high standards of professionalism, in the service of hard work, inclusion and equity. Ainscow's life's work bears the hallmark of all these northern qualities just as the city's buildings are made up of Victorian tile and brick. In the past, I have found his definitive and progressive approach to student inclusion informative and inspirational for my own work when, a few years ago, I entered that field of scholarship and practice for the first time.

When you see at Ainscow at work, what you find behind the irony and self-deprecating wit, is a deep respect for the dignity of people, all people, whatever their circumstances. He sees decency where others see only deficit, community even among abandoned buildings and run-down rental properties, where others can see only chaos. He believes in and writes about the power of people to find and own their own solutions with outside help and support, rather than having one solution after another externally imposed upon them by privateers, bureaucrats, and well-meaning (and less-than-well-meaning) do-gooders.

So when the Greater Manchester Challenge was first conceived and he was asked to be its Senior Adviser, Ainscow passionately believed that most of the answers to the problems of the north-west resided in the north-west itself. The solution he and his team devised, therefore, can be expressed in a twisting of the title, but not the plot, of a classic movie, into Northwest by Northwest.

Ainscow suffers no fools and is critical, where appropriate, of the misguided measures of central government and the previous efforts of the citywide London

Challenge. This is his critique of government policy and also his constructive response.

> They tend to all start from an instinctive assumption that schools – and by implication teachers – are the main source of the problem. Consequently, massive efforts have been made to deal with these perceived deficits though a combination of top down interventions, accountability measures and changes in governance arrangements.
>
> The argument that develops in this book starts from a very different set of assumptions. In essence, it builds on the idea that within schools and the communities they serve there are untapped resources that can be mobilised in order to transform schools from places that do well for many children and young people so that they can do well for all of them.

Ainscow and his colleagues were prepared to learn from anything that could help them when they set about their work – from years of their own research on school improvement, from the Harlem Children's zone in New York, from the successes and frustrations of the London Challenge, and even from the wisdom of a Yorkshire novelist. The London Challenge, they noted, had tended to bypass Local Authorities when finding ways for schools to work together – unlike, incidentally, the London Boroughs of Tower Hamlets and Hackney which significantly improved performance by working together as an Authority (Hargreaves and Shirley, 2012; Fullan and Boyle 2014).

In the down-to-earth words of one of the officers on the initial planning committee, 'Look, this is simple. The job of schools is to improve themselves. Our job is to make sure this happens'. The Challenge had no single strategy for bringing its principles to life. Recently turned around schools became the 'keys to success' in helping other schools. Some schools were organized in quadrants of different types and at different stages of development. A Jewish school assisted a predominantly Muslim partner. A Catholic school prayed for a good inspection result for its secular counterpart.

Hidden capacity was capitalized on, knowledge was moved around, and old enmities were overcome in the pursuit of the higher purpose of the whole area's regeneration. In all this 'the involvement of the local authorities was necessary and inevitable'.

This is one of the most extraordinarily powerful books on school improvement and positive systemic change I have ever read. And it bears a message that the world needs to acknowledge: working with the community, not against it; investing in professional and community capital; reviving rather than removing local community and democracy; collaborating with competitors; and being pragmatic about means in the pursuit of ideologically unshakeable ends.

Through Ainscow's own insights about and experiences of leadership, his big picture view of evidenced-based change, his many years of experience along with his moral courage to endure monumental uncertainty and complexity in a period that must sometimes have inflicted almost unbearable stress, he has now reached a point where he is able to document, make sense of and communicate in a lucid and prudent way, all that there is to be learned from this remarkable system change.

Ainscow talks about and also instantiates in glorious, no-nonsense detail the importance of knowing your people, building leadership capacity from within, moving around what we already know, striving for a higher moral imperative, and regenerating the communities that the creative destruction of twenty-first century capitalism and its predatory educational marketeers seems determined to destroy.

This remarkable book offers hope and a strategy, not hope as a strategy. It is a book that school leaders and system leaders everywhere should read and feel emboldened by. If the public parks of Manchester need a new bench for all its citizens to use, they should inscribe Ainscow's name upon it thus: 'Well done, lad: you did your best and made things better for our families.'

Andy Hargreaves
Brennan Chair in the Lynch School of Education, Boston College,
Adviser in Education to the Premier and Minister of Education of Ontario

References

Fullan, M. and Boyle, A. (2014) *Big-city school reforms*. New York: Teachers College Press.

Hargreaves, A. and Shirley, D. L. (2012) *The global fourth way: The quest for educational excellence*. Thousand Oaks, CA: Corwin Press.

Hargreaves, A., Boyle, A. and Harris, A. (2014) *Uplifting leadership: How organizations, teams, and communities raise performance*. San Francisco: Jossey-Bass.

PREFACE

I first began drafting this book in early 2011, as the project that is its main focus – the Greater Manchester Challenge – was drawing to a close. The fact that I was so closely involved in that initiative explains, at least in part, why it has taken so long to complete the book. Simply put, I found it difficult to step back from what had been such a consuming experience in order to tell the story and draw out the lessons.

Writing the book has provided me with a most unusual opportunity to give an account of a large-scale improvement initiative, looked at from the inside. As a result, it necessarily involves an autobiographical strand that runs through the text, as I set out to reflect on and make sense of what I have learnt. This has required me to draw together ideas from the two 'worlds' in which I experience my professional life: firstly, the world of education policy and practice; and, secondly, that of educational research. Fortunately, being a Gemini, I found it relatively easy to move between these two very different contexts. Indeed, in my mind, they are completely interconnected.

From my first world, I draw on the experiences of our efforts to bring about improvements in the work of over 1,100 schools, in the ten local authorities that took part in the Greater Manchester Challenge. This led me to collaborate with hundreds of teachers and local authority officers, plus many other stakeholders. To them all I owe a vote of thanks for the contributions they made to the progress that was achieved. I must also thank the members of the excellent team of Challenge Advisers who worked on the initiative: Yvonne Birch, Kate Daley, George Gyte, Maureen Haddock, Paul Harwood, Cath Howe, John Hull, Janet Woods, Jim Tarpey, Wendy Marshall, Gena Merrett, Andrew Morley and Wendy Parmley. Working closely together for over three years, we became friends as well as colleagues.

Our work in Greater Manchester was supported by a group of splendid civil servants. Three in particular – Inderjit Dehal, Holly Guest and Jenny McWalters – became fully integrated into the team and also became members of our circle of friends. As I explain in the text, there was also an important contribution from our Minister, Beverley Hughes MP (now Baroness Hughes of Stretford), who helped to shape the strategy and provided inspirational leadership. Later on, this role was taken on with much enthusiasm by Diana Johnson MP. I also gained considerably from regular discussions with my counterparts in the other two City Challenges, Sir Mike Tomlinson in London (followed by David Woods) and Sir Geoff Hampton in the Black Country.

Moving into my other world, that of university academics, I use the book to show how I attempted to draw on the findings of a programme of research carried out with colleagues over many years at the University of Manchester. In drawing on this extensive programme I must acknowledge the contributions of many Manchester colleagues, particularly Chris Chapman, Alan Dyson (even though he still sees everything in black and white), Peter Farrell, Sue Goldrick, Helen Gunter, Andy Howes, Kirstin Kerr, Olwen McNamara, Susie Miles, Peter Mittler, Daniel Muijs, Dave Tweddle, and Mel West. So many of the ideas I use in this book arise from their various contributions and I cannot overstate the debt I owe to them all.

Beyond Manchester, I must mention the inspiration and advice I have taken from other colleagues in the academic world. Particularly significant in this respect are Tony Booth, Sir Tim Brighouse, Michael Fielding, Andy Hargreaves, David Hargreaves, David Hopkins, Ben Levin and Judy Sebba. A special thanks must go to Kyriaki Messiou for her personal support, advice and frequent challenges. I also draw on research I am currently involved in with my colleagues at Queensland University of Technology: Suzanne Carrington, Barbara Comber, Lisa Ehrich, Jess Harris, Val Klenowski, Judy Smeed, Nerida Spina and Leisa Brandon.

Finally, I want to acknowledge the important contributions of Denis Mongon, who died just a few weeks prior to the completion of this book. Over many years Denis was somebody I relied on for advice. There are many ideas and, indeed, sections of text in this book that are there because of his influence. He is much missed by me and by many other colleagues.

Mel Ainscow
Manchester
August 2014

1

STRUGGLES FOR EQUITY IN EDUCATION

Oakwood High School serves a public housing estate in the North of England, where the residents are mainly from economically disadvantaged backgrounds. For years the school has had a dreadful reputation in the area because of low student attendance, bad behaviour and poor performance on national tests and examinations. However, the school year 2009–10 saw a sudden and dramatic improvement. Student attendance improved significantly, and in the national examinations taken by English students at the age of 16 the overall school performance improved by over 20 per cent.

Across the city, about eight miles away, Victoria Grammar School, serves a very different community. Students are selected for the school as a result of tests taken at the age of 11. In the main they come from relatively better off families; indeed, some could be described as wealthy. The performances of its students in national examinations are, predictably, outstanding, making it an attractive choice for aspirational parents, many of whom move into the area in the hope that their youngsters will gain a place.

The rapid progress made at Oakwood arose, to some extent at least, as a result of its partnership with the Grammar School. Through this unusual relationship, involving the crossing of various social boundaries, new energy and expertise was made available to Oakwood. Commenting on what happened, the headteacher of the Grammar School explained:

> I spend about three days a week over at Oakwood and one of my assistant heads works 50 per cent of the time with the senior leadership team there to build capacity. It was apparent from the outset that the team at Oakwood had the skills to move the school forward but its members were not forged into a team and were not made accountable.

She also commented on the benefits gained for her own school, not least in respect to the opportunities it had provided for some of her staff to address new professional challenges.

This story is one of many examples of how school-to-school partnerships of various kinds can help to stimulate improvements in practice and expectations. These unusual relationships were encouraged through a three-year initiative known as the Greater Manchester Challenge, the purpose of which was to improve outcomes for children and young people across the city region, focusing in particular on those from low income families. The budget for the project was £50 million and I had the role of Chief Adviser.

In this book I provide an account of what this involved. In so doing, I add to the growing literature that attempts to make sense of the successes of the City Challenge initiative in England, first of all in London and then later in the Black Country (in the West Midlands) and Greater Manchester (i.e. Ofsted, 2010; Hutchings *et al.*, 2012; Hutchings and Mansaray, 2013; Barrs *et al.*, 2014; Claeys, Kempton and Paterson, 2014; Greaves, Macmillan and Sibieta, 2014; Kidson and Norris, 2014). What is distinctive about my contribution is that as a participant observer I am able to explain what happened from the inside. This has enabled me to draw lessons that will, I believe, be useful to those in other parts of the world who are interested in system level change.

As I will explain, this does not result in the sorts of simplistic and prescriptive recommendations that too often permeate the literature on school improvement. Rather, my insider stance enables me to engage with matters of detail that draw attention to local complications that can act as barriers to change processes. This leads me to formulate a strategic framework that can be used to analyse existing arrangements in order to develop powerful improvement approaches. More specifically, this framework helps to pinpoint resources that can be mobilized in order to overcome the barriers that exist through collective efforts that involve many stakeholders. I argue that this is a *different way of thinking* about how to develop school systems that are more equitable, one that requires an engagement with the social and political factors that are fundamental to the way these systems work. The flexible and responsive nature of this approach means that it can be adapted for use in different national contexts.

Strengthening social capital

Central to the way of thinking that I present are attempts to develop new, more fruitful working relationships: within and between schools; between schools and their wider communities; and between local and national government. A helpful theoretical interpretation that can be made of these strategies is that, together, they help to strengthen *social capital*. In other words, they create pathways through which expertise and lessons from innovations can spread.

In recent years, the work of Robert Putnam has been influential in making the idea of social capital a focus for research and policy discussion. He explains:

Whereas physical capital refers to physical objects and human capital refers to the properties of individuals, social capital refers to connections among individuals – social networks and the norms of reciprocity and trustworthiness that arise from them.

(Putnam 2000, p.19)

Writing about the more recent situation in the United States, Putnam states that 'what many high-achieving school districts have in abundance is social capital, which is educationally more important than financial capital' (p. 306). He also suggests that this can help to mitigate the insidious effects of socioeconomic disadvantage.

Reflecting on his work with schools serving disadvantaged communities – also in the United States – Payne (2008) comes to a similar conclusion. Thinking specifically about school contexts that are characterized by low levels of social capital, he argues:

Weak social infrastructure means that conservatives are right when they say that financial resources are likely to mean little in such environments. It means that expertise inside the building is likely to be underutilized, and expertise coming from outside is likely to be rejected on its face. It means that well-thought-out programs can be undermined by the factionalized character of teacher life or by strong norms that militate against teacher collaboration.

(p.39)

Mulford (2007) suggests that by treating social relationships as a form of capital, they can be seen as a resource, which can then be drawn on to achieve organizational goals. There are, he explains, three types of social capital, each of which throws further light on the processes that could be developed within an education system. The first of these is 'bonding social capital' – this relates to what can happen amongst work colleagues within a school. 'Bridging social capital' is what can occur between schools through various forms of networking and collaboration. And finally, 'linking social capital' relates to stronger relationships between a school and wider community resources.

As I explain in subsequent chapters, the work of the Greater Manchester Challenge involved a series of interconnected strategies that fostered stronger social capital of all three types. This helped to break down barriers within schools, between schools, and between schools and other stakeholders, in order to facilitate the sorts of mutual benefit that I have mentioned. However, it is important to recognize that, within the context of changing and, at times, contradictory national policies, the gains made through such approaches were often hard won, and remained fragile and therefore easily lost. Here, continuing tensions regarding priorities and preferred ways of working between national and local policy makers, and, indeed, between schools and local authorities, were factors that continued to create barriers to progress. So, for example, some of those near to central government remained preoccupied with achieving short-term gains in test and examination scores in ways that created barriers to efforts for promoting sustainable improvements. Coupled with this was a mistrust of local authorities – the staff of which were often seen as part of the problem, rather than part of the solution – and doubts about the need to have separate strategies that fit particular contexts.

Self-improving school systems

Current efforts in many countries to create schools that can reach all students effectively have often failed to deliver (Giroux and Schmidt 2004; Wilkinson and Pickett, 2009; OECD 2010; Schleicher, 2010). Whilst they may have raised the bar, they have not closed the gap. In this book I present a different way of thinking about this task, one that is led from within schools.

In thinking about what is meant by the idea of a self-improving school system I draw on the work of two distinguished scholars, both of whom share the same surname. From Andy Hargreaves I draw on what he and his colleague have described as 'the Fourth Way' (Hargreaves and Shirley, 2009, 2012). This is based on what they see as the limitations of three previous ways of thinking about educational change:

- *The First Way* was characterized by state support and professional freedom. In this context, innovation was encouraged and practised, but was often random and inconsistent.
- *The Second Way* attempted to achieve more cohesion and consistency by focusing on market competition and educational standardization, approaches that were imposed at the expense of professional autonomy.
- *The Third Way* attempted to combine the best of state support and market competition, and balance professional autonomy with accountability. However, it was limited by its emphasis on performance driven targets and testing.

Reflecting on these earlier formulations led Hargreaves and Shirley to conclude:

> Educational standardization has dumbed down our curriculum and burdened our schools with bigger government and overbearing bureaucracy, and has not enabled us to adapt flexibly to the future. These old ways of educational change in the 20th Century are ill suited to the fast, flexible and vulnerable new world of the 21st century.
>
> *(Hargreaves and Shirley, 2009, p. x)*

As a consequence, they argue that a Fourth Way is now needed. Having analysed examples of school change from various parts of the world that have helped them in developing their new formulation, they argue that this:

> brings about change through democracy and professionalism, rather than through bureaucracy and market forces. It transfers trust and confidence back from the discredited free market of competition among schools, and reinvests

them in the expertise of highly trained and actively trusted professionals. At the same time, it reduces political bureaucracy while energizing public democracy. This means a fundamental shift in teachers' professionalism that restores greater autonomy from government and introduces more openness to and engagement with parents and communities. The Fourth Way, therefore, means significant change for everyone – governments, parents, and teacher unions alike.

(p. 72)

Within the Fourth Way, teachers set shared targets, rather than attempting to meet the targets demanded by others. In this way, it is argued, democracy plus professionalism replaces bureaucracy and the market – it is less about government and more about democracy. Within the Fourth Way, the government is not there to drive and deliver, but to steer and support. Finally, in the Fourth Way, responsibility comes before accountability, because it is collective responsibility for performance that ultimately will lift the system. As a result:

> The Fourth Way pushes beyond standardization, data-driven decision making, and target-obsessed distractions to forge an equal and interactive partnership between the people, the profession, and their government. It enables educational leaders to 'let go' of the details of change, steering broadly whenever they can and intervening directly only when they must – to restore safety, avoid harm and remove incompetence and corruption from the system.
>
> *(Hargreaves and Shirley 2009, p. 71)*

Whilst not suggesting that the project that is the main focus of this book was driven by these ideas, my analysis of the lessons that can be learnt from what happened most certainly was. In particular, my conclusion as to what is needed to foster the development of self-improving school systems is based on the argument that we need to go 'beyond standardization, data-driven decision making, and target-obsessed distractions to forge an equal and interactive partnership between the people, the profession, and their government.'

Related to this, my analysis also makes extensive use of David Hargreaves's conceptualization of what a self-improving system would look like. In a series of what he describes as 'thinkpieces' written for the National College for School Leadership in England, Hargreaves presents a set of important ideas that are crucial to the conclusions I arrive at in this book (Hargreaves, D. H., 2010; 2011; 2012a; 2012b). He argues that there are four 'building blocks' for the development of a self-improving system: capitalizing on the benefits of clusters of schools; adopting a local solutions approach; stimulating co-construction between schools; and expanding the concept of system leadership. He further suggests that in order to move forward these building blocks have to be strengthened, so that schools collaborate in more effective forms of professional development and school improvement.

Writing about the changing policy context in England in 2010, which saw the election of a new government, Hargreaves argues that:

> increased decentralisation provides an opportunity for a new vision of school improvement that capitalises on the gains made in school leadership and in partnerships between schools. It would usher in a new era in which the school system becomes the major agent of its own improvement and does so at a rate and to a depth that has hitherto been no more than an aspiration. It is essential that such a change would enhance parental confidence in the quality of schools and the effectiveness of teachers, on both of which better educational outcomes depend.
>
> *(Hargreaves, D.H., 2010, p, 4)*

This book looks at the practicalities of putting this thinking into action on a large scale, within a changing policy context that, so far, has proved to be less favourable than the one implied here by David Hargreaves. Indeed, as I will illustrate, it proved to be a context in which the Fourth Way thinking envisaged by Andy Hargreaves and Denis Shirley was mixed up with a contradictory and confusing mix of assumptions related to their other three Ways.

Educational equity

The two schools referred to at the beginning of this chapter – Oakwood High and Victoria Grammar schools – illustrate the central challenge facing the English education system and, indeed, many other systems around the world. Though the two are both state funded, circumstances to do with massive inequality between different communities mean that each has young people with significant differences in respect to the support they have available to their learning. As a result, Oakwood is working against the odds, whilst the teachers at Victoria engage with students who seem to have everything going for them.

In their influential book, *The Spirit Level*, Wilkinson and Pickett (2009) seem to have situations like this in mind when they argue:

> Although good schools make a difference, the biggest influence on educational attainment, how well a child performs in school and later in higher education, is family background… Children do better if their parents have higher incomes, and do better if they come from homes where they have a place to study, where there are reference books and newspapers, and where education is valued.
>
> *(pp. 103–5)*

My primary professional concern is with the challenges that are created by these types of inequality. Specifically, my focus is on finding more effective ways of creating school systems that can 'reach out' to all children and young people, whatever their personal characteristics and family circumstances (Ainscow, 1999). Within the international community this has been the focus of the Education For All movement, promoted since 1990 by the United Nations organizations to extend educational opportunities, particularly in developing countries (UNESCO, 2010). Meanwhile, in the developed world, international monitoring systems have enabled countries to compare the stage of development of their education systems in relation to this agenda, albeit with reference to a relatively narrow set of outcomes (OECD, 2010).

For many years I have had opportunities to work within education systems – in my own country and elsewhere – in exploring how the agenda of equity can be moved forward. In this book I build on these earlier experiences in order to draw out lessons that may have implications for the work of others who have similar concerns. This leads me to argue that schools have a greater potential for improvement than is currently being used. This being the case, the best way forward is to make better use of available expertise. In this way, schools and education systems can become self-improving. I will argue that such an approach requires a major shift regarding ways of thinking about the development of education systems. This has implications for the thinking and actions of everybody who has a stake in schools.

At the core of the book is my account of a three-year effort to transform the education system of the city region of Greater Manchester, in the United Kingdom. As I will explain, my involvement in this initiative enabled me to work with others in an attempt to put into practice ideas that had emerged from decades of working on development and research projects in my own country and internationally. This experience threw light on the complexities involved. As a result, I was forced to rethink the nature of the task.

Before explaining what this involved, however, I summarize the contexts in which my work is located, first of all internationally and then in terms of England.

International trends

Throughout the world children enter schools from different backgrounds, have different experiences of education, and leave with very different results. In many countries the poorest children tend to lose out most starkly, achieve the worst results and attend the lowest performing schools (Giroux and Schmidt, 2004; Wilkinson and Pickett, 2009; OECD, 2010). The influential Programme for International Student Assessment (PISA) shows that an achievement gap between rich and poor pupils exists in all the OECD countries. For example, students from more socio-economically advantaged backgrounds outperform students from average backgrounds by the equivalent of one year's worth of education (OECD, 2010). A fundamental challenge for policy makers and practitioners is, therefore, to find ways of breaking the links between disadvantage, educational failure and restricted life chances.

The extent of this gap between the achievements of students from rich and poor families varies significantly between countries (UNESCO, 2010). So, for example:

In a world-class system like Finland's, socioeconomic standing is far less predictive of student achievement. All things being equal, a low-income student in the United States is far less likely to do well in school than a low-income student in Finland. Given the enormous economic impact of educational achievement, this is one of the best indicators of equal opportunity in a society.

(Mourshed, Chijioke and Barber, 2010, pp. 8–9)

On a more optimistic note, international comparisons in relation to literacy indicate that the best performing school systems manage to provide high-quality education for all of their students:

Canada, Finland, Japan, Korea and the partner economies Hong Kong-China and Shanghai-China all perform well above the OECD mean performance and students tend to perform well regardless of their own background or the school they attend. They not only have large proportions of students performing at the highest levels of reading proficiency, but also relatively few students at the lower proficiency levels.

(OECD, 2010, p. 15)

The implication is that it is possible for countries to develop education systems that are both excellent and equitable. The question is: what needs to be done to move policy and practice forward in relation to this agenda? The ideas developed in this book will be relevant to colleagues in many countries that are grappling with this challenge.

The context of England

England is a useful context to consider when thinking about the issue of equity, as noted in a 2007 OECD study which reported that the impact of socio-economic circumstances on young people's attainment was more marked in the United Kingdom than in any other of the 52 countries considered.[1] A review of data carried out by our Manchester team on the national situation illustrates some of the complexities that exist (Kerr and West, 2010). It suggests that:

- on average, poor white British students – both boys and girls – are more likely than other ethnic groups to continue to underachieve;
- of the minority ethnic groups, Chinese and Indian pupils are generally the most successful and African-Caribbean pupils the least;
- poverty – as indicated by eligibility for free school meals – is strongly associated with low attainment, more so for white British pupils than for other ethnic groups;
- children from homes with single and/or unemployed parents, and parents who have few educational qualifications themselves, often do less well at school.

These patterns are echoed by studies that have examined the performance of schools and their pupils at various stages of education across the UK. Summing this research up, Goodman and Gregg (2010) say: 'Children from poor homes are nearly a year behind when they start school and two years behind by age 14', and they 'tend to have a far less positive view of learning, of school and of themselves'.

When looking at what happens after age 16, we see that educational inequalities are at their starkest in relation to those young people who are not in education training or employment (Kerr and West, 2010). They are most often those with: a history of persistent truancy, use of drugs and alcohol, a disability, mental health issues, criminal and anti-social behaviours, and poor educational attainment. Teenagers from certain backgrounds are also at greater risk. So, for example, amongst all 16 year-olds nationally, seven per cent are unemployed and not involved in further forms of education. Yet this rises to 11 per cent amongst those from the poorest socio-economic groups, 13 per cent amongst those with a disability, 22 per cent amongst those excluded from school, 32 per cent amongst those who are persistent truants and 74 per cent amongst teenage mothers. Those most likely to truant or be excluded from school include young people of Caribbean heritage, 'looked after' children and those categorized as having special educational needs.

Although such statistics identify broad patterns, different factors often interact to compound the links between social disadvantage and education. For example, children with low attainment tend to come from poorer families. These families tend to live in deprived urban areas, where there are high levels of ill-health, poor housing and overcrowding, unemployment, and a whole host of other factors associated with poor educational outcomes. We also know that it is not just levels of poverty in these areas which impact on schooling – neighbourhood dynamics are also important (Lupton, 2003; Kerr, Dyson and Raffo, 2014). For example, in some areas of inner city social housing, and in neighbourhoods with many Asian heritage owner-occupiers, examination results are consistently better than would be anticipated based on indices of poverty. By contrast, some of the areas with the worst performance are those where predominantly white pupils live on large, city-overspill, public housing estates. Such neighbourhoods, although struggling academically, are often not identified as being acutely poor or disadvantaged.

A variety of studies also suggest that underachievement cannot simply be explained by children and young people's backgrounds, but that the type of school they attend, the mix of pupils in the school, where the school is located, and their experiences of teaching and learning in the school, are also important (Duncan and Murnane, 2011; Clifton and Cook, 2013). Annual reports from the national inspection agency, Ofsted, have consistently signalled that schools in deprived areas are more likely to be judged inadequate than those in more affluent areas. However, in 2013 the Chief Inspector reported that many low achieving pupils from poor backgrounds were an 'invisible minority' in schools rated good or outstanding in quite affluent areas (Ofsted, 2013). This suggests that school and non-school factors may well combine to lower the attainment of children and young people who are already disadvantaged by their backgrounds. Summing this up, Benn and Millar (2006) argue that one of the biggest problems the country faces is 'the gap between rich and poor, and the enormous disparity in children's home backgrounds and the social and cultural capital they bring to the educational table' (p. 145).

English policy developments

Recent years have seen intensive efforts by successive governments to address such concerns. These efforts have been part of an intensification of political interest in education, especially regarding standards and the management of the state system (Whitty, 2010). During the period of successive Labour governments (1997 to 2010) this led to a series of highly centralized national strategies to strengthen practices of teaching and leadership. At the same time, competition between schools was seen to be one of the keys to 'driving up standards', whilst at the same time further reducing the control of local authorities over provision.[2]

More recently this competitive emphasis has been intensified as increasing numbers of state schools have been encouraged – and, in some instances, required – to become 'academies'. These 'independent state schools' are in many ways similar to the charter schools in the USA and free schools in Sweden (Meyland-Smith and Evans, 2009). Such changes are intended to 'liberate' schools from the bureaucracy of local government and establish a form of market place. In this way, it is intended that families will have greater choice as to which school their youngsters will attend (Adonis, 2012).

In this uncertain and confusing policy context, progress is monitored through national tests, the results of which are available to parents in order to assist them in choosing schools (Muijs *et al.*, 2011). In addition, schools are regularly inspected by a national agency, the Office for Standards in Education (Ofsted). The outcomes of inspection are published in a report, which is a public document. If a school is judged as failing (or likely to fail) to provide an acceptable standard of education, it is made subject to 'special measures'. Underachievement and low levels of attainment amongst students, a high proportion of unsatisfactory teaching, and ineffective leadership, are seen as the most consistent features of failing schools (Nicolaidou and Ainscow, 2006).

However, there are those who feel that the system is more likely to identify schools in challenging circumstances as 'failing', while schools in more affluent areas are likely to be given the benefit of the doubt (Benn, 2012). In addition, Ofsted has been judged by some to have had a harmful effect on schools (Tomlinson, 2005). On the other hand, research by Allen and Burgess (2012) contradicts this view suggesting that 'failing' an Ofsted inspection leads to far greater pupil progress within a school than passing an inspection.

Interventions

As attention has been drawn to the greater impact of socio-economic circumstances on the progress of students in England there has been a heightened concern to respond. It is, therefore, hardly surprising that the last 20 years have seen successive governments taking steps aimed at improving the quality and performance of schools, particularly those serving disadvantaged communities. The review of research evidence carried out by members of our Manchester team (Kerr and West, 2010) led us to classify these interventions into four overall types: general interventions, targeted interventions, within-school interventions and structural interventions.

General interventions

General interventions aimed to improve the overall quality and effectiveness of schooling, particularly in relation to the strengthening of leadership and teaching. The underlying assumption was that (at least part of) the reason for inequities in educational outcomes lies in the limited effectiveness of some schools. Improving schools in general is therefore seen as a way of improving the outcomes for disadvantaged pupils, leading to an improvement in 'life chances'.

This type of intervention was particularly popular in England during the late 1990s and early 2000s. It was most evident in the National Literacy, Numeracy, and Key Stage 3 strategies, which were subsequently incorporated into the National Strategies. The implementation of these was rather unusual – in effect a set of system wide improvement approaches commissioned from a private organization and supported by teams of consultants employed nationally, regionally and within each local authority. As improvements in test and examination scores tended to tail off, however, the efficacy of these one-size-fits-all approaches was increasingly questioned. The decision to phase out the National Strategies was announced in a 2009 White Paper on developing twenty-first century school systems.

Targeted interventions

These approaches were aimed directly at improving the performance of specific schools in areas of socio-economic disadvantage. Once again, an underlying premise was that ineffective schools are a key source of inequitable outcomes. In England, such schools have sometimes (following inspection) been subject to direct interventions and regular monitoring, coordinated by the local authority. But a wider range of targeted interventions involved the identification of schools facing challenging circumstances and the focusing of additional programmes and resources on them.

Several such initiatives involved the setting up of collaborative arrangements between schools, as in the Education Action Zones, the Excellence in Cities programme, and through the Leadership Incentive Grant (Ainscow and West, 2006). Arguably the most significant example of this approach, however, was the London Challenge, which focused on raising attainment of disadvantaged learners, whilst at the same time improving the overall performance of all London schools. The perceived success of this intervention led to the extension of the City Challenge approach, including the developments that are the main focus of this book. It also influenced the approach used in a more controversial initiative, the National

Challenge, which targeted over 600 'under-performing' secondary schools, which were overwhelmingly located in areas of socio-economic disadvantage.

Within-school interventions

Whilst the first two types of intervention focused on improvement at the whole-school level, this third type was aimed at improving outcomes for under-attaining groups *within* schools. These approaches were therefore based on the premise that schools demonstrate differential levels of effectiveness for different groups of pupils. In English national policy documents, such approaches were usually referred to as being focused on 'closing the gap' between high and low performing pupil groups. So, for example, there were interventions that specifically focused on the undera-chievement of boys, particularly those from white working class backgrounds; learners from certain ethnic backgrounds; bilingual learners; children in public care; travellers; gifted and talented; and children defined as having special educational needs. In addition, attention was given to improving access to university education amongst students from disadvantaged backgrounds. The Aim Higher programme, for example, involved local authorities and universities working closely with schools to help raise aspirations and open up pathways for these young people.

Structural interventions

Seeking to boost educational performance in areas of high social and economic deprivation through changes in system structures and governance arrangements has been, in some ways, the most radical type of intervention. So, the last ten years or so have seen the creation of various new categories of school, such as federations, trusts and academies, followed more recently by the idea of free schools, which legally are another form of academy.

What is interesting here is the way tackling social disadvantage has become con-flated with improving school performance. If a school was identified as 'underper-forming' against national averages – and, unsurprisingly, the great majority of such schools are situated in the areas where levels of social deprivation are highest, and levels of physical and economic well-being lowest – it could be federated with a more successful school; or given trust status, so as it could draw on support from other educational and community organizations; or it could be closed down and re-established as an academy.

A federation is a shared governance structure, involving the joining together of two or more schools (Muijs et al., 2011). Federated schools can retain separate budgets and staffing, share some resources whilst keeping others separate, or com-bine governing bodies within a fully integrated structure. Thus they can be located on a continuum, from voluntary, informal 'soft' federations through to statutory, formal 'hard' federations, which are in effect single employers. There were also many examples of secondary schools collaborating with each other, but not for-mally federating.

Trust schools were introduced under the 2006 Education and Inspections Act. This allowed all schools to form trusts by working with external partners. Later, the government pledged to accelerate the introduction of National Challenge trusts, in order to deal with underperforming schools.

Academies are 'independent state schools' and, as noted earlier, are in many ways similar to the charter schools in the USA and free schools in Sweden. Although they are state funded, they may be sponsored by a private company, faith groups or other educational establishments, including universities and further education colleges (RSA, 2013). The relationship between the Secretary of State and individual academies is outlined in a school funding agreement, which is a legally binding agreement. Academies enjoy increased autonomy in comparison to maintained sector schools, including flexibility with regard to teacher pay and conditions. Their introduction has raised controversy throughout their existence, and the debate about their efficacy and desirability has remained fierce in the media, as well as amongst members of the research community (see various chapters in Gunter, 2013).

Since the election of 2010, the impetus around the idea of an 'education marketplace' has speeded up dramatically and by mid-2014 the majority of secondary schools in England had become academies. These schools operate outside the remit of the local authority and are responsible for setting their own admission criteria, though the authority retains a duty to coordinate and administer the allocation of places and ensure that there is sufficient supply. Very few academies have, thus far, exercised the autonomy available to them with regard to admissions and the vast majority continue to admit children according to criteria set by the local authority.

Impact

Predictably, government statements have frequently pointed to improvements in test and examination scores, arguing that the impact of these various interventions has been significant (Whitty and Anders, 2012). The research community, however, holds a variety of views, and there are some who argue that there has been very little impact, particularly amongst learners from disadvantaged backgrounds, and that the apparent improvements in measured performance are not supported by detailed analysis of national data (e.g. Tymms, 2004, Meadows et al. 2007; Sammons, 2008).

Meanwhile, it has been argued that the development of the educational marketplace, coupled with the emphasis on policies fostering greater diversity of schools, has created a quasi-selective system in which the poorest children, by and large, attend the lowest-performing schools (Ainscow et al., 2012). Consequently, the low achieving and, many would argue, the least advantaged schools, fall progressively further and further behind their high-performing counterparts. In terms of these effects, through selective advantaging and disadvantaging of schools, those policies that have generally led to increased standards have also increased rather than decreased disparities in education quality and opportunity between advantaged and less privileged groups. The policy priority, therefore, is to find ways of continuing to improve the education system but in a way that fosters equity.

Conclusion and chapter summaries

This introductory chapter has introduced the main themes of the book, including the concern to develop self-improving school systems in order to promote equity. It also summarized the international context for this agenda before focusing in more detail on the situation in England, where the school system reflects the inequalities that are the feature of the country.

Over the last 20 years or so, successive British governments of different political orientations have made educational reform a priority. This has led to a plethora of centrally driven interventions. Whilst the nature of these responses has varied significantly, they tend to all start from an instinctive assumption that schools – and by implication teachers – are the main source of the problem. Consequently, massive efforts have been made to deal with these perceived deficits though a combination of top-down interventions, accountability measures and changes in governance arrangements.

The argument that develops in this book starts from a very different set of assumptions. In essence, it builds on the idea that within schools and the communities they serve there are untapped resources that can be mobilized in order to transform schools from places that do well for many children and young people so that they can do well for all of them. It also shows how an engagement with evidence of various forms can act as a catalyst for such developments, not least by making the familiar unfamiliar in ways that challenge taken for granted assumptions as to what is possible.

In Chapter 2, I describe the development of a large-scale initiative, the Greater Manchester Challenge, that set out to make progress in relation to the quality of schooling provided for all children and young people, particularly those from disadvantaged backgrounds. In so doing, I begin the process of explaining the social complexities that come to the surface as those who get involved in such a development bring their particular views of what an effective education means and the ways in which improvements can be achieved. The chapter explains how an overall strategy evolved, the main purpose being to move thinking and practices around.

The subsequent chapters look more closely at how the various strands of activity within the strategy evolved. In each case, I explain how earlier research that I had carried out with my colleagues had offered potential starting points for these developments. Frequent reference is also made to lessons learnt from the experience of the London Challenge, which had commenced five years earlier than the Greater Manchester initiative.

In Chapter 3, I explain the intensive efforts made to achieve rapid improvement in some 200 or so schools that came to be seen as the 'Keys to Success', an approach that had been originally formulated in London. The chapter explains how, gradually, it became apparent that the most powerful approach for these schools was to partner them with other schools that had the capacity to support their improvement. None of this is straightforward, however, and the chapter goes on to explain the crucial role of the team of Challenge Advisers who became skillful in brokering, coordinating and monitoring such school partnerships.

Chapter 4 continues the theme of encouraging schools to support one another. It explains how 'Families of Schools' were created in order to promote widespread involvement in a collective effort to improve the work of some 1,150 schools across Greater Manchester. Whilst this led to positive experiences that benefitted many children and young people, some schools remained reluctant to get involved. Much was learnt about the strategies that are needed in order to achieve such a large-scale effort to encourage schools to cooperate. Most importantly, it became clear that an engagement with data of various kinds is a means of moving such partnerships to a deeper level that involves both the sharing of expertise and exper- imentation with new ways of working.

Recognizing the importance of factors beyond schools, Chapter 5 describes how efforts were made to mobilize the wider community in supporting improve- ment efforts. The ongoing analysis of the context revealed what seemed like an endless range of possibilities in this respect, starting of course with the families of the children and young people. Efforts were also made to involve local businesses, universities, sports clubs, arts organizations, voluntary bodies and religious groups. Once again it became apparent that there were many untapped resources that needed to be drawn on. In this respect, the chapter illustrates the frustration of many community groups at their failure to break down what seem to be barriers of various kinds to their greater involvement in the work of schools.

A concern that existed right from the outset of the Greater Manchester Challenge was with sustainability. The evidence from many other large-scale efforts to improve school systems is that even when things appear to go well the momentum eventually disappears and what positive impact occurs fades. Chapter 6 describes the efforts made to avoid this outcome by creating a leadership strategy that sought to involve headteachers themselves in coordinating the improvement strategy. With this in mind, some 170 or so strong headteachers were formally designated as having a systems leadership role. The chapter explains how they increasingly took on shared responsibility for strengthening the strategy, so much so that by the end of the formal period of the Challenge a group of them had set up a non- profit-making agency that continues to coordinate school-to-school collaboration across Greater Manchester.

A central issue that becomes apparent throughout the book relates to the social and, at time, political complexities that exist when trying to involve so many stake- holders in sharing responsibility for the progress of every student, in every school, across a large education system. Chapter 7 looks at this issue in detail, focusing in part on the dilemmas I faced as the 'public face' of the Challenge and, at the same time, the person accountable for the effectiveness of its strategy. Particular tensions occurred between representatives of national and local government, and of course there was the difficulties involved in getting senior staff in schools involved. However, perhaps the greatest challenge within the Challenge related to the roles of local authorities. Indeed, as the idea of a self-improving system led by those within schools gained wider support, the question was frequently asked as to whether there was any role for local authorities. This chapter describes efforts made within the ten authorities to rethink their contributions, including the pain that this sometimes created as well-established senior people were asked to make fundamental changes in their thinking and practices.

Each of these six chapters concludes with recommendations that I make as a result of reflecting on what happened in Greater Manchester. Chapter 8 draws these ideas together in order to propose a different way of thinking about how school systems can become more equitable. Central to this is a strategic framework that starts with the need to analyze contexts in order to develop strategies that suit particular circumstances. More specifically, this helps to pinpoint barriers to progress, and resources that can be drawn on to address these challenges. The implication of this is that what the book offers is not a toolkit of techniques that can be moved from place to place, but a way of thinking that should be used flexibly in response to local circumstances. What this involves is illustrated by accounts of developments in Wales, Australia, and England since the election of the coalition government in 2010.

All of this leads me to argue that the approach I recommend is flexible enough to be used in other national contexts. Furthermore, I conclude that it will be particularly relevant in those countries where an increased emphasis on school autonomy is leading to a dangerous fragmentation of provision that may further disadvantage young people from low income families.

Notes

1 It should be noted that the four countries that make up the United Kingdom (England, Northern Ireland, Scotland and Wales) each have their own education policies.
2 There are 152 English local authorities. They are democratically accountable for providing a range of services for their local communities, including education.

2

A CITY CHALLENGE

Over many years I have argued that the most important factor that will enable us to achieve more equitable schools is the collective will to make it happen. Occasionally, those who have heard this have suggested that it might be an unrealistic aspiration. As I understand it, their point is that in unequal societies – such as Australia, Chile, the UK and the USA – it will never be possible to get everybody pulling in the same direction. Whilst recognizing the power of this argument, I remain convinced that it should be possible to mobilize everybody who has an interest in education to work together for the common good. Perhaps somewhat idealistically, I also take the view that a system of schools that treats every child fairly is, ultimately, in the interests of everybody – an argument that is made so convincingly by Wilkinson and Pickett (2009).

Between 2007 and 2011, I had a remarkable opportunity to explore what this involves on a grand scale when I was asked to take the lead on an initiative to improve the performance of schools within the city in which I was born, Manchester. In this chapter I summarize the story of what happened. In subsequent chapters I analyze these experiences in order to draw lessons as to what is needed to develop school systems that can be effective for all of our children. In so doing I explain the ideas that I took to this task based on the research I had carried out previously with various colleagues. This leads me to reflect on the difficulties involved and how these might be overcome.

Getting involved

In the summer of 2007 I received a telephone call from a civil servant with whom I had worked closely on a previous national project. She explained that the government was planning to introduce an initiative to address low standards in schools across the ten local authorities that constitute the conurbation of Greater Manchester.

She went on to explain that, whilst her approach was to be regarded as being informal, she wanted to know if I would consider taking on the role of leadership in what was to be known as the Greater Manchester Challenge.

Eventually, the post was advertised formally as follows:

> The Government is seeking a Chief Adviser for Greater London schools, and a Chief Adviser for Greater Manchester schools, to offer advice and leadership in the drive to raise school standards in each city region. Each city challenge is a programme lasting until at least 2011 to improve educational outcomes for young people, delivered in partnership between Government, schools, local authorities and all those working to raise education standards in the cities.

Linking the proposal to what had happened in London between 2003 and 2007, the advertisement went on to define the initiative as being a 'partnership' between the different stakeholders. It also explained the nature of the Chief Adviser role:

> The London Challenge has operated since 2003, and the Government has recently decided to extend it for at least 3 more years, and to develop its scope. The Greater Manchester Challenge will be designed on the successful principles of the London Challenge, but will be tailored to the city's needs and challenges. The challenge will incorporate all aspects of the school system including teachers, pupils, leaders and the local as well as national strategic partnerships within the education system.

The advertisement went on to outline the person specification for these appointments:

> you will have a proven track record of leading change and raising educational standards in an urban area. We invite tenders from high calibre individuals with demonstrable experience and track record of strategic engagement and delivery at a very senior level. You will have the capacity to motivate and inspire heads, governors, teachers and school support staff. You will be able to demonstrate a successful track record of strategic leadership and of delivering change in schools. Exceptional influencing skills and an approach capable of engaging stakeholders across a wide range of organisations both in the public and private sector are essential.

It was explained that the Chief Adviser would 'bring a strategic and co-ordinated approach to schooling in the City Challenge area', and work closely with the Chief Advisers in London and in another initiative in the Midlands (the Black Country Challenge) to ensure a coherent City Challenge model and sharing of best practice. The role was also to advise and report to Ministers on the development and delivery of the strategy, and work closely with the City Challenge team and the Office of the

Schools Commissioner to design and implement the City Challenge strategy, encourage innovation, choice and diversity, and change in the workforce and curriculum. There was also mention of the need to work effectively with others, e.g. local authorities, institutions, business and charitable foundations, to 'enable visible transformation of education'.

On 9 October 2007, following a formal interview with representatives of central and local government, my appointment as Chief Adviser (and a similar arrangement for the Black Country Challenge, in four local authorities in the West Midlands, which had subsequently been advertised) was announced in a press release from the Department for Children Schools and Families (DCSF),[1] as follows:

> The Government today announced the Chief Advisers who will lead around a £78 million campaign to raise standards in schools across some of the most deprived areas of Greater Manchester and the Black Country. Professor Mel Ainscow is the Chief Adviser of the new Greater Manchester Challenge, around a £50 million programme over three years, and Professor Sir Geoff Hampton is appointed as Chief Adviser of the around £28 million Black Country Challenge. Both programmes will boost standards in primary and secondary schools in the regions, where there is a history of under achievement among young people.

The press release also included a statement from the Minister of State for Children, Young People and Families, and Minister for the North West, Beverley Hughes MP, with whom I was to work closely over the next couple of years. She commented:

> I am delighted to welcome Professor Ainscow as the new Chief Adviser for Greater Manchester. Mel is renowned for his work on raising the achievement and attainment of all children and young people but particularly those from more disadvantaged backgrounds, which is what this programme will be specifically addressing. I am confident that he will be a major force in helping us to break the cycle between deprivation and low achievement in the region.
>
> The Greater Manchester Challenge will build on our experience in London, where highly targeted investment in disadvantaged areas has brought dramatic results. I am confident that we can repeat this success in Greater Manchester and support the work already being done by our educational partners locally.

I was quoted as saying:

> I am delighted to be part of this important opportunity to improve the quality of education for all children and young people across Greater Manchester. There are lots of good things going on in schools in Greater Manchester. The task now is to spread the best practice to all schools.

> For me personally this is the culmination of many years in education, as a teacher, headteacher and university academic. I was brought up and went to school locally and I feel very committed to ensuring that the Greater Manchester Challenge makes a big difference.

The press release concluded with a summary of what was to happen next, once again making mention of the idea of partnerships:

> Both campaigns will be delivered in partnership with education stakeholders in the regions, including local authorities and schools. Their target will be to turn around major school problems faced by the regions to achieve:
>
> • A sharp drop in under performing schools
> • More outstanding schools
> • Better results for disadvantaged children.

It was noted that detailed plans would be developed over subsequent months and that the main elements were likely to include:

• Intensive support for schools where there is the biggest opportunity to break the link between deprivation and educational underachievement. This will mean support for around 50 primary and 50 secondary schools in Greater Manchester and 30 primary and 30 secondary schools in the Black Country in challenging circumstances. Schools may receive a package of support including: expert advisers, student coaching and mentoring, help for students with English as a second language.
• Greater Manchester and Black Country leadership strategies led by school leaders for school leaders. Headteachers of successful schools will work with weaker schools to improve their leadership teams.
• A tailored package of support to cut underachievement. This is likely to include: professional development for teachers, pupil coaching and help for groups of children at risk of underperforming.
• An analysis of the key issues across both regions. Schools will also be put in 'families' to benchmark themselves against similar schools and share best practice.
• Local solutions to local problems. In London, this has included help with children moving school and a system for helping parents choose a secondary school.

As things developed, this initial list of elements was to begin a process of debate, negotiation and, at times, dispute, regarding how best to go about the initiative that continued over the following three years. Through the chapters that follow I describe examples that are intended to give a flavour of what all of this involved. In so doing, I aim to explore the oft-quoted remark that *school improvement is technically simple but socially complex*. In other words, it is relatively easy to work out what needs to happen; the real challenge is to get those involved to agree to do it.

The October 2007 press release went on to present background information regarding the success of London Challenge, noting in particular that Ofsted had reported that London schools had improved 'dramatically' and that the capital had recorded its best ever GCSE results in 2006, showing London state school pupils leading the rest of the country for the third year running. This was followed by what were referred to as the 'top ten facts' about London Challenge, which, it should be noted, had only focused on secondary schools up to 2007. These facts were listed as follows:

- London achieved its best ever GCSE[2] results in 2006. 58.3 per cent of students attending maintained London schools achieved five good GCSE grades, up by 3 per cent points over 2005 and ahead of the national figure of 57.5 per cent.
- More London students are mastering the basics with 45.8 per cent achieving five good GCSE passes including English and maths, up by 2.8 per cent points over last year compared to a 1.7 per cent point increase to 44.1 per cent nationally.
- Almost one in three London schools achieved outstanding results of 70 per cent or above 5 A$\star$ to C in 2006.
- Improvements in the number of students gaining five good GCSE passes have been achieved in all but one of London's boroughs. Many improvements have been seen in schools facing significant challenges.
- All London boroughs improved their results including English and maths in 2006.
- 19 London boroughs reported increases of 4 per cent points or more including English and maths, and 30 boroughs boosted their five A$\star$ to C passes by 2 per cent points or above.
- 8 London boroughs are in the top 20 most improved local authorities in the country between 1998 and 2006.
- For the second year running more than 50 per cent of students in inner London schools obtained five good passes compared to 32 per cent in 1997. 61 per cent of pupils in outer London achieved the benchmark in 2006.
- 22 London schools are in the top 100 in the country showing sustained improvement in English and maths over the last three years.
- No London borough is now below 43 per cent. In 1997, nearly two thirds of London boroughs were achieving below this level.

My starting points

As will become clear in subsequent chapters, much of my earlier work – both as a practitioner and researcher – related closely to the overall agenda of the Challenge. Having worked as a teacher and then headteacher, I had gone on to be a local authority adviser. In all these roles my central interest had been focused on students experiencing difficulties in schools, many of whom were from economically disadvantaged backgrounds. When I moved into university work – first at Cambridge and then later in Manchester – my agenda as a researcher remained largely the same.

At the formal interview for the post of Chief Adviser for the Greater Manchester Challenge, I summarized these earlier experiences using a PowerPoint slide in terms of a suggested rationale, as follows:

- **Schools know more than they use.** We need to make better use of existing expertise and creativity across the ten authorities.
- **The expertise of teachers and educational leaders is largely unarticulated.** In order to access the reservoir of unused expertise, we need to create a common language of practice for sharing ideas.
- **Evidence is the engine for change.** We can use it to create space for rethinking and to focus our attention on overlooked possibilities for moving practice forward.
- **Networking is socially complex.** Successful networking will require new relationships within and across the ten authorities.
- **Leadership must foster inter-dependence.** Therefore, we need forms of leadership that will encourage trust, mutual understanding and shared values.

During the interview, I used another slide to make some suggestions, based on our earlier research, as to how effective networking might be achieved in the form of the following 'ingredients':

- **Ownership.** In contexts where collaboration pays off, partner schools – particularly heads – have reasonable control over the agendas that are to be the focus of the activities.
- **Levels of involvement.** Whilst the commitment of heads and other senior staff is essential, best practice seems to involve forms of collaboration that exist at many levels.
- **Practical focus.** Focusing on real world issues, particularly those to do with the core business of teaching and learning, seems to provide the best type of vehicle for working together effectively.
- **Making time.** Effective networking requires flexible management arrangements that provide staff with opportunities to learn from one another
- **Commitment to values.** Networks that are more sustainable involve a deeper level of partnership around common beliefs and values.
- **Shared responsibility.** Successful networking leads to changes in organizational cultures and, therefore, demands the sharing of responsibility through new forms of collaborative leadership.

As I tell the story of what happened in Greater Manchester, I show how this thinking was further refined as I experienced the reality of putting it into practice. I will also explain how this helped me to understand the social and political complexities of what this involves.

The context

Before explaining how things developed, however, it is important to get a sense of the context in which the initiative took place. The Greater Manchester city region comprises ten local authorities: Bolton, Bury, Manchester, Oldham, Rochdale, Salford, Stockport, Tameside, Trafford and Wigan. It is home to a population of some 2.5 million people and at the outset of the Challenge it had over 600,000 children and young people. Across the city region, there were approximately 1,150 schools and colleges.

The city region is a conurbation of several once independent towns and cities, which grew rapidly during the industrial revolution. Each has a strong sense of identity, expressed historically by the existence of magnificent town halls and, more recently, through loyalty to local sports teams. In this sense, the idea of Greater Manchester has limited meaning for most of its citizens.

The economy of the city region was built around the cotton and coal industries, and Manchester has often been described as the world's first industrial city. However, in the latter part of the twentieth century, both of these industries declined dramatically, and the region began to struggle economically. During the 1990s, the region turned the corner and started to prosper again, although in some districts it is still left with the challenges of a legacy of half a century's industrial decline (Manchester City Council, 2009).

The area is diverse in a number of ways, with extremely high levels of poverty. Children and young people come from a range of ethnic and cultural backgrounds, with a high proportion whose families have Asian heritage. Nearly 16 per cent have a first language other than English. In 2012 it was reported in the national press that 153 languages are spoken within the city of Manchester and that over 60 per cent of children are bilingual. This means that the city is rivalled only by New York and Paris for its ethnic and linguistic mix.

Greater Manchester was given administrative shape in the local government reforms of 1974, with the urban areas of South East Lancashire and North East Cheshire being joined together to form the ten Boroughs of the Metropolitan County. The County lost its administrative status in 1986, but the ten Metropolitan Boroughs continued to work closely together and became increasingly active in finding ways to co-operate. Eventually, in 2011, this led to the creation of what became known as the Greater Manchester Combined Authority.

The city region is often referred to as the economic engine of the North West and is the largest economy outside of London (Manchester City Council, 2009). At the start of the Challenge, in 2008, it was anticipated that over the following 15 years, over 132,000 new jobs would be created and that economic growth would be above the UK average. There are industry specialisms in sectors such as ICT and digital communications, financial services and life sciences and a growing creative industries sector, which was further strengthened by the BBC's relocation to Salford Quays. This success has been built on a critical mass of highly skilled and specialist people; close proximity to the highest performing research and teaching universities outside the so-called Golden Triangle of Oxford, Cambridge and London, with a student population of 100,000; world class sporting and cultural facilities; strong civic leadership; and a growing reputation for entrepreneurialism.

Despite these successes, there remain significant challenges. The city region's high value and high performing economic centres are geographically close to some of the most deprived communities in the country. At the time of the launch of the Challenge, over 430,000 people were either unemployed or economically inactive. There was also a significant shortage of skills across the city region, resulting in skills gaps and deficits for employers, and restricted employment and career progression opportunities for its residents. The qualification profile for the working age population lagged behind the national and regional average.

Given these circumstances, the overall aims of the Challenge were to raise the educational achievement of all children and young people across the ten local authorities, and to narrow the gap in educational achievement between learners from disadvantaged backgrounds and their peers. The approach that developed emerged from a detailed analysis of the local context, using both statistical data and local intelligence provided by stakeholders. This drew attention to areas of concern and also helped to pinpoint a range of human resources that could be mobilized in order to support improvement efforts.

Recognizing the potential of these resources, and drawing on lessons from London Challenge, it was decided that networking and collaboration – within and between schools – would be the key strategies for strengthening the overall improvement capacity of the system. In the rest of this chapter, I describe the setting up and development of the initiative, and the gradual emergence of its overall strategy. In so doing, I begin to explain some of the difficulties involved, not least the tensions regarding priorities and preferred ways of working between national and local policy makers, and, sometimes, between schools and local authorities. I will describe how many of those near to central government remained preoccupied with achieving short-term gains in test and examination scores in ways that created potential barriers to efforts for promoting sustainable improvements. Coupled with this was their mistrust of local authorities and doubts about the need to have separate strategies that fit particular contexts. At the same time, within the ten local authorities there was an understandable uncertainty about the motives and agendas of what was proposed, despite the rhetoric of partnership referred to earlier.

Learning from London

After being appointed as Chief Adviser, I was keen to learn as much as possible about what had happened in London since 2003. Whilst there was considerable documentation, there was little written from an independent perspective. Discussions with academic colleagues working in London confirmed the view that I had picked up from policy makers and practitioners that considerable changes had occurred in relation to the way that secondary schools across London went about their business and, as I have indicated, that there was certainly evidence of improved performance in national tests and examinations. However, doubts were expressed about the extent to which these improvements had made a significant difference to students from the most disadvantaged backgrounds.

A key contact for me was Tim Brighouse, who led the London Challenge. Indeed, I remained in regular contact with him over the following years in order to draw on his experience. In September 2007, Tim shared with me a draft of a chapter that subsequently appeared in an edited book (Brighouse, 2007). In that chapter, he told the story of the first five years of the London Challenge and presented his reflections on what had occurred. In so doing, he quoted from the foreword to the prospectus for the programme, 'The London Challenge; Transforming London Secondary Schools', which included a passage setting out the origins and intentions of the scheme:

> This great city needs and deserves a truly world-class education system, which serves every community and enables every person in the city to fulfill their own individual creative potential. That is what the proposals published in this document are intended to achieve.
>
> London already does have some world class universities, some world class colleges and some world class schools. It has some world class teachers and some world class educational facilities. And the educational performance of London's schools has improved significantly in recent years. Fewer than 11 per cent of children in inner London achieved 5 good O levels in 1987 – more than 40 per cent achieve the equivalent now.
>
> But there are still far too many schools which are failing to inspire and lead their communities and far too many areas where educational aspirations are low. Too many parents are anguished and fearful, rather than proud or confident, when choosing their child's secondary school. And there are far too many who feel that either expensive private education or lengthy journeys across the city from home to school are the only satisfactory answer.
>
> This situation is unacceptable and it is the reason why we are determined to establish an education system which is truly world class everywhere in London. That system has to be founded more on creativity and diversity which is the city's strength, rather than uniformity. It has to provoke and challenge rather than accepting mediocrity. And it has everywhere to stimulate excellence and establish world standards. In short the exhilarating achievement which characterises some London schools must become the trademark of all London schools.
>
> Though the Government is allocating more resources to London, and we are prepared to allocate still more, I do not fundamentally believe that London's educational problems are problems of resources. It is much more about significant and radical reform that will mobilise the vision and leadership

of the London educational community to achieve educational excellence. We need to make a visible and radical break with the past to transform aspiration and create a culture of achievement.

To that end, Tim went on to set out what he saw as three essential components:

First we have to focus on the two areas of London where we consider the problems to be greatest. These are the north London group of three local authorities (Haringey, Hackney and Islington) and the south London group of two (Lambeth and Southwark). In these areas we need to establish an educational organisation and systematic drive for excellence which rewards success and does not tolerate failure. We have to develop a diverse system of academies and specialist schools which ensures that parents have a choice between excellent alternatives.

Second we have to work exceptionally closely with schools which are failing to reach acceptable standards and to take whatever decisions are necessary to raise the quality of these schools, so that their local communities can have full confidence in what they can achieve.

And third we must strengthen, across the whole of London, the standing of London's education. We must celebrate and enhance the quality of London's teachers and create better educational opportunities for students. We will create a new and better deal for students, teachers and headteachers – so that London becomes seen as a highly attractive part of the country in which to study and teach.

In the chapter, Tim also commented on his frequent use of the phrase 'world class', which he argued, drew attention to the 'pre-occupation in the developed world with producing ever higher standards of educational outcomes in a quest to be economically competitive and in the knowledge that unskilled jobs are disappearing and that those that remain are increasingly filled by immigrants'.

It is important to note at this stage that London Challenge had the active involvement of a government Minister. In the early period this had been Stephen Twigg, who was later followed by Andrew Adonis. As I have noted, in Greater Manchester this role was taken by a Minister who was Member of Parliament for one of our local areas. As the story of the Challenge evolves through subsequent chapters, the presence of this high status political leadership should not be overlooked.

London Challenge

Bearing all of this information in mind, in late 2007 I spent some days working with London Challenge colleagues. This included attendance at the fortnightly meetings of the Challenge Advisers, as well as shadowing some of them as they visited their 'Keys to Success' schools; that is, schools designated as requiring more intensive support.

The meetings were in two parts. One of these involved civil servants in updating the Advisers on current policy developments. The other part of the meeting was described as the 'professional hour'. This was a time when strategies were debated and opportunities provided to share experiences from the field. During one of these discussions, an Adviser whispered to me: 'We like to try quirky things you know'. This confirmed for me the importance of the Advisers having freedom to use their extensive experience to assess situations and try out novel ways of moving schools forward.

I found out that, typically, each Adviser worked with four or five Keys to Success schools, remembering, of course, that at this stage the focus in London was only on the secondary sector. I also heard that most of these schools had established a project board, which usually included the headteacher, the chair of governors and a local authority officer. The meetings of these boards provided opportunities for the Challenge Advisers to keep up to date with implementation processes. In this respect, it was evident that the writing of field notes following school visits was seen as an important strategy, not least in helping the civil servants to keep an eye on developments in the field.

One factor that concerned me was to do with how the Keys to Success schools were designated and announced. It was evident that Tim Brighouse's role had been crucial in this sense, not least in getting across to these schools their crucial strategic role in kick starting system-wide improvement. In this sense, the choice of the title, 'Keys to Success', was, in my view, a masterstroke. In Chapter 3, I explain how we developed the idea in ways that fitted the circumstances we met in Greater Manchester.

Visits with Challenge Advisers to some of the Keys to Success schools gave me further insights into how this worked on the ground. So, for example, one of the secondary schools I visited was in a very poor area, with over 50 per cent of its students entitled to free school meals. It was described to me as having been 'in and out of categories', referring to the fact that over many years it had experienced a series of painful inspections. Apparently at one stage the school had been closed for two weeks because a man was living in the roof!

A package of support had been organized for the school, mainly from another school, that provided coaching for heads of subject departments and regular inputs of strong teaching provided by a group of advanced skills teachers.[3] Meanwhile, I was told that a major problem was that the headteacher and local authority staff had been reluctant to confront the fact that there were a number of poorly per-forming senior staff, one of whom was the deputy head. In this situation, the Challenge Adviser had eventually insisted that formal action must be taken and, by the time of my visit, a new deputy was in place, somebody who had been located via the well-established London Challenge networks.

Reflecting on visits such as this, I saw a pattern of activity that seemed to be relevant to the challenges we were about to face in Greater Manchester. For me, the key to it was the skill of the Challenge Adviser in working with a school's senior staff to assess the context. What was also important was the freedom they were given to act quickly and decisively, albeit within a context in which they were held accountable for their schools' progress. In this way, the Adviser was then in a position to determine the nature of any external support that might be needed. Then, through the combined knowledge base that existed within the London Challenge team regarding where relevant expertise was likely to be available, the Adviser was in a position to commission appropriate support, whether that be from another school or some other external agency.

One source of information regarding sources of support was provided through the Families of Schools data system, within which schools across London were grouped on the basis of the profiles of the communities they served. In this way, schools could compare their current levels of student achievement with those found in similar schools. And, in so doing, they could locate schools with relevant strengths that they might choose to approach for support. My instinct was that more could be made of this approach by actively orchestrating arrangements through which schools within a Family might work together. In Chapter 4, I explain what we learnt about using this approach.

Through the Adviser's involvement in the process of assessing the context and formulating a plan of action, he or she was in a position to evaluate whether other, more drastic actions were needed in order to secure the school's improvement. And, of course, in some instances this might mean a decision that the head, or other senior staff, did not have the capabilities to lead the process. In such situations, individual Advisers could draw on the experience of their colleagues in determining appropriate ways forward. The fact that they carried the authority of a Minister also gave them a mandate to insist that local authority staff make use of their statutory powers to intervene.

I also learnt about the way London had developed its own leadership strategy. This was led by headteachers with support from the National College for School Leaders, and had introduced the concept of successful headteachers working as consultant leaders, providing support for schools experiencing difficulties. Another idea that was then emerging was that of 'teaching schools', a concept that was later to become part of English national policy.

Through my discussions it became evident that a small number of committed heads were, in effect, driving all of these efforts to develop system leadership across London, including George Berwick, the head of Ravens Wood School in Bromley, whom I knew from my days in Cambridge. Writing in my diary in October 2007, I noted: 'Greater Manchester needs a George'. As in turned out, we had the good fortunate to have the involvement of Janet Woods, a former primary head whom I had worked with on a number of earlier local authority led activities. She took on this role, using a rather different but equally effective style.

My sense was that the London Challenge strategy was largely bypassing the 33 local authorities, apart from the support provided to five that were seen as a cause for concern. Indeed, in discussion, several of the Advisers gave the impression that they saw the authorities as an irrelevance. One said, 'We do not ask the permission of LAs before we act'. Another commented, 'It's the challenge to the schools that matters'. Reflecting on this, I remained of the view that, as far as Greater

Manchester was concerned, the involvement of the local authorities was necessary and inevitable, not least in respect to developing an approach that would have a chance of being sustainable. At that stage, however, I had little appreciation of how difficult this would prove to be, as I explain in Chapter 7.

Considering what was to happen a few years later, it was interesting that at that stage in London the newly-emerging academies were seen as being outside the remit of the Challenge, partly because they had access to additional funding to support their development. Whilst this policy stance also applied in Greater Manchester as far as the Keys to Success programme was concerned, academies were actively involved in many of the other Challenge initiatives, not least the work of the Families of Schools.

Reflecting on these experiences, in the *Times Educational Supplement* (8 February 2008), I was quoted as saying, 'There are things we are bringing up the M6[4] and it would be foolish not to take advice from London, but we have our own circumstances to deal with.' The article explained that the underlying problems of poverty were similar in the two areas but had to be dealt with in different ways.

Setting up the Challenge

During the early months of the Greater Manchester Challenge, prior to the formal launch in April 2008, the absence of a defined way of working led to something of a policy vacuum. Sometimes this was filled by what seemed to me to be rather premature events organized by the National College, at which a variety of speakers from outside the region gave their versions of what should happen. These were usually not well received, by headteachers in particular. This reinforced in my mind the message I had picked up in London that our strategy had to be determined and taken forward by local people, rather than based on the thoughts of external experts.

From the outset it was decided that there would be two civil servants stationed in the Manchester office of the DCSF. A number of others would travel up from London on a weekly basis. It was also agreed that a Steering Group should be formed, made up of five representatives of the local authorities (four directors and one chief executive), a representative from the further education sector, and a small number of civil servants. The Minister attended occasionally and I chaired the meetings. Interestingly, the Minister wanted there to be another steering group made up of students, but sadly this never happened.

As I explain in Chapter 7, the Steering Group was a context in which many of the tensions that existed between representatives of national and local government were played out, particularly during the first two years or so. In this context, I found myself playing the roles of negotiator and peacekeeper. At the same time, I saw it as a means of getting high level buy-in for our developing strategy, such that I could state, authentically, that what we were doing had been formally agreed. The difficulties that did occur mostly arose when group members attempted to engage with matters of detail, particularly in relation to the use of funding. Thinking about this at the time of the first meeting of the group in late 2007, I noted in my diary:

> The Steering Group must not get bogged down in detail. We need to pro-
> vide them with reports and invite their thoughts on the overall strategic
> vision.

The overall agenda for the Challenge was set out in a vision document, titled
'Raising the bar, closing the gap'. This provided an overview of the strategy, a
description of the context and what was for me a worrying list of 'pledges'. These
consisted of intended outcomes that, as far as I could determine, had been generated
through consultation with colleagues within the DCSF, many of whom wanted to
argue for their particular areas of concern. Despite the frequent reference to partnership during the announcement of the Challenge, at this early stage there was
little heard of the views of the local authorities, nor of practitioners in the schools.

Crucial to our strategy was the appointment of the team of Challenge Advisers
whose work was to follow the pattern established in London. These were to be
highly experienced practitioners – mainly former headteachers – who each had a
track record of leading educational improvement in challenging contexts. This
message was indicated in a national advertisement in October 2007, which stated:

> The Advisers will work with primary and secondary schools in the most chal-
> lenging circumstances ... The aim will be to rapidly raise attainment where
> necessary and seek long term and sometimes radical solutions to improve the
> life chances and opportunities for pupils. Successful Advisers will be allocated
> approximately five to ten schools across the City Challenge areas. They will
> be accountable to DCSF but will work closely with Local Authorities and
> School Improvement Partners (SIPs).[5]

The advert went on to say:

> We expect the school Advisers to provide resource of between 75 (guaranteed
> minimum commitment) – 125 days per year. However, should an Adviser wish
> to take on the additional Primary Lead, Behaviour Management and/or the
> English as an additional language advisory function then these will be consid-
> ered as additional days. Please note that the exact timing and phasing in of
> resource will be reviewed and agreed with the Department on an ongoing basis.
>
> We invite tenders from high calibre individuals and companies with demon-
> strable experience and track record of strategic engagement and delivery at a
> senior level over many years. Examples of past experiences could be but not
> limited to headship, Senior LA Advisor, HMI experience or equivalent.
>
> To be eligible for the school Advisers positions, you will have a proven
> track record of expertise in working with primary and/or secondary schools
> in the most challenging circumstance, to raise education standards in terms of
> improving attainment at relevant Key Stages, narrowing attainment gaps,
> improving the quality of teaching and learning and building capacity so that
> improvement is sustainable.

Over the following months a series of interviews took place with a panel consisting of a civil servant, a local authority officer and me. By late 2007, an initial group of eight Advisers had been appointed and we held our first meeting at the University of Manchester in February 2008. These half-day meetings were to continue on a fortnightly basis for the following three years.

Contextual analysis

By the time the team of Advisers got together, an initial analysis of the Greater Manchester school system, carried out by colleagues in the DCSF, had provided a crude baseline against which progress was to be measured. Interestingly, this was not all bad news since it became clear that recent years had seen some improvement in test and examination results. For example, in the GCSE examination taken by most English young people at the end of year 11, the percentage attaining 5 or more A★ to C grades had risen by 20 percentage points between 1997 and 2007, which was greater than the increase nationally of 17 percentage points.

Nevertheless, real challenges remained, particularly in some of the more deprived local areas of the city region. For example, Table 2.1 shows the variation in improvement in primary school tests across the highest and lowest performing Greater Manchester local authorities between 1997 and 2007. It indicates that in the lowest performing authority there had been only a seven percentage point increase in the number of pupils attaining what the government referred to as 'the recommended level' in maths in the ten-year period.

The initial analysis also indicated that, across the city region, 10,000 children and young people attended schools that were 'weak', according to Ofsted's categorization (i.e. as a result of inspections), 10 schools were 'in special measures', and a further 14 had a 'notice to improve'. Commenting on this, the vision document argued that it was 'unacceptable that so many children and young people are in schools where the standard of education and provision is inadequate. In addition over 3,500 children and young people attend schools below the new Key Stage 2 floor target and the Key Stage 4 floor target'. It was also noted that a further area of concern was low attendance and persistent absence. In fact, the Greater Manchester average attendance was slightly above the national average, with absence in 2006 at 8.2 per cent, falling to 7.9 per cent in 2007.

Alongside this initial contextual analysis, my early discussions pointed to potential resources that might be drawn on to support our strategy. For example, there were four universities, who through their 'Aim Higher' partnership were working

TABLE 2.1 Percentage increase in number of primary age pupils attaining recommended level between 1997 and 2007

	English	Mathematics	Science
Lowest performing authority	11	7	12
Highest performing authority	23	22	25

together in helping schools to raise aspirations amongst students from disadvantaged backgrounds. We also had the involvement of Future Leaders, a national programme that sought to 'grow' a new generation of potential heads for urban schools. Linked to this, we had seen the introduction in the city region of Teach First, a charity that was committed to get top graduates to spend two years teaching in urban schools. Such initiatives were potentially important and I saw it as part of my role to engage them in our overall strategy for the city region.

Engaging stakeholders

In order to engage stakeholders across the education system, between November 2007 and April 2008, the Minister and I carried out a series of school visits, one in each of the ten local authorities. These visits were also intended to inform local media of the Challenge. Each visit included a short tour of the school, orchestrated by the headteacher, discussions with groups of children, and meetings with parents. Finally, there was a meeting with senior representatives of the local authority, including politicians, to share ideas about how the Challenge should proceed.

In all these contexts, the Minister demonstrated a remarkable capacity to engage with stakeholders in an informed and supportive way. Prior to each visit she received extensive written briefings from civil servants regarding the context we were to visit and the people involved. It was very clear that she read this material closely and sometimes civil servants would complain to me informally that she was not satisfied with the extent of the briefing material.

The first of the visits illustrated the nature of the difficulties that we were facing in respect to some of schools in challenging circumstances. Not an extreme case in respect to the levels of disadvantage in its local community, the school nevertheless was performing poorly in terms of factors such as attendance, which stood at 91.8 per cent, and levels of attainment on the national examination taken by most English students around the age of 16. The school was housed in a dreadful series of buildings, spread across a field. Competing for students with two other local schools that had much better reputations, its numbers were falling rapidly. It was also experiencing difficulties in attracting teachers. As far as we could make out, the local authority seemed to have had no success in turning round this sad situation and, despite protests from some of the parents, was planning to close it down.

Many of the visits further reinforced in my mind the view I had that most of the expertise we needed was readily available in the schools of Greater Manchester. We saw, for example, splendid examples of how schools serving relatively poor districts were providing children with rich educational diets, including fabulous art, drama, music and science experiences, and, in so doing, achieving levels of attainment that were reflected in the league tables and through the judgements of inspectors. We also heard about the ways that some schools were working closely with families and local communities to support these efforts. At the same time, I had a growing sense in many parts of the city region that local authority staff were not mobilizing this expertise in order to help move the system as a whole forward. In some instances, too, there were strong indications that local authority staff were failing to intervene in schools that were clearly in difficulty. In the case of one authority, it was also evident that headteachers had little or no confidence in the Director of Children's Services, whom they felt was even scared to attend their meetings. Despite having a relatively large staff of officers, its record for school attendance (students and staff) and student attainment was amongst the worst in the country.

One local authority stood out in this respect. On all sorts of indicators of school performance it appeared to be successful, so much so that it was annually one of the top authorities in the country. What was noticeable in that authority was that it had a relatively small number of officers who appeared to know the schools well and who were quick to step in when they spotted trouble. Significantly, their usual response in such situations was to connect the school to another that was known to have strengths in the areas that needed improving. Unsurprisingly, senior officers in this authority had been reluctant to get involved in the Challenge, arguing that they should be allocated their proportion of the budget to support the further development of their effective practices.

As things developed the work of this particular authority was used as a role model to inspire the rethinking of practices in the other nine and, as I explain in Chapter 7, some of its officers provided direct support to certain of the other authorities that were experiencing difficulties in supporting their local schools. In this important sense, our emphasis on school-to-school support was mirrored by the encouragement of cross-border cooperation at the authority level.

An emerging framework

It was immediately obvious to me that the goals that had been laid out in the vision document would necessitate reforms at all levels of the education service. This being the case, the aim was to encourage experimentation and innovation, rather than simply doing more of the same. Significantly, there was government approval for taking this approach, as signalled by the active involvement of the Minister.

The Challenge set out to take advantage of new opportunities this provided, not least as a result of adopting an approach that drew on the strengths that existed in different parts of the city region. These included possibilities for: tackling educational issues that cut across local authority boundaries (such as, declining school performance at the secondary school stage, the development of personalized learning pathways for older students); linking educational issues to broader social and economic agendas (such as, population mobility, employment, transport, housing, community safety, health), and the freer exchange of expertise, resources, and lessons from innovations.

As I have explained, the overall approach of the Challenge emerged from an analysis of the local context, using both statistical data and local intelligence provided by stakeholders through a series of both formal and informal consultations. This drew attention to areas of concern and also helped to pinpoint a range of human resources that could be mobilized in order to support improvement efforts.

Recognizing the potential of these resources, it was decided that networking and collaboration – within and across schools – should be the key strategies for strengthening the overall improvement capacity of the system.

During a period of unprecedented centralization in the English education system this approach was somewhat unusual, to say the least. One of my concerns, therefore, was to get this message across to colleagues in the field, particularly those in the schools and local authorities. Building on what I had learnt in London, I felt that use of language was crucial in this respect. Consequently, we adopted some of the concepts used in London, such as 'Families of Schools' and 'Keys to Success', that helped to signal that a different approach was being developed.

In a similar way, and in an attempt to create the sense of a common purpose, it was agreed that the focus of Challenge activities would be on 'three As'. These were that all children and young people: should have high *Aspirations* for their own learning and life chances; are ensured *Access* to high quality educational experiences; and *Achieve* the highest possible standards in learning. These terms were then incorporated into the Challenge logo.

The emphasis on collaboration and experimentation was further signalled by other carefully chosen language used to talk about the Challenge – formally and informally – at meetings and through a monthly newsletter sent out to schools. For example, frequent mention was made of the importance of 'moving knowledge around', recognizing that 'most of the expertise that is needed is here in Greater Manchester', and 'getting behind those in schools who can make things happen'. I also reminded people that 'this is not about doing more of the same', encouraging people to understand that we did have a degree of freedom to experiment, albeit within a context where were all under pressure 'to deliver'. For example, in one of our early newsletters to schools I wrote:

> Taking forward this massive agenda is a major commitment that requires the collective commitment of everybody involved in education across Greater Manchester. At the same time it opens up new opportunities for creativity and innovation.
>
> As we have stressed from the outset, the Greater Manchester Challenge is not about doing more of the same. Rather it involves processes of experimentation in order to find more effective ways of reaching out to all children and young people. If we can work together the possibilities for improvement are endless. This is why I hope that everybody who reads this Newsletter will want to get involved.

These themes were further explained in a discussion paper I prepared in early 2008 for the first meeting of the Challenge Advisers and civil servants. In it, I set out the direction that we were proposing to take, based on discussions that had taken place over the previous few months, both in London and with stakeholders in Greater Manchester. The content of what was the first of many such discussions papers was as follows:

This paper sets out to stimulate discussion amongst partners regarding the overall strategy for the Challenge. In it, I have attempted to draw together ideas that have been put forward during recent consultations. In so doing, I have kept in mind the overall purpose, which is to improve educational outcomes and life chances for all young people in Greater Manchester.

Opportunities. The Challenge sets out to develop a strong culture of learning in all schools that will lead to a sharp drop in underperformance, not least in relation to English and maths. This will require a focus on narrowing the attainment gap between learners from advantaged and disadvantaged backgrounds. It will be linked to efforts to raise aspirations and improve life chances for all young people, in particular amongst vulnerable groups. It is intended that all of this will lead to a significant increase in the number of schools that are outstanding in terms of their capacity to achieve positive outcomes for all of their students.

These ambitious goals will require the development of powerful strategies for breaking the link between disadvantage and educational underachievement. They will necessitate reforms at all levels of the education service. This being the case, the aim must be to encourage experimentation and innovation, rather than simply doing more of the same.

In thinking about the development of the strategy, it will be important to take advantage of the new opportunities that are provided as a result of adopting an approach that draws on the strengths that exist in different local authorities.

The paper went on to suggest that the emerging strategy – which would draw on lessons from the London Challenge, as well as evidence from international research on urban school improvement – should involve three linked strands of activity. These were explained as follows:

Strand 1: Intervening directly. This will take the form of a series of rapid and intensive efforts to bring about significant improvements in relation to schools and groups of learners that are currently underachieving. These will include:

1.1 Keys to Success schools – This will be a bespoke programme of support for schools facing particularly challenging circumstances. It will be led by a team of expert advisers who will work closely with headteachers in analysing their school contexts and designing relevant improvement plans. Linking with local authority staff and school improvement partners, these Challenge Advisers will broker appropriate external support in order to strengthen school leadership teams, improve teaching, raise student aspirations and improve outcomes for young people,

1.2 More intensive support – Where there is found to be a need for more intensive support, the Challenge Adviser will facilitate the creation of an improvement board. This board will mobilise support and coordinate improvement efforts. Usually these schools will also be linked with a partner school that can offer additional support. As far as possible, the Challenge Advisers will work closely with local authority staff on these activities in ways that are intended to strengthen local expertise.

1.3 Targeted support for disadvantaged students – Focused on all schools in the region, this will involve efforts to narrow achievement gaps between disadvantaged and other students through bespoke solutions related to the 'Every Child Matters' agenda.[6] Specifically, there will be a focus on ensuring that all young people leave school with functional skills in English and maths, understanding how to learn, think creatively, take risks and handle change. Examples of outstanding practice in relation to this agenda will be identified and used to stimulate and support improvements efforts in other contexts.

1.4 Raising aspirations – A key goal must be to raise the aspirations and expectations of all children, young people and families, not least amongst gifted and talented students from disadvantaged backgrounds. Specific activities will involve listening to the voices of students, seeing them as partners in learning, and mobilizing them in taking action to create more inclusive learning contexts within their schools. These initiatives will build on excellent practices that already exist within some schools in the region. At the same time, extensive use will be made of the media to provide the wider community with positive messages of the way that schools in Greater Manchester are making a difference to the life chances of young people.

1.5 Leadership development – These activities will be specially designed to support improvements across the Challenge. They will include: 'consultant leaders' coaching less experienced headteachers; a 'teaching schools' programme, whereby high performing schools (or, in some instances, departments) are deployed to offer direct support to schools facing leadership challenges; professional programmes for middle leaders and succession planning to develop the next generation of leaders; and programmes designed to meet specific local needs, such as the 'Investing in Diversity' scheme in London, which supports the development of leadership skills and aspirations amongst teachers from ethnic minorities.

Strand 2: More effective networking. Both within and across schools and local authorities, this will be central to the strategy of the Greater Manchester Challenge. In this way, emphasis will be placed on making far more effective use of the best practice that already exists within the region. Activities that will help to encourage and strengthen networking include:

2.1 Families of Schools – This is a data tool for primary and secondary schools that will allow them to compare themselves against others with similar students and to share best practice. Previous experience in London has shown that the Families serve as a powerful starting point for a range of work covering targeted student interventions, school-to-school collaboration and teacher professional development.

2.2 Area-wide solutions – Efforts will be made to develop more effective solutions to problems that exist across the local authorities. For example, within Greater Manchester it may be necessary to find ways of ensuring that parental choice is not disadvantaging certain groups of learners. In London, such approaches helped local authorities create: a city-wide admissions system; a prospectus for 14–19 provision; and a quality control system for supply teachers.

2.3 Theme groups – Various working groups involving relevant staff from across the local authorities will be established. These groups will be set up to encourage innovatory activities in relation to key themes within the Challenge, such as the use of data, responses to vulnerable groups, raising expectations amongst students and families, responding to gifted and talented students from disadvantaged backgrounds, the use of student voice as an improvement strategy, and supporting the participation of new arrivals and bilingual learners.

2.4 Improving learning – A key goal must be to 'raise the game' of all teachers across Greater Manchester, focusing directly on the improvement of learning. Use will be made of 'lesson study', a systematic procedure – well established in some Asian countries – that, under the right conditions, can be powerful in improving the effectiveness of the learning experiences that teachers provide for all of their students. Lesson study involves groups of practitioners in planning a lesson together and then observing the responses of students as each member of the group teaches the lesson. Networks of schools will be encouraged to set up lesson study groups in order to spread expertise and encourage greater experimentation regarding teaching and learning.

2.5 Working with partners – Through the Challenge, efforts will be made to coordinate the efforts of different partners that have the potential to contribute to better educational outcomes for disadvantaged students. In particular, there will be a need to strengthen the interface between schools and other services, including children's centres and further education provision. Strong links will also be made with the work of the National Strategies, Teach First, Future Leaders and Aim Higher initiatives. The local universities will be key players in this respect, and particular efforts will be made to strengthen partnerships between higher education and secondary schools.

Strand 3: Aiming for sustainable development. Ensuring that improvements continue is a predictable problem for all educational improvement efforts. The Challenge will address this problem by:

3.1 Working with local authorities – Through the involvement of its highly experienced team of Advisers, it is intended that the Challenge will help to build the capacity of local authorities to foster improvements in urban education. These efforts will focus on ensuring that education services are designed around the needs of each child, with the expectation that all learners will achieve high standards. Networking arrangements between the authorities, involving staff at different levels, will assist in ensuring that best practices are shared across the region. Where appropriate, groups of local authorities will be provided with support in order to create 'collaboratives' that will strengthen their pooling of expertise and resources

3.2 Supporting school improvement – Each authority will be asked to formulate its own plan for using the Challenge to strengthen arrangements for supporting school improvement, particularly in relation to schools facing challenging contexts. These arrangements must challenge assumptions that students' chances of success are linked to socio-economic background, gender or ethnicity. A think-tank of senior school improvement staff will meet regularly with colleagues from the Challenge in order to review progress on these plans and to support one another in experimenting in order to create more effective practices

3.3 Involving families and communities – Emphasis will be placed on strengthening the roles of families as co-educators in raising aspirations and improving achievement, building on existing good practices across the authorities. A communication strategy will be developed in order to draw community attention to the efforts being made to improve the quality of education provided for all children and young people. The direct involvement of the Minister and local MPs will be important in reinforcing the high status of these efforts. Occasional celebration events will be used to publicise successes.

3.4 Linking school improvement to community development – Research suggests that effective urban school improvement requires close links with developments in communities, and with external political and economic institutions. With this in mind, the aim will be to work closely with the Chief Executives and their senior colleagues in the ten authorities in order to connect the work of the Challenge to larger overarching plans for 'place shaping'.

3.5 Developing plans for the development of provision – The Schools Commissioner will lead on developing a conurbation-wide plan to ensure that the whole area offers a diverse range of provision – such as academies, trusts, all-through schools and various forms of federation – in order to transform schools suffering intractable problems that have been unable to improve their performance. The Challenge will support these radical moves in order to ensure that they contribute to overall improvement efforts across all schools and colleges in their areas.

Looking back, it strikes me now that the paper incorporates an interesting and, at times, uneasy mix of ideas derived from my own experience – including my involvement in London – alongside others that related to the policy agenda of central government.

The strategy

During the first year of the Challenge various methods were introduced in order to 'move knowledge around'. And by the middle of the second year of the initiative, the team of Advisers, civil servants and I had formulated a diagram that illustrated how these elements were linked. This was used to help stakeholders have a sense of our overall strategy (see Figure 2.1).

In what follows I summarize the elements of the approach, the details of which are explained in subsequent chapters.

Keys to Success

In terms of schools working in highly disadvantaged contexts, we found that school-to-school partnerships were the most powerful means of fostering improvements. Most notably, what we referred to as the Keys to Success programme led to striking improvements in the performance of some 200 schools facing the most challenging circumstances. There was also evidence that the progress that these schools made helped to trigger improvement across the system, not least as a result of the carefully brokered support provided by other schools, as explained in Chapter 3. Importantly, we saw how such partnerships – usually involving pairs or trios of schools – can benefit all the schools involved, leading me to argue that by helping others you help yourself. At the same time, I explain that it is important to recognize that such arrangements are difficult to organize. Indeed, where poorly conceptualized and managed, they can simply lead to lots of talk and little action that makes a difference to the learning of children and young people.

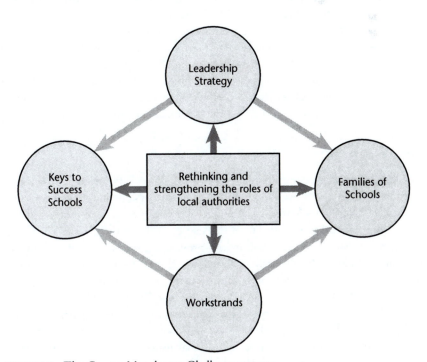

FIGURE 2.1   The Greater Manchester Challenge strategy

As the Keys to Success programme grew in strength, it became necessary to introduce other arrangements for helping its impact to continue and, indeed, to widen its influence across the system. With this in mind, new initiatives emerged, such as 'Stepping Up', 'Closing the Gap' and 'Good to Great', explanations of which are also provided in Chapter 3.

Families of Schools

In an attempt to engage all schools in the city region in processes of networking and collaboration, Families of Schools were set up, using a data system that groups schools on the basis of the prior attainment of their students and their socio-economic home backgrounds. There were 58 primary Families and 11 secondary, each of which had between 12 and 20 schools from different local authorities. The strength of this approach is that it groups together schools that serve similar populations whilst, at the same time, encouraging partnerships amongst schools that are not in direct competition with one another because they do not serve the same neighbourhoods.

In Chapter 4, I draw out lessons from these activities regarding how networks of schools can be made effective, recognizing once again that such approaches can easily become talk shops. In this respect, I argue that data is a crucial factor in creating networks that are more likely to lead to action amongst the school partners. So, the performance of schools within a Family could be compared in terms of the overall attainment levels of their students and the improvements that have occurred over the previous three years.

Such varied performance amongst Family members offered possibilities for using differences as a resource to stimulate the sharing of expertise. It also provided the stimulus for joint efforts to innovate. Within the Challenge, the aim of this was to: improve the performance of every school within a Family; increase the numbers of outstanding schools; reduce the gap between high and low performing groups of learners; and improve outcomes for particular vulnerable groups of students.

The work strands

In talking about the various strategies for moving knowledge around, many head-teachers reported that it was important that the partnerships and networks that we created involved schools from different local authorities. Indeed, one secondary head commented that, for him, all of this had been the 'game-changer'. This suggests that cross-border collaboration can provide a mechanism for encouraging innovation – although, as I have suggested, sometimes it can simply lead to time-consuming meetings that have little direct impact on learners in classrooms.

As part of the Challenge we introduced a series of what we referred to as 'work strands' in an attempt to use cross-border collaboration to inject further innovation and pace into the system. Each of these initiatives was led by one of the local authority partners and focused on educational issues facing all local authorities, linking school improvement efforts to broader social and economic agendas.

Looking back now, I feel more effort should have been put into strengthening this approach as a means of drawing on wider community resources in support of schools. In Chapter 5, I describe some of the initiatives that occurred in order to suggest what else might be done in this respect. In so doing, I draw attention to the extensive resources within an urban conurbation such as Greater Manchester that can be drawn on to support the efforts of schools to improve the life chances of all of their students. First and foremost, of course, there are the resources of family members. Beyond these are resources in local businesses, sports and arts organizations, community and faith groups, the media and institutions of higher education. My argument is that if we are to find ways of giving all young people more options in their lives we need to involve the resources that exist within the wider communities.

The leadership strategy

Moving an education system forward such that it makes better use of the energy and expertise that lies dormant to varying degrees within schools, between schools and beyond schools, involves major changes in thinking, practice and relationships. It follows that this will not happen by chance. Rather, it has to be managed and led. Within the Greater Manchester Challenge, headteachers were seen as having a central role in this respect, acting as what Hopkins (2007) refers to as 'system leaders'. That is to say, they were invited to accept responsibility for the progress of other schools as well as their own. The good news is that our experience suggests that many successful headteachers are motivated by the idea of taking on such roles.

By the end of the Challenge, there were some 170 or so outstanding headteachers designated as system leaders.[7] Increasingly, over the three years of the initiative, they drove forward improvement efforts across the city region. In addition to their involvement in the Families of Schools and the partnerships set up to support Keys to Success schools, they explored other mechanisms for making better use of the expertise that exists within the schools.

In describing these developments in Chapter 6, I explain how my colleagues and I saw them as an important means of addressing our major concern regarding the challenge of sustainability, knowing that this had been a problem in many other large scale urban improvement projects. As I will explain, at the time of writing, over three years after the end of the Greater Manchester Challenge, there is strong evidence that the processes involved are still continuing.

Rethinking the roles of local authorities

The creation of a system for improvement that is driven by schools themselves, and that involves cooperation between schools and other community organizations, begs questions regarding the roles of local authorities. Indeed, it raises the possibility that the involvement of a middle level administrative structure may not even be necessary.

The experience of Greater Manchester suggests that local authority staff can have an important role to play, not least in acting as the conscience of the system – making sure that all children and young people are getting a fair deal within an increasingly diverse system of education. In order to do this, they need to know the big picture about what is happening in their communities, identifying priorities for action and brokering collaboration. This required significant structural and cultural changes, with local authorities moving away from a command and control perspective, solely focused within their own boundaries, towards one of enabling and facilitating collaborative action across the city region. At times, local authority colleagues found these changes challenging, particularly during a time of reducing budgets.

In Chapter 7, I explain how the strengthening of cross-border cooperation at many levels provided contexts within which mutual support could be provided in addressing these concerns. In this way, officers and support staff at various levels were able to assist one another in addressing new policy demands. This involved moments of tension and, sometimes, conflict that arose from the different views that existed as to what direction to follow in order to rethink the roles of local authorities. Whilst, at times, these arose as a result of differences between senior colleagues within schools and local authorities, the actions of representatives of central government were also a factor in creating power struggles. All of this throws light on the changes in thinking and practice that are needed at that national level in order to foster the conditions within which self-improving systems can develop.

Assessing the impact

After three years the impact of the Challenge was significant in respect to overall improvements in test and examination results and, indeed, the way the education system carries out its business. So, for example, by 2011, Greater Manchester primary schools outperformed national averages on the tests taken by all children in England. And, in the public examinations taken by almost all young people at 16, in 2011 secondary schools in Greater Manchester improved faster than schools nationally, with the schools serving the most disadvantaged communities making three times more improvement than schools across the country. Importantly, the two local authorities with the lowest levels of attainment were the ones that showed the greatest progress between 2007 and 2011. Significantly, both authorities had a mix of community and faith schools, alongside a range of sponsored academies. During the same period, the number of schools below the government's floor standard[8] decreased more than it did in other areas of the country. In addition, the proportion of 'good' and 'outstanding' schools, as determined by the national inspection system increased, despite the introduction of a more challenging framework.

An independent evaluation of the City Challenge programme in the Black Country, Greater Manchester and London concluded that, overall, it had been successful in achieving its objectives (Hutchings *et al.*, 2012). Commenting on this, the authors of the report argue:

Clearly a great many factors contributed to these improvements, including national policies and strategies and the considerable efforts of headteachers and staff. However, these factors apply everywhere in the country. The most plausible explanation for the greater improvement in Challenge areas is that the City Challenge programme was responsible. The vast majority of stakeholders at all levels who contributed to this evaluation attributed the additional improvements that have been made in these areas to the work of City Challenge.

(p.vi)

The evaluators concluded that the strategic factors contributing to its success were the time-scale; the focus on specific urban areas; flexibility of approach; use of expert Advisers and bespoke solutions; school staff learning from practice in other schools; and the programme ethos of trust, support and encouragement. At the same, it should be noted that others have offered alternative possible explanations for the positive impact, including Greaves, Macmillan and Sibieta (2014) who point to the positive impact of the increase in the proportion of pupils from ethnic minorities in London and Manchester.

The evaluations that have taken place have also noted that City Challenge has had a very wide range of legacies nationally, as signalled by the content of a White Paper issued shortly after the election of the new, coalition government (DFE, 2010). This sets out the government's vision for a self-improving education system, stating that:

Our aim should be to create a school system which is more effectively self-improving... It is also important that we design the system in a way which allows the most effective practice to spread more quickly and the best schools and leaders to take greater responsibility and extend their reach.

(p.73)

On 11 June 2011 the Secretary of State for Education, Michael Gove, gave a speech where he argued that, in order to address the issue of educational underperformance, particularly amongst disadvantaged groups of learners, there is a need to develop a 'culture of collaboration'. With this in mind, he noted that it was good to see the development of more networks of schools and the expansion of teaching schools, and to see how efforts are being made to 'embed the success of the Greater Manchester Challenge'. Echoing similar ideas, in a speech in 13 November 2012, the then Shadow Secretary of State, Stephen Twigg, also made reference to building on the progress in Greater Manchester, emphasizing in particular the idea of 'evidence-based collaboration'.

A further impact of City Challenge has been the emergence of locally led arrangements to continue the practices that had been developed (Hutchings and Mansaray, 2013). In each of the three areas, organizations with a strong focus on schools learning from each other have been created to take forward the Challenge approaches. In London and Greater Manchester these are led by groups of head-teachers. Meanwhile, other organizations have adopted aspects of the Challenge approach to school improvement, including some local authorities that have encouraged school-led partnerships; groups of faith schools; and a growing number of academy chains (Claeys *et al.*, 2014). Commenting on such developments, a report from the House of Commons Education Committee (2013) concludes:

> Partnership working and cooperation between schools has long been part of the education landscape, whether encouraged by government or not. Nevertheless, in recent years and alongside the changing role of local authorities, school partnerships and cooperation have become an increasingly important part of what has been referred to as a 'self-improving' or 'school-led' system. This has been seen particularly in the successful London Challenge and City Challenge programmes which led to significant improvements in the schools in the areas involved. It has also been a key driver behind the rapid expansion of the academies programme.
>
> *(p. 7)*

In a review of the longer-term impact of City Challenge, Hutchings and Mansaray (2013) conclude that the improvements have been sustained in London and Manchester, but less so in the Black Country. However, they argue that all of the areas have benefited from important legacy activities. The review identifies a number of reasons behind the continuing impact of each of the Challenges, such as the timescale of the programmes, the continuity of the personnel involved and the extent to which those in the area felt 'ownership' of the Challenge. Importantly, the authors note that 'the challenges were comprehensive area-based initiatives that tackled all elements of schooling. It cannot be assumed that taking certain elements in isolation will be as effective as the combination of elements' (p.42).

Hutchings and Mansaray go on to suggest that, in the Challenge areas, the legacy has included a more outward-looking approach; more effective processes and strategies; higher expectations of pupils; stronger coaching skills among middle and senior leaders; and a greater awareness of what to do to improve further. While this is a substantial record, the authors note that the current arrangements and structures for school improvement still have considerable limitations. Most important among these is fragmentation and lack of structure, which may result in vulnerable schools not getting the support they need. All of which points to the need for coordination of further efforts to support the maturing of self-improving systems, a theme I address in Chapter 7.

Drawing lessons

Within such a large scale and socially complex project, it is, of course, difficult to make causal claims in respect to the particular factors that led to improvements, especially within an initiative that incorporated such a wide range of strategies. It is also the case that I walk a delicate line here in using measures such as test scores and inspection reports to describe the success of the intervention, given the concerns I have about their reliability and perverse impact. On the other hand, whilst recognizing the dangers of narrowing our view of what education is about, a focus on attainment is justifiable because it undeniably has important consequences for life chances (Kerr and West, 2010).

All of this draws attention to the highly contentious nature of improvement in schools, since, as my colleagues and I have argued:

> One person's view of an improving institution may be another's vision of educational hell. This means that we cannot understand improvement in education without considering the values underlying the changes we would like to take place.
>
> *(Ainscow, Booth and Dyson, 2006, p. 11)*

Bearing this in mind, the argument I develop in the chapters that follow is informed by the notion of 'school improvement with attitude'. For me this means a deep commitment to equity which leads me to challenge many assumptions about school improvement and educational reform that imply a simple 'what works' formula (Ainscow, 2013). Rather, I offer a different way of thinking about system-level improvement, one that involves an analysis of particular contexts in order to develop strategies that make better use of available energy and expertise in order to give every child 'a fair go', as my Australian colleagues would say. My suggestion is that this way of thinking offers more promise than suggestions that seek to impose externally generated, one-size-fits-all improvement mechanisms.

There are, however, some rather obvious questions that can be asked about my analysis, not least in relation to my status within the Challenge initiative. As a researcher, I was provided with a remarkable opportunity to put into practice ideas that had emerged from years of investigating ways of developing more equitable schools and education systems. At the same time it placed me in a position of having privileged access to information regarding the way decisions are made within an education system, from the levels of government ministers and senior civil servants, through to that of teachers in the classroom. All of this provided frequent reminders of the social and political complexity involved when trying to bring about changes in the way that a system does its business.

On the other hand, as the person charged with the task of championing the Challenge, how far can my interpretations be trusted, not least because my efforts to collect data about the processes involved were largely carried out in an incidental way? My response to this concern is that, whilst readers must take it into account in determining the weight of my argument, they should recognize that my 'insider' stance enabled me to experience things in ways that researchers rarely do. It is also worth adding that, throughout the three years, a small group of my academic colleagues acted as critical friends, reading the frequent discussion papers I prepared in order to stimulate debate with stakeholders within the project, and offering their more detached views.[9] In particular, I invited them to challenge the interpretations I was making and to draw my attention to any evidence that I was falling into the trap of becoming an agent of central government.

Another obvious question relates to the large amount of funding involved: £50 million over three years. So, how far were the successes of the Challenge the result of the investment of additional money into the system? And, how viable are the approaches I am recommending without extra resources? This remains an area of debate within my mind. Certainly, the project involved a lot of additional finance. On the other hand, over the previous decade or so, far more money had been invested in the system through a plethora of national improvement strategies that had led to very little improvement in the overall performance of schools across the city region.

Keeping these caveats in mind, in the chapters that follow I reflect on statistical data compiled as part of the formal monitoring of the impact of the project, my archive of documents, and qualitative evidence collected through numerous informal observations and conversations recorded in my research diary, plus more occasional formal interviews with stakeholders, in order to draw out some lessons. At the same time, my participant observer perspective leads me to throw light on the social and political complexity involved in using these lessons.

Conclusion

This chapter has provided an overall account of the developments that occurred during the three years of the Greater Manchester Challenge, showing how pathways were created to move knowledge around and encourage joint efforts to encourage experimentation with new ways of working. It has also summarized the overall impact, which was impressive in a number of senses. At the same time, it is important to note that there remain areas of the system that are matters of concern, not least the continuing low achievements of many youngsters from disadvantaged backgrounds. Nevertheless, there are important lessons to be drawn from this intensive effort to move an urban education system forward. These are, I suggest, lessons that can drive improvements in different national contexts.

The first of these lessons is that **education systems have untapped potential to improve themselves**. Therefore, ongoing contextual analysis is needed in order to identify areas of concern and the human resources that can be used to support improvement efforts in relation to these issues. This emphasis on collaborative inquiry also generates evidence that can be used to facilitate collaboration within and between schools, as well as helping to kick start experimentation with new practices. It does this by making the familiar unfamiliar, as policy makers and practitioners are confronted with different perspectives on their usual working practices. As I will explain, all of this has important implications for roles and relationships at different levels of an education system, as well as for national policies.

Notes

1   Following the General Election of 2010 this was renamed the Department for Education (DfE).
2   This is the national examination taken by almost all young people at around the age of 16.

3 These were formally designated as a result of their expertise as having a role in supporting teacher development.
4 The motorway that links London and Manchester.
5 These were consultants employed by local authorities to provide professional challenge and support to a school, helping its leadership to evaluate its performance, identify priorities for improvement, and plan effective change.
6 Launched in in 2003, this was an important policy initiative in relation to children and children's services.
7 This is now part of a national scheme where outstanding headteachers are designated as National or Local Leaders of Education (N/LLEs). As such, they are expected to provide support to other schools.
8 This is the minimum standard set by government, below which schools are subject to some form of intervention.
9 Chris Chapman, Alan Dyson, Peter Farrell, Denis Mongon and Mel West acted as my critical friends throughout the project and, in so doing, contributed many ideas to the analysis presented in this book.

3

KEYS TO SUCCESS

Predictably, the process of contextual analysis that we began at the outset of the Greater Manchester Challenge drew attention to many schools across the city region whose performance – as measured on tests and examinations – was a cause for concern. Most but not all of these schools had experienced difficulties with Ofsted inspections and, as a result, had been placed in one of the two categories that during that period signalled the need for some form of formal intervention, i.e. 'special measures' or 'notice to improve'.

Building on the experience of the London Challenge, we decided to designate some of these schools as the 'Keys to Success'. As I indicated in the previous chapter, the use of this language was intended to signal a move away from deficit terminology, such as 'failing schools' or 'schools in challenging circumstances', that imply that low performance in tests and examinations arise from poor school practices, and/or dysfunctional families and communities.

Our idea for the Keys to Success schools was that by supporting their rapid improvement we would be able to create a ripple effect across the entire education system. With this in mind, our intention was to bring about rapid improvements in these schools such that others would take note. The big question was, how could we do this? Here, earlier research carried out by our University of Manchester team offered some useful leads.

Turning schools around

Much of our earlier research had focused on schools – typically, but not exclusively, those in urban contexts – where progress has been difficult to secure (Ainscow and West, 2006). Through these experiences we had seen how some schools demonstrated that it is possible to break out of the cycle of low expectations and attainment. This being the case, we had looked more closely at schools in which progress had been sustained over a period of years in order to learn more about factors that are associated with success (West, Ainscow and Stanford, 2005). To this end, we set out to find out what these schools had done, and about what it was, in the views of those involved, that had 'made the difference'.

Many of the headteachers we interviewed indicated that the main catalyst for improvement was fear of school closure, brought on by falling rolls, a history of poor performance in examinations, and the impact of negative local press coverage on the image of the school. Indeed, they felt that these pressures from outside had provided helpful levers for change, even though they often had a darker side.

Dilemmas and challenges

Headteachers were keen to argue that improving test scores is not the same as improving the quality of schooling. In this respect there was considerable reference to the strategic and, sometimes, moral dilemmas they faced in relation to their improvement efforts. In particular, they talked of tensions they had experienced between the need to raise standards, as measured by aggregate test and examination scores, and their concern as educators to focus on the needs of all of their students. So, for example, one head explained:

> Two years ago, although our A to C scores weren't impressive, our five A to Gs were over 90 per cent... So, last year we put more effort into the five A to Cs and our five A to G rate dipped. Actually, we saw this as a bit of a failure. No one really noticed and actually we got all these congratulations for the big improvements.

In talking about these concerns, some heads drew attention to more worrying effects, not the least an increase in student exclusions. For example:

> People think that when you are improving exam results that it will necessarily improve the quality of schools, and I think in many cases it does. But I think one of the consequences for us has been that there has been a fantastic increase in exclusions

The heads also talked about a series of challenges that they had had to face in order to move their schools forward. Many felt that the most significant of these was related to the need to raise the expectations of staff, students and parents. One head talked about 'making students believe in themselves, when they and their parents doubt or don't have good expectations of their academic ability'. The same person referred to the need to challenge the 'what do you expect' culture among some teachers. Another head commented:

> You see, staff and students were down trodden – the school had been slated in the national and local press. My challenge was to raise their self-esteem

and self-image, which is not an over-night job... There were hard decisions about having to release people because we were overstaffed, to tell
people they are not good enough for the job. All of those things were
challenges, but nothing compared to changing the ethos of a community
that didn't think that it was any good and didn't have any right to be any
good

Some of the heads also faced significant difficulties when it appeared that their own
expectations clashed with those of parents. For example:

Challenging parents' perceptions was really difficult because I came in with,
you know, a clear view of the school and a very clear view of where I wanted
it to be. What I didn't expect, [was] that the parents didn't want it to change...
They were quite comfortable with the cosy school.

This need to raise expectations by challenging existing values and beliefs left some
headteachers anxious about possible implications for people's lives. They were conscious that their efforts were adding yet further pressure on staff, pupils and parents
who were already under stress. Commenting on these worries, one head said:

The regime in schools has changed... Especially for the kids who come
from extremely deprived backgrounds, such as ours, that can have greater
consequences than in other [circumstances]... The school agenda is different from the children's and parents'. The stress that this brings to children
and their parents is significant in some cases. Sometimes, the parents and the
child would prefer not to have to deal with that stress, beg us to move their
child down a set, unhappy about the extra work lessons and the extra
homework. I hadn't appreciated, really, the extent to which there was stress
in their lives normally... Many of those young people's lives and families
are lived in terrible, terrible stress. It's not just a matter of teaching the kids.
It's almost caused a change in the whole family's approach to what education is about.

Related to the importance of raising expectations, most of the heads saw the need
to get their colleagues to set appropriate targets as the second most significant challenge they faced. Mostly, they saw this in terms of expectations during lessons.
Indeed, many talked of the challenge of making sure that there was a continuous
emphasis on the improvement of teaching and learning. Talking about this, one
head explained that here 'teachers wanted to do good for the kids, but...didn't
quite realise that the kids could stand a bit more rigour'. Linked to this emphasis on
teaching and learning was the challenge of getting children to work outside of the
classroom on academic tasks and activities.

Issues to do with the wider context of the school also posed significant
challenges for many headteachers. For example, some talked about the pressures

brought about because their schools were surrounded by selection systems that 'creamed off the best students'. In addition, many of the schools faced falling rolls because of their poor image in the community; and most felt vulnerable to receiving the least able and most difficult children under local admission arrangements. Some of the schools were surrounded by areas of significant social deprivation; indeed, one head referred to a 'drugs-and-guns culture'. Many needed urgent improvements in the quality of their physical environments and, in some cases, there were also difficulties arising from split-site operations.

The recruitment and retention of staff posed particular challenges, especially where schools were known to be in difficulty and in areas where living costs are high. The labels of 'special measures' or 'serious weaknesses' tended to add to such difficulties. Some heads linked these difficulties to issues of funding. One argued that 'schools such as this are not funded appropriately'. Another felt that 'fragile funded projects are not particularly helpful', and that 'the strings attached' may inhibit schools' ability to respond appropriately to local issues and concerns. Commenting further, the same head explained: 'We incorporate very positively these government initiatives, but quite often they stymie and restrict what you want to do'.

Improvement strategies

In general terms, four inter-connected strategies were identified by a majority of the headteachers as being the most successful in raising achievement in the schools. These related to: changing the culture of the school; focusing on teaching and learning; reviewing the school day; and the purposeful use of data. At the same time, many of the heads were keen to explain that no one strategy could be regarded as the reason why their schools had improved. For example:

> I changed a thousand things to do with the school by 1 per cent. Now I think we spend more time improving one thing 1,000 per cent. The list goes on forever. Because if you're talking about raising standards the list goes to the toilet brushes, the cleaning, the food the children eat, the way staff conduct themselves. The list is endless really.

Most of the heads talked in detail about their efforts to change what they saw as being the culture of their schools. They mainly described this in terms of changing values and beliefs. This involved building relationships, strengthening morale and raising expectations. Here, it was rather noticeable that there was a concern for staff to distance themselves from notions of 'caring for' their pupils. There was also a determination amongst the headteachers to assert that their schools' business was the education of children, enabling them to meet the criteria of success as recognized nationally. Interestingly, this emphasis was even evident amongst the few that maintained that they focused on caring for the child.

A careful reading of what the heads actually said suggests that, in fact, many schools *had* increased their emphasis on what might be considered social development. It struck us that, perhaps, this apparent contradiction arose from their concern to convey the extent to which they privileged teaching and learning as *the* focus of their schools. In practice, many of the strategies intended to build relationships, morale and expectations, appeared to be strongly linked to this overall focus on teaching and learning. In this sense, the concern to foster social and emotional development can be seen as a necessary feature of successful teaching.

The focus on improving teaching and learning was seen by many of the heads as also being closely related to the needs of staff. This included a requirement to redefine roles and responsibilities, such that there were new interpretations of working relationships, management arrangements, teams and duties amongst both senior staff and teachers. Headteachers specifically tried to ensure that they were able to appoint teachers of the highest quality who were suited to the school. This also meant that those who were not perceived to be willing to take on necessary changes would be encouraged to 'move on'.

There was also a striking appreciation of the need to support teachers and, indeed, other staff, so as to enable them to operate successfully. Many of the heads were concerned to create 'a happy place' to work, 'a place where they (staff) would want to be', not least because recruitment and retention posed such difficulties. In the same way, some heads encouraged their staffs to take a similar view in relation to the pupils. In particular, they explained that they wanted teachers who would spend time talking to the pupils, both formally and informally. Indeed, this emphasis on talking to and listening to students was seen as a key strategy for school improvement. It was hardly surprising, therefore, that many of the heads saw this as something of a priority in relation to their own use of time. One head explained, 'If the kids know that you are listening and are acting on what they say, it makes a significant difference to their attitudes to school...' She added, 'It's also useful as a lever for challenging staff attitudes'.

Some heads also talked about the importance of fostering the teachers' professionalism, such that they knew that their expertise was respected and that they were trusted to conduct themselves in the best interests of the students. Emphasis was placed on developing systems that allowed members of staff to teach without interruptions. At the same time, strategies were used to challenge teachers to think about their ways of working. Here, target-setting and engagement with data were seen as being particularly important. Research evidence was used in some schools, to develop teachers' understandings of how children learn. What we see, then, is evidence of a balanced use of pressure and support, although in these schools more strategies were directed at challenging teachers than at supporting them.

The use of data was seen by all of the heads as a key factor in the improvement of teaching and learning, the curriculum, and the culture and image of the school. Of course, the way that data are used is vital in this respect. For example, one head commented that this was about:

develop[ing] a climate where people believed [that] what they were doing was having an effect – data was very useful here, target-setting – and also changing expectation, demonstrating progress. The value-added measures were crucial; then you could talk to students and show it to inspectors.

Data were also used to agitate for improvement whilst, at the same time, appearing to be non-threatening. For example:

I also have a tactic that I use with the teaching staff where I can read off data on GCSE results which shows how pupils have performed in an individual subject and how that same group of children has performed across all the other subjects. And then I can say to a head of department, you are half a grade or a grade below in your subject. And then if they say to me, 'Well, I don't get the best pupils', I say to them, 'No you may not, but still looking at the same group of children, they have achieved better in other subjects, so there are questions about yours'.

Data were also seen as a means by which the headteachers could demonstrate and, indeed, celebrate achievements:

scores tell us what the kids should be getting, [this] meant that the teachers could see what they were doing and that was crucial. Staff could see some recognition and the value they had added which was a very good thing for them… giving staff the confidence to take risks.

In the main, the headteachers attributed the success that their schools had enjoyed to the hard work of staff and students. Once the hard work started to effect positive changes, most found that 'success breeds success', and early successes, in particular for new headteachers, were significant in improving and maintaining achievements. One head explained, success became 'a big loop that feeds back on itself… Very difficult to get going' but 'once on a roll it becomes easier'. Another argued that it is 'a virtuous cycle' that 'is self-perpetuating… Now we haven't got the battles that we had. The critical mass is with us'.

It seemed that with success in motion, a 'feel-good' factor becomes present that strengthens staff and pupil confidence to achieve more. Expectations were raised, and this seemed to underpin improvements. One head suggested that for the staff in these schools, 'the past is scary' and they 'can't afford to go back to square one'. Success, on the other hand, generates visible, measurable returns in terms of the school's possibilities:

Once on a roll it becomes easier, not necessarily in terms of rigour that the staff give to it, but in the quality of the intake, of course. Having got your results up and parents having confidence in the school leads to higher attainers joining the school…. The sixth form becoming academic, not a small vocational offer, giving the kids something to reach for, and seeing the students picking up A levels and going on to university, pushes the brighter ones into doing well.

Headteachers explained that they had used every opportunity to celebrate positive achievements. This involved 'making sure everybody feels good about themselves' and that 'the students feel part of the success'. One head talked of a commitment to 'working in the tradition of success: very formal achievement evenings, celebrities in, parties, press cuttings, showing that successes are valued'.

All the heads felt that the leadership team has an important and significant role in protecting and building on past achievements. They must lead in acknowledging the hard work of staff and pupils, as well as the eventual successes. It is crucial that they keep both the staff and the pupils 'on board', ensuring that all staff and pupils know the current vision, direction and strategies of the school as it develops. Leadership also needs to be at the centre of strategies to project and protect the ethos of the school. This includes valuing the staff and pupils, encouraging 'friendly' competition amongst them, keeping the focus on teaching and learning, with attention to detail and rigorous monitoring, reviewing and evaluation. The performance management of teachers needs to be underpinned by a commitment to continuing professional development for all teachers and thoughtful induction for new teachers to the schools. Teachers need to feel supported and allowing flexibility in their teaching arrangements seems a significant way to show them support.

It is also the task of the leadership team to ensure that new avenues and opportunities for the school are explored. In particular, it is important to establish the principle that other people's ideas are welcomed and valued, and, for example, that the school development plan belongs to everybody in the school. At the same time, the school, and specifically the leadership team, has to ensure 'you don't stand still', are 'turning attention to those other things that are not yet hitting the mark' and 'focusing on each year group, constructing a programme for them within the overall ethos of improvement'.

The heads argued that the use of data had become an increasingly important way of sustaining progress. While schools are data-rich, there is evidence of them recognising the need 'to be discriminating on target-setting; there's so much data around these days, so it is a question of which data gives the best predictions'. The schools had become more adept at using data to supplement national test results with their own internal assessments – and trust their own data more as they 'build up a historical database' on the profiles of the schools' particular students. In this way, target-setting had become a systematic means of maintaining progress by encouraging both staff and students to set and check on progress towards short-term goals.

Whilst the contribution of the leadership team is clearly vital, many of the heads also looked to middle management as an 'engine for change'. For example, one head suggested: 'Results come from the subject departments, so it is making sure

that middle-management is strong and supports those working within those departments. Sustainability has come through working with departments'.

In thinking about sustainability, some of the heads emphasized the importance
of retaining a hard core of teachers. This is necessary, they argued, to safeguard the
consistency of approach within the school. Of course, teacher retention is also
important, because recruitment can be an issue for schools in challenging circumstances. One head explained:

> And, in terms of sustainability, some of the pressures of inner city schools
> make people reluctant to apply to us. So it's not just the social context,
> because many teachers will put up with that. What they are worried about is:
> 'Is this school vulnerable? Will I get inspected every two years? Will I be
> criticized because my lessons are not up to scratch when I know that I am
> having to work really hard with families with behaviourally challenged
> children?' And the pressure in terms of judging us in exactly the same way as
> schools in more affluent areas are judged. That is going to militate against
> getting the really good teachers into our schools.

Heads felt that staff must feel truly involved in the decisions made and the activities
going on in the school, and given responsibilities that make them feel challenged.
Supporting and motivating staff through acknowledgement and celebration of their
work promotes their sense of being valued. Feedback to teachers needs to be honest
both on good and on less favourable features of their work, as this is an important
part of sustainability. Teachers also need space to take risks, experiment and seek
ways to 'reinvent the wheel' in the quest to find the best ways to teach the children
in their charge. These efforts need to be set within a context where teaching and
learning matters have a high profile, and pupil input is encouraged, such that pupils
see themselves as partners in learning and are prepared to extend themselves as well.

It was notable, too, that many headteachers also spoke about the 'constant pressure' that was placed on students to ensure that they met their targets. There was an
admission that 'the pressure is intense… The boys have nowhere to hide… We
know unless we keep the pressure on we're not going to achieve'. Further, 'if you
are being taught the same way all the time, you're not going to be an effective
learner. Things going on after school, Easter classes … all put in the melting pot
means that there is quite a varied way of learning your stuff. That does keep the
motivation going'. These strategies also provided important avenues for students to
gain new experiences, which furthered their motivation to achieve and increased
their expectations.

Drawing lessons

This earlier research provided vivid illustrations of the pressures that exist when
schools are put under pressure to improve. It also brings into focus the many dilemmas faced by school leaders as they attempt to do what they believe to be best for

their students and staff within an education system that is dominated by high-stakes testing and accountability.

So, then, what are the implications of these experiences for practice in the field? In particular, what did this suggest about the ingredients that needed to be incorporated into improvement strategies within the Greater Manchester Challenge?

All but one of those interviewed were in their first headship and had been appointed to schools confronted by a bewildering range of difficulties. Whilst these difficulties were generally understood within the school, and sometimes (for example, in the case of special measures) had been signalled clearly to the wider community, practical plans to address the difficulties had not, in most cases, been developed. Indeed, it seems that while understanding the difficulties is a vital precursor to the development of effective strategies for dealing with them, this very understanding can in itself become a disempowering force. When the full list of problems has been drawn up, and staff members are able to enumerate the many barriers to progress, simply contemplating these can paralyse even the most enthusiastic of teachers. Consequently, in the heads' descriptions of the circumstances from which they started, we noted a sense of helplessness that needs to be overcome before progress is possible. Our feeling was that the first, important achievement of these heads was to move the school community on, beyond this 'helplessness', into the realization that things could change. The ways heads went about this, inevitably, varied from school to school.

Of course, research of this kind must attempt to identify common elements, as it seeks to identify the ingredients that combine into success. However, useful as it is to know what these ingredients are, it is equally important to recognize that they do not readily come together into any one 'recipe' that will transform the school. I therefore feel that a note of caution is necessary here. Yes, there do seem to be common ingredients, but these need to be mixed in different proportions and added in a different order according to the school's circumstances. This suggests that possibly the most important attribute of a headteacher in a school facing challenging circumstances is an ability to analyse the context as quickly as possible, as suggested by Harris and Chapman (2002). My feeling, therefore, is that the strategies highlighted through this earlier research need to be seen as a bank of ideas that may help headteachers to develop their own actions plans for their own circumstances, but certainly not as a list of things to do.

Keys to Success

Building on this 'bank of ideas', as well as drawing on successful experiences in London, something like 200 schools took part for various periods in the Keys to Success process over the three years of the Greater Manchester Challenge. Initially schools tended to be reluctant to join what was seen as some kind of 'club for failing schools'. However, as success stories started to spread across the city region this began to change. Indeed, for some schools the title 'Keys to Success' became a badge of honour, with some signalling the fact on their websites and letterheads.

Further impetus to all of this came about as word got around that some of these schools were now being invited to be the strong partner supporting another school facing difficulties.

Admission to the programme resulted from a process of negotiations between Challenge Advisers, civil servants and local authority officers. This was usually referred to as 'triage', a term used traditionally to describe the priority setting that occurs in relation to medical emergencies and disasters. Sometimes this led to disputes when those involved had different assessments of the situation in particular schools. As the Challenge Advisers got closer to the contexts, however, they were in a stronger position to judge the quality of recommendations made by their local authority colleagues.

In many cases, of course, evidence from test and examination results, plus the outcomes of inspections, meant that the decision was relatively straightforward. Nevertheless, there were situations where there were warning signs that a school was in rapid decline, including some that had good reputations in their communities. Our concern was that some of our local authorities' officers did not have sufficient knowledge of their schools to make such assessments.

The interventions in the Keys to Success schools were developed as result of a close analysis of existing practices that looked to define why progress was not occurring, whilst at the same time locating examples of good practice to build on. The approach used in each school was unique – often referred to by the Advisers as 'bespoke' – based on a detailed analysis of the local context and the development of an improvement strategy that fitted the circumstances. In general terms, the focus was usually on the sorts of factors mentioned in our earlier research: strengthening teaching and leadership practices, pupil tracking systems, and raising expectations amongst staff, students and parents.

The Advisers had a central role here, working alongside senior school staff in carrying out the initial analysis and mobilizing external support. In many instances, an improvement board was created which met regularly in order to ensure momentum was maintained. Usually the membership of these boards consisted of the head, chair of governors, a local authority representative and the Challenge Adviser.

During the first year of the programme, following a tendering process, in the secondary sector we employed a private company whose task was to mobilize relevant support in relation to the improvement plans that emerged for each school. This approach had been seen to be effective in London but in our case it was disappointing. So much so that at the end of the first year of the initiative the contract was not renewed.

Meanwhile, it became increasingly apparent that much of the progress made in the Keys to Success schools was achieved through carefully matched pairings (and sometimes trios) of schools that cut across social 'boundaries' of various kinds, including those that separate schools that are in different local authorities. In this way, expertise that was previously trapped in particular contexts was made more widely available. This led the Advisers to place increasing emphasis on this approach. In so doing, they also refined their own skills in making the approach work, becoming, as

I sometimes joked, a kind of dating agency for the city region. As we hoped, it also became clear that the progress that these schools made helped to trigger improvement across the system.

Crossing boundaries sometimes involved what seemed like unlikely partnerships. For example, a highly successful primary school that caters for children from Jewish Orthodox families worked with an inner city school – one of the largest in the city region – to develop more effective use of assessment data, and boost the quality of teaching and learning. This school has a high percentage of Muslim children, many of who learn English as a second language. Over a period of 18 months, the partnership contributed to significant improvements in test results, and throughout the school the majority of students reached national expectations for their ethnic groups. It also led to a series of activities around wider school issues, such as the creative arts and the use of student voice, where the two schools shared their expertise. The headteacher of the Jewish school commented:

> It's been a totally positive experience, built on mutual respect. This (the partner school) is a great school and the learning is definitely a two-way process.

Another unusual partnership involved a primary school that had developed considerable expertise in teaching children to read, supporting a secondary school in another local authority where low levels of literacy have acted as a barrier to student progress. Describing what happened, the head of the primary school commented:

> Together we have developed the use of a letters and sounds phonics strategy to support improvements in literacy among the three lowest English sets in Year 7, including students with special educational needs. We had seen real impact using a more multi-sensory approach to the teaching of phonics within in our own school and I couldn't see any reason why it shouldn't be used to similar effect with older students.

She went on to talk with enthusiasm about the professional development opportunities all of this had provided for her own staff. News of the success of this particular partnership was spread around the city region and soon there was a queue of secondary schools waiting for similar support.

A striking feature of the partnerships that were most effective was the sense of joint responsibility that developed between the schools, such that there was a shared commitment for the success of one another. I was reminded of this when I was told the story of a Roman Catholic secondary school in a relatively privileged district that supported a poorly performing school in another authority, where many of the students came from economically poor homes. Apparently, on the day that the second school was being inspected, a senior member of staff in the partner school suggested to her headteacher that they should pray for their colleagues. Whilst I am not qualified to comment on the effectiveness of this approach, the good news was the inspection resulted in a positive report!

Using evidence

Whilst increased collaboration of this sort is vital as a strategy for developing more effective ways of working, the experience of Greater Manchester shows that it is not enough. The essential additional ingredient is an engagement with evidence that can bring an element of mutual challenge to such collaborative processes.

We found that evidence was particularly essential when partnering schools since collaboration is at its most powerful where partner schools are carefully matched and know what they are trying to achieve. Evidence also matters in order that schools go beyond cosy relationships that have no impact on outcomes. Consequently, schools need to base their relationships on evidence about each other's strengths and weaknesses, so that they can challenge each other to improve.

In order to facilitate this kind of contextual analysis, various strategies and frameworks were devised to help schools to support one another in carrying out reviews. In the primary sector, this involved colleagues from another school acting as critical friends to internally driven review processes; whilst in secondary schools, subject departments were involved in 'deep dives', where skilled specialists from another school visited to observe and analyse practice in order to promote focused improvement activities.

We found that the power of these approaches is in the way they provide teachers with opportunities to have strategic discussions with colleagues from another school. For example, in one primary school such conversations helped senior staff raise attainment and build leadership capacity. The school was judged 'satisfactory with good features' as a result of an inspection in 2007, but the following year its test scores in mathematics dipped dramatically. Eighteen months after enlisting support from another school, attainment was significantly higher. The headteacher explained:

> The rise in standards is largely down to quality conversations between senior leaders at our school and another primary school in the neighbouring borough. This has reinvigorated leadership, helped set direction and boosted confidence going forward.

In describing her involvement, the headteacher of the partner school explained:

> I feel my school has benefited a great deal too. The main impact has been for me and the senior leadership team, as I have been able to have challenging and confidential discussions about the strategic direction of the school and make changes in the way members of the leadership team work together. This has, in turn, given me the confidence to distribute leadership more effectively and delegate with confidence.

Through such examples we saw how boundaries to do with cultures, religion, age group of students and selection could be crossed in order to facilitate the exchange of expertise. We also saw how the differences between schools triggered changes in thinking and practice, sometimes regarding quite routine matters. For example, the head of one secondary school saw the display in her school's reception area in a new light as a result of her first visit to her partner school. The deputy head of another secondary school mentioned how staff from the school they were supporting noticed the way teachers dressed.

Significantly, many of these examples also indicated that such relationships can have a positive impact on the learning of students in both of the partner schools. This is an important finding in that it draws attention to a way of strengthening relatively low performing schools that can, at the same time, help to foster wider improvements in the system. It also offers a convincing argument as to why a relatively strong school should support other schools. Put simply, the evidence is that by helping others you help yourself.

Refining the process

As the Keys to Success programme developed we saw many examples of schools that had previously been in difficulty taking off. This being the case we felt a need to refine the approach in order to vary the levels of support made available. We were also conscious of the need to offer support for other schools that had not been signposted as a cause for concern but where there was a sense of coasting, or where there were worries that some groups of students were being overlooked.

With these concerns in mind, the Advisers worked with civil servants and local authority staff to categorise schools in relation to the levels of support needed. In this way, a smaller proportion of schools were designated as needing the intensive involvement of Challenge Advisers for a longer period, whilst others were offered additional resources as a result of recommendations by their School Improvement Partner.[1]

Meanwhile, other strategies were devised to encourage further groupings of schools for the purpose of mutual support. For example, one approach, known as 'Stepping Up', was developed as a co-operative learning cycle to support groups of three primary schools in a peer inquiry process to secure rapid improvement. The approach was used flexibly to suit particular circumstances. Consequently, various versions were developed. The instructions for one of these were as follows:

> The Stepping Up process is a tight, robust inquiry-based activity to secure actions for improvement. Whilst the participants in the process need to be flexible, it would be important that they are necessary people to impact on the change to be brought about. As a starting point the team should include: a peer headteacher, members of the school leadership team and an experienced external consultant. As appropriate, it would be useful to involve pupils, staff, governors and parents. Once the team has been established they will then follow what is a three-stage process. The following is provided as a guide to this process but this is likely to be refined to respond to each individual context.

Stage 1: Colleagues in the review team meet to agree the focus for the visit, based on an evaluation of key documentation. Having agreed the focus, there is a further discussion to decide how information is to be gathered during the visit. Where will the team go, what will they look for? Who will they speak to, what documentation will they look at, and where might their focus be when speaking to children and looking at their work?

Stage 2: In conducting the visit it is absolutely vital that team members do not work in isolation. Time should be made for conversations whilst information is gathered, observations made and ideas exchanged. At the end of the day it is anticipated that all members of the team should have gained an individual impression of practice within the school. At this point these impressions should be written up. On behalf of the team, the peer leader will work with the headteacher to produce a joint summary of outcomes of the process. This will be a position statement on current achievement, the quality of teaching, the behaviour of the pupils and the effectiveness of leadership.

Stage 3. A further reflective session then takes place with the school leadership team. This is an opportunity to reflect on the position statement, review and refine the issues and actions to be addressed.

The roles of Challenge Advisers

In working with the Keys to Success schools, our aim was to 'get behind people' in these communities, on the assumption that if they were to improve they would improve themselves. As I have explained, analysis of context was crucial in this respect, the purpose being to build on relative strengths within these schools and address areas of their work that were a cause for concern.

As noted in the previous chapter, the team of Challenge Advisers was a crucial factor in this respect. Once appointed their task was to develop ways of working that were appropriate to the idea of a self-improving system. Here I drew lessons from the work we had carried out previously in one local authority, where we were privileged to be able to observe closely the work of its team of school improvement officers (SIO) as they worked together in order to improve the work of schools (Ainscow, Howes and Tweddle, 2006).

During the three years of our involvement in that authority there was clear evidence that its school improvement strategy paid off. Test and examination results rose across all phases of the service, with improvement rates in the Key Stage 2 tests[2] among the highest nationally. And whilst over the period up to 15 schools either required special measures or were designated as having serious weaknesses as a result of Ofsted inspections, these figures were eventually reduced to just two with serious weaknesses. In addition, some schools that had previously been in crisis subsequently received positive inspection reports. As a result, in its inspection report on the local authority, Ofsted stated, 'This is a remarkable, unique record that is not paralleled elsewhere in the country'.

In order to make sense of what all of this involved we developed a typology of the roles that we saw the authority's team of SIOs taking on. These were as follows:

- **The face of the local authority:** Here they appeared as a figure of authority, useful in dealing with personnel issues, and in reassuring or challenging governors, staff or parents. In this respect we noted many examples of the role taken by SIOs in addressing sensitive personnel issues in schools.
- **The sounding board:** This was where the SIO could be seen as a respected, trusted colleague to whom headteachers, in particular, could relate the details of a situation and so create an opportunity for consideration of various options for action. In some such situations the SIO seemed to act as a counsellor, a person able to give appropriate attention, especially to a head involved in complex, emotionally demanding situations.
- **The model:** SIOs were sometimes seen as professionals with a breadth of experience, who through their practice communicated possible ways of achieving certain goals. For example, we were told that some heads tended to ignore the potential of data in forming an understanding of their school, being more naturally inclined to spend their time as a key figure in the school community. So the SIO role would involve working alongside them on such aspects, to realise the potential.
- **The challenger:** This involved SIOs in taking on the role of questioner, with a brief to push through to greater clarity on a management issue. In the view of one head, the SIO who worked in her school was astute enough to probe through to the 'reality behind the rhetoric'. She explained how in going through plans or records, where previously advisers would have been quite content to listen and go away believing the good news, the SIO would ask questions and probe more. In this particular case, the head invited the SIO to challenge her, to push her in a school in which it would be easy to be complacent.
- **The link:** Sometimes the role became that of providing a 'postal service', dropping things off to schools. Often SIOs seemed to simply drop in and out of schools in this way, keeping a certain low level of contact which might be useful in all sorts of ways, not least in picking up incidental information about what is happening. Indeed it struck us that often providing a postal service might be a kind of excuse.
- **Supporter:** Here we saw the SIO as a person taking the side of the school against external threats. With regard to Ofsted inspections, in particular, the SIO sometimes took a role in the preparation period. There was no doubt that this was widely appreciated by many of the heads.
- **Interested friend:** Several times the SIO was mentioned as someone who would come to events such as concerts or presentations, and be informally involved in the life of the school as community. Always heads associated this with building relationships with staff.

The approach to school improvement developed within the particular authority involved a complex set of interconnected strategies, implemented by the team of hard-working and committed SIOs. In this sense, much could be learnt from what they did and how they did it. Having said that, our close involvement led us to believe that a deeper analysis was needed in order to understand the full significance of what had occurred over the three-year period.

As I have previously mentioned, it is sometimes argued that school improvement is technically simple but socially complex. In many ways this applies to this account. There is no doubt that staff within the local authority were remarkably creative in inventing ways of working that stimulated and supported change within schools. However, we remained unconvinced that simply teaching new people how to use these approaches, or, indeed, lifting them in order to reproduce them in a different context, would have the powerful impact that they clearly had within the particular context. The problem with such an approach is that it overlooks the social processes of learning that enabled the strategies to have their powerful impact. Consequently, we reflected further on our evidence in order to seek a deeper understanding of what was involved in these 'social processes of learning'.

The SIOs in our study saw themselves as supporting and, where necessary, challenging school-led improvement strategies. However, all of this was set within a wider context of relationships and procedures that meant that they had developed a deep knowledge of what went on in the schools. In this way they were able to engage senior school staff in detailed discussion of improvement strategies, bringing to bear their detailed knowledge of particular people (staff and pupils), contexts, policies and practices. The SIOs knew their schools, and that it was this knowledge which made their interventions authentic. In terms of our team of Challenge Advisers this was, for me, a central message.

The work of the Challenge Advisers

My leadership of the Challenge Advisers in Greater Manchester was much informed by what I had observed within this particular authority, not least the emphasis placed on teamwork. It was also clear that, as in the London Challenge, members of the SIO team had been encouraged to use their extensive experience to analyse the situation in individual schools and develop strategies that they believed would fit those circumstances. In so doing they were trusted to make appropriate decisions as to the best way forward, where necessary stepping out of the conventional ways of making things happen. One of our mantras, 'this is not about doing more of the same', was a useful reminder in this respect. I also occasionally reminded the team of that comment made to me by one of the London Advisers: 'We like to try quirky things'.

This meant that as far as the Keys to Success schools were concerned, Advisers were given considerable autonomy to make decisions regarding what forms of support should be made available. They also had a political mandate to make things happen, as well as access to resources that they could use to lever change.

And, of course, all of this was part of an arrangement whereby they were also held accountable for achieving progress.

In some instances, the Advisers came to the conclusion that circumstances in a school meant that, even with additional support, improvements were unlikely to occur. In such contexts, their task was to recommend or, in some cases, demand, that the local authority used its legal powers of intervention. This might lead to changes in leadership, and/or the suspension of the school's governing board, to be temporarily replaced by an interim executive board charged with supervising next steps. Sometimes, too, this triggered what was referred to as a 'structural solution', such as a federation with another school, or a re-designation of the school as a sponsored academy. This latter response became even more of a feature during the final year of the Challenge, with the arrival of the new government. As a result of such situations, the political nature of our work became much more apparent as we came under pressure regarding national policies, not least the growing emphasis for schools to become academies. I will return in Chapter 7 to some of the difficulties this created.

Each Challenge Adviser had a civil servant who was jokingly referred to as their 'minder'. The two met occasionally to discuss the Adviser's range of contributions. Whilst this was generally carried out in a supportive way, where there were concerns regarding the quality of an individual's work this was made clear. In a few instances the contracts of certain members of the team were not renewed and over the period of three years a total of 15 advisers were involved at various stages. In a few cases, Advisers worked on both the London and Greater Manchester Challenges at the same time, including two specialists: one related to the improvement of behaviour and the other for English as an additional language. This proved to be a helpful way of sharing experiences and lessons between the two contexts.

As far as drawing down finance for supporting schools was concerned, the arrangements were summarized in a set of notes prepared by civil servants dated June 2008, which stated:

> Advisers will be able to draw on support up to a certain amount without needing to get this cleared by DCSF first. For support packages exceeding this amount a bid form will need to be submitted by the Adviser to their relevant DCSF minder. In exceptional cases, where significant support may be required for an individual school which exceeds £75k, this will need to be signed off by the Minister. A full submission will need to be prepared for the Minister, for which we will rely on a detailed, compelling input from Advisers.

The notes went on to add:

> The Minister has made it clear that she expects local authorities to contribute to all packages of support. She will expect us to indicate what support is already provided by the local authority, in addition to support from the National Strategies, as appropriate.

The same note suggested two key questions that Advisers should ask after every school visit. These were:

> 1. *Did I make a difference through my visit to the school's effectiveness, or did I merely distract and disturb?* Always leave the school feeling better and more energized as a result of a visit. This emphatically doesn't mean becoming an 'uncritical friend', but using challenge and support in the best professional sense. It involves the feeling that there is a way forward, there are solutions to very difficult issues, that the head and the school are not on their own.
>
> 2. *What more could I do?* The acid test for any Adviser is always to deliver promptly on any promises made during a visit but this might mean using our collective wisdom better. Certainly we ought to keep bringing good practice to the school, connecting them to other schools, and reminding them of all the opportunities presented by the Challenge.

Supporting change

As I have emphasized, the style of the approach used by Advisers to support the process of change varied from school to school. Nevertheless, there was an overall pattern that guided these interventions. This was helpfully summed up in a paper written towards the end of the initiative by one of the primary team, who worked on both the London and Greater Manchester Challenges. In it he wrote:

> The following is a brief reflection on the process I engaged with while working as a Challenge Adviser. Whilst it is written as a linear process, in practice it was never like this. That said, I feel the following is a useful and authentic guide to what happened when working with challenging schools.
>
> **Step one: a review process using key documents and data.** This involved working with senior local authority colleagues to carry out a review to ensure the right schools were targeted for involvement. Having identified schools for involvement, I carried out a review, using statistical evidence, inspection reports, local authority and internal evaluations, to achieve an overview of the quality and effectiveness of individual schools. Detailed reports were completed with suggested key targets established as a starting point for conversations with each school's leadership team.
>
> **Step two: establish a rigorous and challenging evaluation for improvement process.** This involved me in working with the leadership of each school in carrying out an inquiry in order to establish improvement targets, proposed actions, intended outcomes, and a timescale for completion. This was supported by systematic quality assurance to ensure standards were being achieved and accountability was real. Due to the nature and speed of change, this was a constant and cyclical activity within the improvement drive. The important goals were to:

- analyse practice to ensure that agreed priorities were the correct ones
- ensure current practice is making a difference to pupil attainment and be aware of the level of impact on different pupil groups
- determine gaps in staff expertise
- be precise about what it was that was making the difference, or was providing a barrier to improvement
- understand where accountability rested and make this explicit for all.

Step three: implement activities to impact on the priority areas. Whilst the targets for all schools tended to fall within the areas of leadership, learning, teaching and community, in each context there was a drive to ensure they were relevant to the particular context and tightly focused. In response to these targets, work with colleagues was crucial, such as staff from within the Greater Manchester Challenge team, the NCSL, and the local authority, in deciding what the support package should be for each school and when it should be deployed. This might include access to:

- national and local leaders of education
- specialist support; for example, specialist leaders in education and our EAL consultant
- a range of continuous professional development for school leaders, teachers and teaching assistants
- a team of leading teachers.

It was particularly important to ensure that the support package was appropriate at each stage of the journey of improvement, adding value and aligned with existing support.

Step four: Support, challenge and manage the development of improvement activities and critical events. This was crucial to ensure that:

- the change process was being managed effectively
- each school turned its plan into actions, making and consolidating progress as appropriate
- there was systematic monitoring of the impact of all aspects of the support package and the contributions of stakeholders
- there was effective monitoring of school performance to ensure targets were being achieved.

Where the support package was providing significant leverage, I would work with key partners to identify places to do more activity. Similarly, if the support package was having little impact, I worked with the local authority, school governors and leadership to challenge and change activity. For example, where a partner school was finding it difficult to make an impact this had to be challenged. Similarly, if a headteacher was struggling to make an impact and was seen to be a barrier to improvement, the governors might be temporarily suspended and an interim executive board set up to help remove the barrier. Where a school had a track record of under-performance for a period of time, some form of structural solution was put in place, which might, for example, involve a federation with another school.

Step five: Effective reporting procedures. These were intended to ensure that stakeholders were informed of all aspects of progress at the individual and authority level. As part of my routine work, after each school visit I completed a 'note of visit', which highlighted progress with specific reference to:

- the quality of school self-evaluation
- progress on achieving priorities in the school's improvement plan
- impact of the support package
- key competence issues and issues for celebration
- recommendations about the next phase of improvement.

Reflecting on his experiences the Adviser concluded:

> We have learnt that whilst, at times, a hands-on approach was necessary, sustainable improvement has been achieved when we have facilitated a group of people, from both within and outside the school, and the local area, working together, in partnership. Improvement has come about due to their collective response. That is, a group of people with the right knowledge and skills, and an emotional connection and commitment to each other, to achieve the intended outcome. It was about 'getting the right people on the bus', in the right seats, at the right time, doing the right things to ensure improvement. This team of people was not fixed, but would adapt to the changing needs of the improvement activity.

Finally, he noted:

> At the outset, many of the schools were impoverished and low in capacity. In such cases, the support package was significant in driving improvement. Initially, the priorities were significant ones but limited in number. As the schools began to improve and internal capacity began to develop, the school team, supported by the Challenge Advisers, began to take on more priorities and drive improvement. In becoming a learning community the schools gradually became higher in capacity, engaging in innovative activity and the support package was limited. In this way we were able to effect change quickly.

As the work with schools developed, the team became gradually more focused on bringing about system-level change. In this connection, another of the Advisers, who had also worked on both the London and Greater Manchester Challenges, wrote a note about the importance of linking activities in Keys to Success schools with efforts to strengthen the way the system works:

> Once contact has been made and relationships are established with relevant local authority officers and advisers, it is important to map the strengths and areas of weakness/gaps in local authority support and challenge arrangements. This is especially the case in areas where capacity and capability to form accurate judgements about the real time progress of schools is vital.
>
> It is equally important to gain knowledge about the capacity of school improvement teams to aid recovery and improvement. So there is an important challenge and support role required of the City Challenge Adviser in relation to those colleagues within a local authority who have key roles that can help or hinder Keys to Success schools. It is important to be 'tough on the task, gentle on the individual' in this respect, being very clear about what our expectations are, and helpful about coaching and role modelling the function of the challenge and support role.
>
> If it is clear that the local authority is unable to provide the necessary support in key areas, then other important activities to be undertaken are brokering and commissioning support. This might often be the case when it comes to supporting improvement in core subjects, as well as English as an additional language work, or behaviour and attendance. At this point it will be important to bring in appropriate City Challenge Adviser colleagues who head up these areas, if available, or contact hub specialist schools who have been trained by City Challenge colleagues to provide relevant support.
>
> However, it is never wise to let up on holding both senior managers in local authorities and in schools to account for real time progress about groups of students at risk of under attaining, or quality assuring the interventions commissioned on a regular basis.

Working as a team

As with our earlier study of the work of the team of SIOs, the London Challenge experience had underlined the importance of Advisers operating as a team. With this in mind, our team met together for half a day fortnightly in the university. Whilst the content of the meetings varied, there were usually two core agenda items: first, a briefing from civil servants regarding overall developments, including updates of policy changes from central government; and second, what was called the 'professional hour', during which members of the team debated the challenges they faced generally, and in respect to particular schools or local authorities. These discussions proved to be tremendous opportunities for collective learning, as the team of highly experienced professionals argued about what actions should be taken. For me personally, it was a privilege to sit back and reflect on the ideas that were generated.

In some instances the challenges presented by certain schools meant that they would occasionally revisit them in order to hear about what progress, if any, was being made. For example, one particular primary school, where overall standards were low in terms of attendance and results on national tests, and where there were also concerns about poor behaviour amongst pupils, was a regular focus of attention. The school had had a succession of headteachers, most of whom had stayed around for short periods. Meanwhile, confidence amongst staff had declined and there were regular disputes between staff and school managers, which led to the involvement of teacher unions. Over a period of two years the Challenge Adviser assigned to the school gradually got to grips with the situation, with support from other members of the team. Interestingly, I have heard that the school has recently been graded 'outstanding' as a result of an inspection.

On some occasions the discussions involved a process of reflection on overall progress with the strategy and what changes might be needed. For example, towards the end the first year of the Challenge I felt the need to provoke a discussion around the theme of 'raising our game'. More specifically, I asked the team to consider how we could:

- achieve consistency whilst allowing space for discretion in relation to what was needed in particular contexts?
- provide an appropriate mix of support and challenge?
- develop responses to urgent, short-term goals whilst at the same time encouraging sustainable improvements?
- make best use of all the available resources?

Alongside the sense of team work that was encouraged through discussions like this at our fortnightly meeting, the contractual conditions under which the advisers were employed was another factor that helped to shape their success. As I explained in the previous chapter, each was employed as a result of a tendering process usually for up to 125 days per year. This meant that their presence was seen as a temporary arrangement to inject new energy and pace into the process of change

Conclusion

The experiences described in this chapter lead me to conclude that **school partnerships are the most powerful means of fostering improvements, particularly in challenging circumstances.** However, this is not a simple strategy to adopt – it can easily become a series of 'talk shops' that lead to little action being taken. It is necessary therefore to learn how to make such partnerships work.

In this respect, the Greater Manchester Challenge has provided many helpful pointers. In particular, it showed how an engagement with evidence of various kinds is crucial, since this can be the catalyst for change, leading those involved to focus attention on overlooked possibilities for moving practice forward. Importantly, it also provided many examples suggesting that such partnerships can be of benefit to both school partners.

A further important factor in the success of the school partnerships is the involvement of outsiders who have the expertise to orchestrate the growth of effective school partnerships. In the case of the Greater Manchester Challenge, the contributions of the team of Advisers were crucial in this respect. The nature of their contractual arrangements and the way they worked as a team were particularly important. Their teamwork was much encouraged by the fortnightly team meetings feature and their occasional joint visits to schools.

Notes

1 Consultants employed by local authorities to support schools.
2 These are the national tests taken by all English primary school children at the age of 11, just before they transfer to a secondary school.

4

FAMILIES OF SCHOOLS

Whilst much of the focus during the early phase of the Greater Manchester Challenge was on improving the performance of the Keys to Success schools, we had to keep in mind the commitment to improve provision for all children and young people, in all of the schools. Consistent with our overall rationale we set out to achieve this goal though processes of networking and collaboration. The big question was, how could we involve over 1,100 schools in such an endeavour?

Once again I had earlier experiences to build on in this respect. These had pointed to the potential of orchestrated networking and collaboration as strategies for fostering system change, whilst also indicating some of the difficulties involved in making this happen.

School-to-school partnerships

For many policy makers, it is an unwelcome yet unavoidable truth that school autonomy within an environment of competition and choice has not brought about significant improvements for all learners in economically poorer contexts. In accepting this fact, policy makers in England have recently been looking to collaboration within networks of schools as a way of embedding school improvement more deeply (House of Commons Education Committee, 2013).

The advantages of formalized networks in a variety of contexts have been well reported (Hill, 2008; Chapman and Hadfield, 2010; Muijs *et al.*, 2011). For example, Wohlstetter *et al.* (2003) studied school networks in Los Angeles and found that the systematic decentralization of resources and power enhanced the capacity of individual schools to reform. In the UK context, some clear benefits have been seen, but the influence of the dominant competitive agenda has meant that not all this networking is collaborative, and it has not often been demonstrably effective in raising pupil attainment across schools (Sammons, 2007).

Previously my colleagues and I had carried out a series of studies that have thrown considerable light on how school-to-school collaboration can strengthen improvement processes by adding to the range of expertise made available (see: Ainscow, Nicolaidou and West, 2003; Ainscow, West and Nicolaidou, 2005; Ainscow and West, 2006; Chapman *et al.*, 2008; Ainscow, 2010; Ainscow and Goldrick, 2010; Muijs, West and Ainscow, 2010; Muijs, 2011). Together, these studies suggest that, under appropriate conditions, school-to-school collaboration has an enormous potential for fostering system–wide improvement, particularly in challenging urban contexts.

For the most part, these studies have focused on situations where schools have been given short-term financial incentives linked to the demonstration of collaborative planning and activity. Nevertheless, they convince us this approach can be a powerful catalyst for change, although it does not represent an easy option, particularly in policy contexts within which competition and choice continue to be the main policy drivers.

Collaboration in a diverse urban area such as Greater Manchester must be about improving the challenging conditions in which many headteachers must create change – not with the unrealistic expectation of a level educational playing field, but by finding ways to add to the sources of support and mutual challenge that school leaders can rely on. Setting up such collaboration demands a level-headed appreciation of some key conditions, such as allowing sufficient time for the relatively slow process of building mutual trust through appropriate shared risks and responsibilities. The reality and implications of this are illuminated in the accounts that are presented in this chapter, starting with an earlier example set in another English city.

An earlier city-wide strategy

Much of the earlier literature on schools collaborating underplays the significance of local context, although there is some research to suggest that what goes on at the district level has a significant role to play in respect of processes of school improvement (e.g. Elmore, 2004). Between 2004 and 2006, my colleague Andy Howes and I carried out a study on behalf of the government of an improvement process known as 'Transforming Secondary Education', in a city in the Midlands where the performance of the school system was a cause for considerable concern. The initiative made collaboration within four networks of secondary schools the main route to sustainable higher achievement (Ainscow and Howes, 2007).

Since collaboration is essentially a social process, we felt that it was important to pay attention to the various perspectives of those involved, including teachers and other members of staff, school leaders, local authority officers and the private company working with them – and to observe and reflect on how they worked together in pursuit of the objectives. Our conclusions were drawn from variations in responses to this process in the various collaborative groupings. These variations suggested that the necessary negotiation of inter-dependent relationships between schools, local authorities and their wider communities requires increasingly skilful and considered approaches from leaders at all levels in the system. The evidence of this study supports the idea that this is particularly true in the general context of competing educational agendas and uncertainty about forms of governance.

Certainly, some features of the local educational context at the beginning of this process were not conducive to the establishment of systematic and sustainable collaborative working. Schools in the city had long competed for pupils and at transition to secondary school, student migration was widespread as more aspirational parents sought out places in relatively high attaining schools. In addition, falling rolls required the closure of two secondary schools during the two years of the project.

In making sense of collaboration we found it helpful to use the metaphor of *creating new paths for improvement* – with headteachers and others constructing these paths as they travelled together. Once made, these paths make further improvement easier, since they facilitate the continued purposeful working together of school leaders, local authority representatives and external agencies. This was a development which effectively harnessed new energy from the school system, creating new forms of governance and accountability, based on the development and consolidation of school-to-school partnerships of various forms. Changes in ethos depended on a release of goodwill and an extension of trust, which was hard to anticipate at the start.

Overall we came to a positive conclusion about the role that collaboration played in creating paths for improvement in this case. Over a relatively short period, secondary schools in the city demonstrated how collaborative arrangements can provide an effective means of solving immediate problems, such as staff shortages; how they can have a positive impact during periods of crisis, such as during the closure of a school; and, how, in the longer run, schools working together can contribute to the raising of aspirations and attainment in schools that have had a record of low achievement. Data showed that attainment levels increased between 2002 and 2004 in all four groupings. There was also strong evidence that collaboration helped reduce the polarization of the education system, to the particular benefit of those pupils who are on the edges of the system and performing relatively poorly, although the impact was uneven.

However, none of what we found applied across the board – each of the 18 secondary schools, and the people managing and developing them, had their own orientations, ethos, and context, and it would be arrogant to assume that their intentions, capabilities and achievements can be summed up in a few pages. Nevertheless, we drew out some lessons that proved to be relevant to what was to happen a couple of years later in Greater Manchester.

Setting up

The project involved the construction of what were referred to as quadrants of schools. Additional government funding (in excess of £1 million) was provided to support the process, and a private company was hired to work alongside the local authority in setting up the project. Whilst whole-hearted involvement in the project could not be mandated, the assumption was that all city secondary schools would participate. In practice, most schools were enthused by the prospect of collaborating in small groups, although a minority of schools were less willing.

A steering group was set up to manage the project. This included the director of education and other senior officers, representative headteachers, experienced staff from another local authority, senior government advisers, and staff from the private company. On a day-to-day basis, the core project team consisted of just two people: a member of the private company (himself a highly regarded local ex-headteacher) and a local authority officer working full-time on the initiative. Early on the private company played an essential role in creating additional capacity for brokering between schools.

Headteachers were consulted extensively over the membership of the quadrants, which were organized not on geographical proximity but in order to bring together schools at different stages of development and with varied levels of examination success. Representatives from schools in another local authority with a history of collaborative working were attached to each quadrant. As I will explain later in this chapter, these features offered leads for what was to develop in Greater Manchester.

The project design featured a 'twin-track' approach. The first track involved short term initiatives aiming at assisting schools in raising standards for all students. In particular, the goal was to meet the government's 'floor target' requirements within two years, according to which all schools were to have at least 25 per cent of their Year 11 pupils attaining five or more A* to C GCSE grades. These initiatives included the production of revision guides in some subjects, booster classes for students just under the attainment targets, and rapid introduction of alternative courses taught with additional staffing in key areas. Some of these initiatives were put in place through coordination between schools at a subject level. Unusually, teachers were paid additional money for attending project meetings out of school. These activities were promoted through collaborative structures and encouraged some sharing of ideas and experiences. However, they entailed very little collaboration between staff in the schools.

The second track was a longer-term strategy based on strengthening collaboration amongst the city's schools. As a relatively small local authority, the city's education department was seen to have insufficient resources to meet all the development needs of schools without input from expertise already located in the schools. Collaboration was intended to facilitate more sharing of resources than had proved possible under earlier schemes, such as the Beacon schools initiative.[1] The implication too was that changing relationships between schools would gradually be mirrored by changing relationships with officers of the education department. With this in mind, a school improvement adviser was allocated to work with each school grouping.

Developing the quadrants

Significantly, the four school groups developed in quite different ways, reflecting their varied contexts and histories. It is helpful to briefly describe these differences, highlighting one or two significant developments in each case.

Quadrant A consisted of only four schools: a strong traditional foundation school,[2] a school that had reopened after failing to improve following inspection, one newly opened school and one marked for closure. They were geographically closer than those in the other groupings, and a particularly close collaboration developed through the sharing of resources. Headteachers decided to manage the group directly, to ensure that activities fitted in with existing school development priorities. They quickly learned that they could rely on each other for support and challenge, as noted by one of the heads:

> The project takes pressure off people… Knowing that you can ring someone galvanizes you to do things sometimes.

At that stage, whilst encouraging collaboration as a general principle, the group only involved teachers where it fulfilled a strategic need that they had identified.

A critical stage for this group concerned the closure of one of the four schools and the 'takeover' of the buildings by a stronger school – which could have caused great conflict. In practice, the help given by the group resulted in the school's final cohort of students attaining more highly than their predecessors in previous years. This is significant in that often school closures lead key staff to move on, leaving a feeling of a sinking ship. The school grouping helped to avoid this by creating a sense of continuity, working together on joint projects, sharing resources, and requiring staff newly appointed to the group to work in the school for the first year of their contract.

The head of the closing school explained that 'we were able to get at a field of staff which we couldn't get at before'. Significantly, too, the school continued to offer some resources in return. The other headteachers were a ready source of support and advice for him ('I'll go to them much quicker than to the local authority if I have an issue') and he was able to offer strong teachers in subjects, such as art, to work part-time in the other schools, to everyone's benefit.

A lot was learnt from this process. The headteacher of the traditional school talked of 'bussing by consent', describing the possibilities for creating a good social mix in all the schools in the group. There was an important ethnic dimension to this, which suggested that increased collaboration amongst schools may be an important way of tackling the ethnic divide building up between schools in the city.

Quadrant B successfully developed a sustainable working pattern as a result of a struggle to be more strategic about collaboration for improvement. The five secondary schools, together with another school from the partner local authority, all worked in different contexts and with varied levels of attainment. The headteachers quickly decided that they were committed to the project and to each other, prioritising their meetings, speaking openly about difficulties, focusing increasingly on teaching and learning, and contributing substantial funds to a communal pot. The decision to appoint and pay for a coordinator at the level of deputy headteacher was critical in creating greater capacity for sustained collaboration after the end of the funded project.

One school was in the special measures category following inspection and benefited from this pot, as the headteacher explained: 'Our thanks to the other schools for the financial support for continuing collaboration – it is extraordinary'. Interestingly again, the school in trouble contributed significantly to the group. In this case, their inspection-driven focus on teaching and learning influenced the other schools to pay more direct attention to classroom processes. All schools had skilful teachers who actively assisted counterpart departments in other schools in the group. This process began through an orchestrated training day and continued through individual contact, encouraged by school leaders.

The group coordinator was involved in making connections, such as facilitating support for particular teachers at the struggling school and linking up with initiatives that were otherwise seen as 'innovation overload'. However, her role was full of uncertainty, going beyond institutional structures and resulting in periodic dilemmas as to where she should place her effort. She more than anyone grappled with the question, 'How do we set something up which is sustainable?' It was this struggle that led to a group application for another government initiative and a consequent reshaping of stated priorities, whilst maintaining the significant relationships that the group had built.

Moving on, *Quadrant C* comprised five schools, one of which was one of the new style 'city academies', another which had already become successful in improving achievement amongst learners from disadvantaged backgrounds, and three schools in challenging circumstances. Collaboration in this group was first and foremost a mechanism for brokering effectively with externally available resources. A particular focus was the 14–19 curriculum, and the production of joint resources for revision and supported self-study. Progress was impeded, however, by the (frustrated) expectation that all schools would participate. One headteacher in particular chose not to engage with the project, saying that it did not address real problems, and that leaders of schools in challenging circumstances did not have time for planning meetings.

Only once the group had agreed to appoint a coordinator was there a significant push forward with activities. As the coordinator said:

> I'm making myself the focus for their loyalty. I'm the person who will be banging on the door complaining if they don't do what they said they would. I'm encouraging them to take part.

The experience of this group supported the argument that collaboration requires the commitment of key stakeholders, and that self-interest is, in practice, a predictable and important component of inter-dependency. This suggests that a necessary (but not sufficient) condition for a successful large-scale intervention based on collaboration is an appeal to self-interest and not simply altruism.

Finally, *Quadrant D* included five secondary schools, four 'facing challenging circumstances' and one that at the outset of the project had been placed in 'special measures' by the national inspection service, Ofsted. The fifth school was a large, highly successful voluntary aided school affiliated to a large church. There was also a special school linked to the group.

Although collaborative activities were slow to materialise, the sense of imposition was a mainly positive factor:

> It was imposed on us, otherwise we certainly would not have seen it as a priority. But you can't make the gelling happen.

New headteachers were appointed to three of the five schools over the period of the project and this slowed down collaboration, but did not prevent it. Initial activities were well received but unfocused. Gradually, however, initiatives involving the sharing of resources between schools took shape. One example concerned English teaching, where the headteachers together paid for and managed a shared member of staff. One of them explained:

> We realised in a group meeting that we were all in dire straights in English. Only one school had a head of English. The headteacher there said I've got an excellent teacher who is looking to move. Our LA adviser knew the teacher, and she managed and facilitated the appointment. It is a middle leader post, and we four schools each share a quarter of the cost.

This was a strategic development for schools whose relatively patchy reputation was making it impossible for them to appoint suitably qualified teachers. It was repeated in other subjects, such as music, where three schools were unable to offer the subject because of a lack of qualified staff, while another school in the group had more than ten music teachers. The group tackled the problem through another initiative to share resources, and coordinated a joint link with influential institutions beyond school in a way that individual schools would find impossible.

Drawing the lessons

The striking observation from these brief accounts is how each of the school groupings that developed from this city-wide project quickly became distinctive. Nevertheless, our analysis of examination results, together with an understanding of what processes were taking place in schools through the project, suggested strongly that there was a positive impact on pupil attainment in all of the quadrants. It is impossible to be sure that this would not have occurred without collaboration, but previous years' results suggested that this was unlikely.

From an early stage there was evidence in some of the quadrants of a critical edge to discussions about priorities and what they really needed to address. However, as one local officer explained, sometimes 'within school groupings, the primary thing is to preserve the harmony of the group'. In some cases explicit challenges were apparent, but this had not been easy to achieve. So, for example, peer review amongst groups of heads proved difficult to engage in initially. However, peer review supported by local authority officers was eventually carried out in all groups, and widely seen as a useful and productive process.

It seems, therefore, that collaboration involves working not with an abstract or distant model of 'good practice', but through learning directly from partner schools what is possible in the context of the inevitable tensions and compromises with which school leaders and teachers have to deal. The stories of the four groups show how headteachers with different priorities tended to emphasize different resolutions of these tensions, and how these differences can be very productive. The different levels of provision for lower and higher attaining pupils in schools in Quadrant A, for example, led to productive exchange of resources and mutual learning, and eventually to a systematic widening of the curriculum on offer through course places for pupils from the other schools. In Quadrant D, the direct link with the special school led to developmental work on areas that might have otherwise received little attention in the push for targets.

As we saw, in two of the school groupings coordinators played an important role in sustaining improvement efforts in the context of competing pressures. It was noticeable, for example, how they were able to create momentum through particular projects, seeking out opportunities, and building allegiances. On some occasions, they were seen to hold back where they judged attempts to engage in collaborative effort to be counterproductive. This led us to conclude that collaboration for school improvement requires someone who can take challenges to a headteacher, or group of heads, and, at the same time, maintain a forward-looking dialogue that helps to expand horizons beyond the individual school.

The evidence of this study offered important pointers for what was needed in Greater Manchester. In particular, it pointed to certain conditions that are necessary in order to make school-to-school collaboration effective. These are as follows:

- the development of relationships amongst schools serving different districts and, in some instances, from another local authority;
- the presence of incentives that encourage key stakeholders to explore the possibility that collaboration will be in their own interests;
- headteachers and other senior staff in schools who are willing and skilled enough to drive collaboration forward towards collective responsibility, coping with the inevitable uncertainties and turbulence;
- the creation of common improvement agendas that are seen to be relevant to a wide range of stakeholders;
- coherent external support from credible consultants/advisers (from the local authority or elsewhere) who have the confidence to learn alongside their

school-based partners, exploring and developing new roles and relationships where necessary.

This earlier experience also led us to conclude that national policy makers would be naive to overlook the influence of what happens at the local level. This is particularly so in urban contexts, where local history, inter-connections between schools and established relationships are always significant. Together with evidence about the limits of school improvement based on individual schools, this particular study suggested that a national education strategy for raising standards for all students, in all schools, requires the systematic and locally organized redistribution of available resources and expertise through a contextually sensitive strategy for collaboration.

Families of Schools

Drawing on the lessons of this and our other earlier experiences – as well as what had happened during the first five years of London Challenge – in Greater Manchester we set up the Families of Schools. Membership of these groups were based on a data system that brought together schools on the basis of the prior attainment of their students and their socio-economic home backgrounds. The aim of this was to engage all schools in the city region in processes of networking and collaboration. Efforts were also made to ensure that special schools and units were involved.

The strength of this approach is that it grouped together schools that serve similar populations whilst, at the same time, encouraging partnerships amongst schools that are not in direct competition with one another because they do not serve the same neighbourhoods. The varied performance amongst Family members offered possibilities for using differences as a resource to stimulate the sharing of expertise and joint efforts to innovate in order to: improve the performance of every school; increase the numbers of outstanding schools; reduce the gap between high and low performing groups of learners; and improve outcomes for particular vulnerable groups of students. With this in mind, the average performance for each Family – both in terms of overall attainment and recent improvement trends – provided a benchmark against which overall goals for each of the partner schools could be set.

Tim Brighouse had formulated the idea of Families of Schools as a result of experiences in Birmingham prior to his involvement in the London Challenge. He explained the rationale as follows:

> If schools really are going to crack the issue of chronic educational underachievement among traditionally disadvantaged groups of pupils, they need two sorts of evidence. The first is reliable data on the scale and varied nature of their attainment gap, and how they compare to other schools in a similar context. The second is reliable research and evidence from other schools about how to improve their performance.
>
> *(Brighouse, 2013, p 70)*

In adopting this approach in Greater Manchester we took it further than had been the pattern in London, where it was mainly used to help schools find suitable candidates for partnership. Our efforts sought to achieve the sorts of benefits I had seen as a result of the quadrants referred to earlier in this chapter. The rest of the chapter analyses these experiences in order to define the conditions that led to higher involvement and a greater impact on student achievement.

Developing the Families

Within the Greater Manchester Challenge there were 58 primary Families and 11 secondary, each of which had between 12 and 20 schools from different local authorities. As I have suggested, the strength of this approach is that it groups together schools that serve similar populations whilst, at the same time, encouraging partnerships amongst schools that are not in direct competition with one another because they do not serve the same neighbourhoods. Many headteachers reported that it was particularly important that the partnerships involved schools from different local authorities. This suggests that cross-border collaboration can provide a mechanism for encouraging innovation – although, sometimes, it can simply lead to time-consuming meetings that have little direct impact on learners in classrooms.

As I explained in Chapter 2, such varied performance amongst Family members offers possibilities for using differences as a resource to stimulate the sharing of expertise and joint efforts to innovate. We found, however, that for this to happen schools had to dig more deeply into the comparative data in order to expose areas of strength that could be used to influence performance across their Family, whilst also identifying areas for improvement in every school. In so doing, they must be wary of the dangers associated with what Simon (1987) refers to as 'satisficing'. Put simply, this involves attempts to meet criteria for adequacy, leading to an acceptance of a merely satisfactory outcome, rather than aiming for the best possible levels of improvement.

With this in mind, the average performance for each Family – both in terms of overall attainment and recent improvement trends – provided a benchmark against which overall goals for each of the partner schools can be set. At the same time, the analysis of data with regard to sub-groups of students (e.g. boys and girls; those eligible for free school meals; minority groups) and different subject areas also enabled a Family to work on the issue of within-school variations. The collective goal was then to move all of the Family members in a 'north-easterly' direction on the performance graph.

In thinking about how to make this happen, we found that it is important to be sensitive to the limitations of statistical information. What brings such data to life is when 'insiders' start to scrutinize and ask questions as to their significance, bringing their detailed experiences and knowledge to bear on the process of interpretation. The occasional involvement of colleagues from partner schools can deepen such processes, not least because of the ways in which they may see things, or ask questions, that those within a school may be overlooking.

Even then, there remain limitations that need to be kept in mind. Statistics provide patterns of what exists: they tell us what things are like but give little understanding as to why things are as they are, or how they came to be like that. This is why qualitative evidence – including 'insider' knowledge – is needed to supplement and help make sense of statistical data. For example, our earlier research had shown how mutual observation amongst colleagues and listening to the views of learners can be a powerful means of challenging thinking and provoking experimentation (Ainscow, Booth and Dyson, 2006). Again, here, there is potential for schools to support one another in collecting and engaging with such evidence in a way that has the potential to make the familiar unfamiliar.

Led by headteachers, many of the Families of Schools proved to be successful in strengthening collaborative processes across the city region. So, for example, primary schools in one Family worked together to strengthen leadership in each school. This included headteachers visiting one another to carry out 'learning walks', during which colleagues had opportunities to reflect upon and debate noticeable differences in practices. Eight schools in another primary Family identified a shared desire to build stronger relationships with the children's homes – for example, parents of children with English as an additional language where there were communication issues, or groups of students with lower attendance.

In one of the primary Families it was immediately obvious from the data that two schools were well ahead of the rest in terms of the performance of their Year 6 pupils on the national tests. A series of meetings of senior staff from most of the schools explored what it was that had led them to make such progress. From the discussions it became evident that both schools had placed considerable emphasis on improving children's writing. Staff in the schools were convinced that this had led to more general improvements in learning. As a result, these schools led a series of professional learning activities to promote similar developments across the Family.

In the secondary sector, schools within one of the Families used a web-based system where students can showcase their work via podcasts, videos and blogs, allowing teachers, parents and students from their own and other schools to view and comment on their efforts. Talking about his school's involvement, a highly respected secondary headteacher commented, 'This is the most powerful strategy for school improvement I have experienced'. Another Family, consisting mainly of schools seen to be relatively successful, set up its own improvement strategy, with senior staff visiting one another's schools in order to do 'health checks'.

Other secondary Families organized various types of master class, where groups of students came together to receive additional coaching in preparation for forthcoming examinations. These were particularly effective when teams of subject teachers from partner schools came together to plan the sessions. In this way, there was additional benefit brought about through the professional development that occurred amongst those teachers involved. Some of these sessions also involved contributions by external speakers brought in to motivate and inspire the young people involved. One group of schools arranged what were known as 'curry evenings', with refreshments provided by a local Indian restaurant.

Some secondary Families got involved in what was called the 'Good to Great' strategy. This involved them in sharing ideas and practices regarding ways of making their schools outstanding in terms of Ofsted judgements. Meanwhile, some worked together around the theme of 'Closing the Gap', looking to explore more effective ways of raising achievement amongst students from economically disadvantaged backgrounds.

Participation and impact

Whilst there was much involvement of schools in these types of activity, involvement in the Families remained patchy and there were concerns that too often those that might most benefit chose not to do so. A striking example of this was a primary school that, much to the surprise of its local authority officers, was placed in special measures following inspection. A new headteacher explained to me that what immediately struck her was that the school belonged to no groups or networks. Consequently, when things started to slide in the school nobody was aware of what was happening. She explained that her previous school had been in an inner city district where schools had collaborated closely for 20 years or more. 'We would have known', she said, 'and we would have stepped in to help'.

Stories such as this reinforced my commitment to the efforts we were making to encourage networking across the city region, as did the rather obvious indications that the most successful schools belonged to many 'clubs'. That is to say, their headteachers saw the value of joining different groupings for different purposes.

The availability of substantial additional funding was, of course, helpful in providing schools with greater flexibility in order to explore different ways of working together. There was, however, a down side. I sensed this at the first meeting of headteachers in one of the secondary Families. The body language of some of the participants indicated a feeling of cynicism about the whole project. Their presence was, I guessed, in recognition that there were resources that could be accessed. The negativity became even more evident when it was made clear that these would only be made available to support authentic collaborative plans.

Our monitoring of what went on as the Families developed suggested certain conditions that had led to higher involvement and a greater impact on student achievement. These are:

- a collective commitment to improve the learning of every student, in every school in the group;
- an analysis of statistical data, using professional insights in order to identify areas that need addressing;

- the pinpointing of expertise within the schools that can be used to address these concerns;
- collaborative activities involving people at different levels, including, in some instances, children and young people;
- a small number of headteachers taking on the role of leading these collaborative activities.

In moving collaboration forward in a way that supports development within a Family of Schools, we found that shared leadership was usually the central driver. This requires the development of leadership practices that involve many stakeholders in collectively sharing responsibility. Often this necessitates significant changes in beliefs and attitude, and new relationships, as well as improvements in practice.

Making the familiar unfamiliar

Our monitoring of the progress of the Families of Schools helped me to refine my understanding of what needs to happen to ensure that such collaborative processes have an impact on the practices of teachers. My thinking in this respect is based on certain assumptions regarding the development of practice that had emerged from our earlier research. These are as follows:

- **Schools know more than they use.** Thus the main thrust of development has to be with making better use of existing expertise and creativity within each school, and across its network of partner schools.
- **The expertise of teachers and school leaders is largely unarticulated.** Therefore, in order to access the reservoir of unused expertise, it is necessary to create a common language of practice.
- **Evidence is the engine for change.** Specifically, it can help to create space for rethinking by interrupting existing ways of thinking and focusing attention on overlooked possibilities for moving practice forward.
- **Collaboration is socially complex.** Successful partnerships require new thinking and, indeed, new relationships that create active connections amongst partners within and across schools.
- **Leadership must foster interdependence.** More specifically there is a need for distributed forms of leadership that encourage the trust that will make openness, risk taking, and cooperative action possible.

Bearing these assumptions in mind, as I observed developments in schools across Greater Manchester I was able to formulate a series of practical suggestions as to how various forms of evidence can be used to promote professional learning, both within and between schools. What is common to these approaches is the way they *make the familiar unfamiliar*. As my colleagues and I have argued previously, these processes create 'interruptions' in the busy day of teachers that can stimulate the sharing of practices and the generation of new ways of working (Ainscow *et al.*, 2006). In this respect, the following approaches can be a powerful catalyst:

1. **Starting with statistics.** Large quantities of statistical information are available in schools regarding attendance, behaviour and pupil performance. These are an essential starting point for school improvement. In recent years the extent and sophistication of such data have improved, so much so that the progress of groups and individuals can now be tracked in considerable detail, giving a much greater sense of the value that a school is adding to its pupils. If necessary, further relevant statistical material can be collected through questionnaire surveys of the views of pupils, staff members and, where relevant, parents and carers. However, as I have indicated, statistical information alone tells us very little. What brings data to life is when 'insiders' start to scrutinize and ask questions together as to their significance, bringing their detailed experiences and knowledge to bear on the process of interpretation. In such contexts, the perspectives of 'outsiders' – colleagues from partner schools – can sometimes draw attention to overlooked possibilities for improvement.

2. **Taking a learning walk.** Learning walks are organized visits around a school's learning areas by groups of colleagues. In some instances, pupils may also be involved. The walks may be pre-focused on an agreed agenda or kept open in order that those involved pick out 'things they notice'. During and following the walk, colleagues are encouraged to reflect on what they have seen in a way that is intended to foster the sharing of ideas and mutual challenge. Another version of this approach involves groups of staff from partner schools in scrutinizing examples of children's work in a way that encourages those involved to reconsider their working definitions of quality.

3. **Mutual observation.** This is an essential element of attempts to improve practices, since research suggests that such developments are unlikely to occur without some exposure to what teaching actually looks like when it is being done differently. Observations can take different forms, depending on the nature of the improvement agenda. So, for example, they may be guided by a relatively focused set of indicators, or, at the other extreme, by a series of open questions or themes. In addition, unexpected events can reveal something of significance to the inquiry. Learning how to observe within classrooms and in a school environment is a challenge – there is always a great deal going on, and it is easy to become distracted. Sometimes it helps to make video recordings, although, again, there are advantages and limitations to this method of data recording. It is useful to be able to replay the recording in order to look at sections in more detail, and it is good for groups of colleagues to discuss a video recording. On the other hand, the video camera can only record what is within the frame and important events may be missed.

4. **Lesson study.** A powerful approach is that of *lesson study*, a systematic procedure for the development of teaching that is well established in Japan and some other Asian countries. The goal of lesson study is to improve the effectiveness

of the experiences that teachers provide for all of their students. The focus is on a particular lesson, which is then used as the basis for gathering evidence on the quality of experience that students receive. These lessons are called research lessons and are used to examine the responsiveness of the students to the planned activities. Trios of teachers work together to design the lesson plan, which is then implemented by each colleague in turn. Observations and post-lesson conferences are arranged to facilitate the improvement of the research lesson between each trial. It should be noted here that the main focus is on the lesson and the responses of class members, not the teacher. The collection of evidence is a key factor in lesson study. This usually involves the use of video recording. Emphasis is also placed on listening to the views of students in a way that tends to introduce a critical edge to the discussions that take place (Messiou *et al.*, in press).

5. **Coaching.** Similar to the idea of lesson study, some schools found it helpful to introduce trained coaches into the teacher partnerships. This is based on the idea that developments in practice require exposure to someone who can help teachers understand the difference between what they are doing and what they aspire to do. The approach incorporates all the elements that research suggests create powerful forms of professional development (Villegas-Reimers, 2003). Specifically, it: is located mainly in classrooms; builds on the expertise available within the school; involves teacher collaboration; helps to develop a language of practice; and uses evidence as a stimulus for reflection and experimentation. The process usually involves four steps: (i) two teachers assist one another in preparing a lesson they will each teach; (ii) prior to each of the two lessons, the teachers meet with a senior colleague, who has been trained as a coach, to discuss their lesson plan; (iii) as the two each teach the lesson their colleagues observe, focusing in particular on students who are thought likely to experience difficulties in achieving the goals; and (iv) following each of the lessons, the coach orchestrates a process of review on what has taken place.

6. **Listening to learners.** Discussions with pupils are another powerful stimulus for professional development (Messiou, 2012). These may be guided by a set of prearranged questions; or, on the other hand, they may take the form of a focused discussion around a set of prompting themes. Interviews may take place with individuals, or in groups. Focus groups are an attractive method, especially when conducting research with children, not least because it is possible to include a larger group of participants. However, there is a danger, particularly with children, that the views of particularly confident individuals may shape the contributions of others.

7. **Seeing things differently.** Beyond conventional observation and interview procedures, there is room for the use of more creative approaches in order to capture the views of others, particularly those of children. Shadowing groups of youngsters through a school day can provide adults with new and sometimes disturbing insights into what it is like to be a learner in their school. For example, in one secondary school it was surprising for staff to discover how some

students go through the whole day without hearing an adult use their name. Such experiences remind us of the subtle ways in which some young people come to feel marginalized. Visual methods, too, can be a particularly powerful way of engaging children (see various chapters in Miles and Ainscow, 2011). So, for example, drawings can be useful as a stimulus for individual or focus group interviews. In a similar way, asking students to take photographs of different aspects of their school experience has proved to be particularly successful in enabling adults, and other children, to see school life through the eyes of the learner who has taken the photograph (Ainscow and Kaplan, 2005).

We found that these strategies for gathering and using evidence can be even more powerful when used within a Family of Schools, not least because outsiders may notice things that insiders overlook. The most successful visits were usually characterized by a sense of mutual learning amongst hosts and visitors. It was noticeable, too, that the focus for these visits often took some time to identify and clarify. Indeed, the preliminary negotiations that took place were in themselves a key aspect of the process. So, for example, during one such visit, the visitors were each invited to observe two children. A simple observation framework, designed by the staff in the host school, focused on children's interactions with peers and teachers. In one case, the children to be observed were chosen by the class teacher on the basis that they were the pupils he knew *least* about in his class. In addition to observations, the visiting teachers were asked to interview the children. Again, a loose structure was devised but the main emphasis was on the visiting teachers following up things that they had seen during observations.

Implications for leadership practice

As I have indicated, in moving collaboration forward in a way that supports the development of all schools and students within a Family, shared leadership was usually the central driver. Often this necessitated significant changes in beliefs and attitude, and new relationships, as well as improvements in practice. The goal must be to ensure that collaboration is between school communities, and not restricted to headteachers, not least because arrangements that rely on one person are unlikely to survive the departure of those individuals who brokered them.

The relationships that existed within a Family of Schools were a critical factor in determining whether or not collaborative arrangements bring benefits. This is why the aim must be to foster social capital, which, as noted in Chapter 1, involves a sense of reciprocity and mutual trust. It requires more powerful, interdependent relationships that can strengthen the capacity of all partner schools to deliver forms of education that respond effectively to student diversity.

In this regard, Michael Fielding's distinction between 'collaboration' and 'collegiality' is helpful (Fielding, 1999). He suggests that collaboration is driven by a set of common concerns, narrowly functional, and focused strongly on looked-for gains. In such contexts, the partners in a collaborative activity are regarded as a resource, or a source of information, rather than as members of a community of practice. In this sense, collaboration can be seen as a plural form of individualism in which participants are typically intolerant of time spent on anything other than the task in hand. On the other hand, *collegiality* is characterized as being a much more robust relationship. It is reciprocal and communal, and is rooted in shared ideals and aspirations, and mutually valued social ends. Collegiality is, therefore, by definition, less reliant upon the pursuit of narrowly defined objectives or gains, but is based on a deeper commitment to exchange and development.

This suggests that, within networks of schools, efforts have to be made to strengthen collaborative activities and understandings, so that these develop towards a genuine sense of shared responsibility for progress. Specifically, the aim must be to develop more collegial relationships, based on a common commitment to improvement across schools, and to principles of equity and social justice. Provided school leaders genuinely feel that they are in control of the priorities that emerge from such a process, our experience in Greater Manchester suggests that there is reason for optimism that this can be achieved.

It is clear, therefore, that the perspectives and skills of headteachers and other senior staff are central to an understanding of what needs to happen in order that the potential power of collaboration can be mobilized. Their visions for their schools, their beliefs about how they can foster the learning of all of their students, and their commitment to the power of interdependent learning, appear to be key influences. All of this means, of course, that the strengthening of these processes will be difficult if those in charge are unwilling or unable to make fundamental changes in established beliefs and working patterns.

Talking about all of this, one headteacher used a rather unusual image to evoke what should happen in an authentic partnership of schools: Article 5 of the NATO Treaty, which states that

> an armed attack against one or more…. shall be considered an attack against them all and consequently they agree that, if such an armed attack occurs, each of them, in exercise of the right of individual or collective self-defence… will assist the Party or Parties so attacked by taking forthwith, individually and in concert with the other Parties, such action as it deems necessary.

Whilst not wishing to promote the idea of schools ganging up to resist a threat to one of their number, the message of shared responsibility that this implies is well made.

Conclusion

The lesson that can be drawn from the accounts presented in this chapter is that **networking is a means of sharing expertise and stimulating experimentation with new ways of working.** However, as we have seen, it does not happen by chance and it is not an easy process to develop, not least because of social boundaries of various kind that hinder the movement of ideas within education systems. This means that pathways have to be created that cross these social boundaries.

Bearing this in mind, the evidence I have presented suggests that more effective networking requires the following ingredients:

- **Ownership:** In contexts where collaboration pays off, partner schools – particularly heads – have reasonable control over the agendas that are to be the focus of the activities.
- **Levels of involvement:** Whilst the commitment of heads and other senior staff is essential, best practice seems to involve forms of collaboration that exist at many levels.
- **Practical focus:** A focus on real world issues, particularly those to do with the core business of teaching and learning, seems to provide the best type of vehicle for working together effectively.
- **Making time:** Effective networking requires flexible management arrangements that provide staff with opportunities to learn from one another.
- **Commitment to values:** Networks that are more sustainable involve a deeper level of partnership around common beliefs and values.
- **Shared responsibility:** Successful networking leads to changes in organizational cultures and, therefore, demands the sharing of responsibility through new forms of collaborative leadership.

It is worth reiterating by way of conclusion to this chapter, that the evidence from Greater Manchester is that networks and partnerships that involved schools serving different neighbourhoods proved to be a 'game changer'.

Notes

1 Beacon schools had been set up previously by the government to disseminate advice to other schools.
2 A policy that at that time enabled schools to have a degree of autonomy from local authority control.

5

MOBILIZING COMMUNITY RESOURCES

In thinking about how the strategies I have outlined so far might be used more widely it is essential to recognize that they do not offer a simple recipe that can be lifted and transferred to other contexts. Rather, they offer an approach to improvement that uses processes of contextual analysis in order to create strategies that fit particular circumstances. In so doing they help to identify barriers to progress and resources that can inject pace into efforts to move things forward. What is distinctive in the approach is that it is mainly led from within schools, with headteachers and other senior school staff having a central role as system leaders. In these respects, the approach is, I believe, as relevant to school systems in Detroit, Hong Kong and Marseilles as it is to Manchester.

All of this has implications for the various key stakeholders within education systems. In particular, teachers, especially those in senior positions, have to see themselves as having a wider responsibility for all children and young people, not just those that attend their own schools. They also have to develop patterns of working that enable them to have the flexibility to cooperate with other schools. It means, too, that those who administer area school systems have to adjust their priorities and ways of working in response to improvement efforts that are led from within schools.

Having said that, it has to be recognized that closing the gap in outcomes between those from more and less advantaged backgrounds will only happen when what happens to children *outside* as well as *inside* the school changes. This means changing how families and communities work, and enriching what they offer to children. As I explain in this chapter, there is encouraging evidence from a range of contexts, including Greater Manchester, of what can happen when what schools do is aligned in a coherent strategy with the efforts of other local players – employers, community groups, universities and public services. This does not necessarily mean schools doing more, but it does imply partnerships beyond the school, where partners multiply the impacts of each other's efforts.

Closing the gap

An OECD report, 'No more failures: ten steps to equity in education' (2007) argues that educational equity has two dimensions. First, it is a matter of *fairness*, which implies ensuring that personal and social circumstances – for example gender, socio-economic status or ethnic origin – should not be an obstacle to achieving educational potential. Secondly, it is to do with *inclusion*, which is about ensuring a basic minimum standard of education for all. The report notes that the two dimensions are closely intertwined, in that 'tackling school failure helps to overcome the effects of social deprivation which often causes school failure' (p. 11)

The report goes on to argue that a fair and inclusive education is desirable because of the human rights imperative for people to be able to develop their capacities and participate fully in society. It also reminds us of the long-term social and financial costs of educational failure, since those without the skills to participate socially and economically generate higher costs for health, income support, child welfare and security.

Despite the efforts made in response to such arguments, in many parts of the world there remains a worrying gap between the achievements of students from rich and poor families (UNESCO, 2010). On the other hand, there are countries that have made progress in reducing this gap whilst at the same time having high standards, as determined by international comparisons (Schleicher, 2010). The implication is that it is possible for countries to develop education systems that are both excellent and equitable. As I noted in Chapter 1, the question is, what needs to be done to move policy and practice forward in relation to this agenda?

Within the international research community there is evidence of a division of opinion regarding how to respond to this question. On the one hand, there are those who argue that what is required is a school-focused approach, with better implementation of the knowledge base that has been created through many years of school effectiveness and improvement research (Hopkins *et al.*, 2005; Sammons, 2007). Such researchers point to examples of where this approach has had an impact on the performance of schools serving disadvantaged communities (e.g. Chenoweth, 2007; Stringfield, 1995). On the other hand, there are those who argue that such school-focused approaches can never address fundamental inequalities in societies that make it difficult for some young people to break with the restrictions imposed on them by their home circumstances (Dyson and Raffo, 2007). Some authors in the United States, for example, cite research that shows racial and socioeconomic achievement gaps are formed before children even enter school (Fryer and Levitt, 2004) and that one-third to one-half of the gap can be explained by family-environment factors (Phillips *et al.*, 1998; Fryer and Levitt, 2004). And talking about reform efforts in the United Kingdom, Ball (2010) argues:

> The over-whelming focus of education policy under New Labour on schools and on 'raising standards' has done very little and perhaps can do no more to close performance outcome gaps between social class groups. I am not saying

that standards have not been raised (what ever that might mean and what ever value in terms of public good that might deliver) but that performance gaps in terms of social class remains enormous… My point is that if we want to understand and explain persistent educational inequalities and do something about them through policy, then increasingly, the school is the wrong place to look and the wrong place to reform – at least in isolation from other sorts of changes in other parts of society.

(p. 156)

Such arguments point to the danger of separating the challenge of school improvement from a consideration of the impact of wider social and political factors. This danger is referred to by those who recommend more holistic reforms that connect schools, communities, and external political and economic institutions (e.g. Anyon, 1997; Crowther et al., 2003; Lipman, 2004; Levin, 2005). These authors conclude that it is insufficient to focus solely on the improvement of individual schools. Rather, such efforts must be part of a larger overarching plan for system-wide reform that must include all stakeholders, at the national, district, institutional and community levels.

An obvious possibility is to combine the two perspectives by adopting strategies that seek to link attempts to change the internal conditions of schools with efforts to improve local areas. This approach is a feature of the highly acclaimed Harlem Children's Zone (Whitehurst and Croft, 2010), a neighbourhood-based system of education and social services for the children of low-income families in New York. The programme combines education components (e.g. early childhood programmes with parenting classes; public charter schools); health components (including nutrition programmes); and neighbourhood services (one-on-one counselling to families; community centres; and a centre that teaches job-related skills to teenagers and adults). Dobbie and Fryer (2009) describe the Children's Zone as 'arguably the most ambitious social experiment to alleviate poverty of our time' (p. 1). Having carried out an in-depth analysis of statistical evidence regarding the impact of the initiative, they conclude:

> high-quality schools or high-quality schools coupled with community investments generate the achievement gains. Community investments alone cannot explain the results.
>
> *(p. 25)*

Recently, some of my Manchester colleagues have instigated a series of initiatives to explore how the thinking that informs the Harlem project might be used in other contexts (Dyson *et al.*, 2012; Dyson, Kerr and Wellings, 2013). In so doing, they have set out to combine a focus on a more or less tightly bounded geographical area within which there are concentrations of people facing marked disadvantages, and the assembly of a range of partners to try to tackle those challenges. Within these efforts, the focus is on improving a wide range of outcomes, rather than on tackling one or other perceived problem, such as high levels of placement in care, or low educational attainment.

Building on lessons from Harlem, they argue that such zones must develop strategies that are doubly holistic in the sense that they should operate both across the childhood and adolescent years, and across all relevant aspects of children's lives.

As the Greater Manchester Challenge developed I was keen to adopt some of this thinking into our strategy, although pressures created by national policies led to frequent strategic dilemmas in so doing, particularly in respect to the need to demonstrate rapid increases in test and examination scores. In exploring all of this I was again guided by our earlier research findings in relation to the idea of area-based developments.

Area-based developments

During the period of Labour governments between 1997 and 2010, extensive efforts were made to develop coordinated area efforts to address the issue of poverty in general and its impact on schools in particular (Kerr, Dyson and Raffo, 2014). Much reference was made to the idea of 'joined up' thinking, leading to efforts to encourage greater cooperation between agencies involved in the lives of children, particularly, education, health and social services.

Over a period of years, we monitored these developments in three local areas, looking specifically at efforts to link school efforts to improve outcomes for learners from economically disadvantaged backgrounds with community action (Ainscow *et al.*, 2006, 2007, 2008). In so doing, we asked why the multiple policy initiatives introduced by successive governments had been unable to break the link between poverty and educational outcomes. This led us to conclude that tensions between the government's dual focus on excellence and equity had yet to be resolved, and that the way forward must lie in creating spaces for the local interpretation of national policies, rather than in top-down control and compliance.

Three districts

Our case study areas were each characterized by high levels of deprivation, but also had some contrasting location, population and administrative characteristics:

- *Area 1* is a former mill town in a metropolitan authority, which has stark patterns of ethnic segregation reflecting the town's two main resident groups – white and Pakistani-Kashmiri. In recent years it has also attracted increasing numbers of European immigrants. Local efforts to coordinate developments had a clear focus on issues in the town – this being seen as an area of great concern within the authority as a whole. There were also ward-based initiatives operating in the town's most disadvantaged areas. The town is geographically quite isolated, and has few large employers.
- *Area 2* is an industrial town in a large two-tier shire authority. It has an almost exclusively white British population and significant areas of social housing. Many of the local opportunities for employment are provided by retail parks,

which tend to offer low paid, low skilled employment. A local partnership had been established which operates at the borough level, and there was a borough-wide partnership board whose remit included extended service provision.

- *Area 3* is an inner city area in a metropolitan authority with a highly diverse multicultural population. This ranges from white working class families traditionally resident in the area, to well established African-Caribbean families, through to international new arrivals – including refugee and asylum seeker families – who tend to be highly transient. Although there are many large employers in the city, they employ few people from the area. The area had a ward co-ordination group, and various service providers had created community forums in order to tap local knowledge – especially with regard to tackling violent crime and the integration of international new arrivals.

In these three areas we explored in some depth why the anticipated synergy between educational improvement and other strategies to address disadvantage largely failed to emerge. Our evidence suggests that unless there are changes to the underlying national model for analysing local issues and holding the various services involved with children to account, local stakeholders will struggle to develop complex area-level responses to inequity. There were, we concluded, deep flaws in the assumption that if each service involved with young people meets its targets, then the net gains will be enough to resolve inequities. This suggests that a model of analysis and response is needed which focuses, in context, on the underlying factors which shape local inequities.

We also reported how education professionals in the three areas were often struggling alone to address the impacts of deep-seated local inequities on what happens to children and young people. We asked how national policies, designed to promote joined-up responses to local inequities, were actually working. More specifically, we considered whether the process of 'joining up' really had the power to tackle inequities in education.

Our research provided a sense of local stakeholders' feelings of powerlessness, and their hopes and fears for emerging models of local co-ordination. In particular, it revealed how the continual pressure to meet nationally imposed targets often undermined local reform efforts, forcing them in line with simplistic analyses and priorities. At the same time, we highlighted many promising developments, where local stakeholders had found spaces within national policy to develop joined up, complex responses to local needs. These concentrated on addressing the *contextual factors* – the dynamics, structures and processes – which underlie local inequities. Through this, local visions for reform, which go far beyond target chasing, had started to be realized.

On the basis of this evidence, we argued that there was more potential than ever before to achieve greater equity within the English education system. In that period, we suggested, multi-agency and collaborative structures were in place to support local developments. The challenge was to ensure that they can deliver – and the local voices we reported provided a powerful steer for achieving this.

Their message was clear: ministers must stop trying to drive reforms through targets, structures and new initiatives. Rather, they must create the conditions in which a credible model for local reform, focusing on the underlying causes of educational inequity, not just its symptoms, can truly be established.

Patterns of development

Despite their differences, a common pattern emerged across our three case study areas as local professionals sought to develop collaborative, multi-agency responses to children from disadvantaged areas. In general terms, it went as follows:

1. Local authority officers had initiated the development of co-ordinating structures. They saw these as a way to bring together a wide range of stakeholders (professional and community based) with the broad aim of enhancing equity, but often did not have a clearly articulated rationale beyond this.
2. These structures tended to have voluntary membership. This meant that some groups of key stakeholders had become self-excluding for a whole variety of reasons, including: a lack of incentive; protecting their own agendas for change and individual capacity; and pragmatic factors such as time.
3. Members still had their own government-determined agendas and targets to meet. New structures have to find ways to accommodate these if they are not to lose further members.
4. These factors limited the capacity of new structures to help develop common understandings and properly co-ordinated responses to local inequities. Indeed, they may reinforce existing divisions and mistrust between stakeholders.
5. As a result, co-ordinating structures often operated as forums where responsibility for tackling different issues was devolved to different services in line with their individual targets. This undermined their capacity to develop complex, integrated responses to local issues.
6. The different stakeholders in the area (whether members of the new structure or not), continued their own searches for new 'solutions' and partnerships to help them meet their own targets.
7. The new structures became ineffective for tackling local inequities. At worst, they became a largely redundant layer of further bureaucracy.

As a result, the emerging collaborative structures in each of the three areas were often not able to provide schools with the support they needed, when they needed it, in their efforts to address complex local issues. In both our inner city and mill town areas, for example, schools were often the first public service that new international arrivals really engaged with. Those schools with spare capacity, in particular, had to provide an immediate response to the needs of children arriving in the area often without any English language. What our evidence suggested was that in areas where there are high levels of transience, and the nature of the most vulnerable groups in the community is constantly changing, other services and coordinating structures are often 'playing catch up' with schools, and may be working from out-of-date analyses of local issues.

Meanwhile, the centralized approaches for school improvement that were current at that time, and the punitive accountability regimes which accompanied these, were also found to be acting as a fragmenting force in these local areas. Understandably, then, headteachers were often more interested in picking and choosing from local networks as they felt could best benefit and enhance the performance of their individual schools, than in acting as 'local leaders' and 'place shapers'. This stance was widely criticized by other service providers who had a wider area-focused remit. Indeed, those working outside education services were clearly frustrated that schools were often unwilling to buy into local strategies, and that the local authority had no mechanism to require them to do so.

In our mill town, for example, schools' reluctance to contribute to local coordination strategies was attributed to their focus on raising institutional performance, rather than looking at wider educational impacts. As the director of children's services commented: 'Good school heads are introverted because of the introverted measurement of standards'. The increased scrutiny of the least successful schools in the area – both by national government and the local authority – was also felt to act as a disincentive for wider collaborative activity.

An academy in our inner city area was in a particularly complex situation in this respect. As a replacement for a 'failing' institution, and serving a highly disadvantaged intake, it was under intense pressure to raise attainments. Its principal was adamant that this was the most important thing the school could do to serve local children, and that its commitment to those children was unshakeable. However, not everyone saw things in this way. Some community representatives we spoke to criticized the school for not being linked into local networks. Meanwhile, others doubted the school's avowed commitment to local children, fearing that, as it became more academically successful, it would stop being 'a local school'. What was clear was that the establishment of an academy outside local governance systems and accountable for meeting centrally-imposed targets had generated suspicions locally that are likely to make collaborative approaches more difficult.

Some implications

Reflecting on these findings, it seemed to us that they pointed to what we saw as a fundamental contradiction in the development of 'joined-up' approaches to inequity. On the one hand, there was a recognition by government that the issues in local disadvantaged areas are beyond the capacity of any one service or institution to address. There was, therefore, every encouragement for 'joined-up working' at local level, and a multiplicity of collaborative structures had sprung up to facilitate the development of coordinated approaches. On the other hand, different services – and, in the case of education, different institutions – remained accountable for priorities and targets that were not devised locally and collaboratively, but that were imposed centrally. As a result, the partners in any collaboration always had at least one eye on how this would affect their capacity to meet the levels of performance expected of them by central government.

In some cases, this meant that the promised collaboration never materialized. Partners absented themselves from meetings, or failed to invite others, or followed their own agendas. At worst, mutual suspicion and hostility made the prospect of collaboration seem remote. These problems were marked in relation to education, where semi- or fully-autonomous schools were driven by mutual competition and, even more, by the dire consequences of failing to meet their targets.

In other cases, 'joining up' happened, but took the form of what we described as *restricted collaboration*, with the following features:

- Partners remain primarily accountable for their individual targets. Collaboration is restricted to areas where there is some overlap between targets, or where partners can offer some mutual support that does not compromise their individual capacity to deliver.
- Since partners' targets are non-negotiable, local priority-setting can do little more than aggregate them. At best, partners can decide collectively which targets will receive additional marginal support – assuming that the competition for this support does not cause the partnership to fragment.
- Since local priorities have to be determined in relation to a national view of what matters, the collaborative understanding of the local situation need be no more than a superficial analysis of how local performance measures up against national targets.
- Local strategies for action may be imaginative and far-reaching – but they do not have to be. All that is needed is a direction of marginal resource and attention to those aspects of performance that are particularly poor in order to make a rapid impact on the relevant indicators.

What was missing from this – in our three case study areas at least – was any more searching analysis of local conditions, or any more strategic approach to collaborative action. Certainly, many of the professionals we spoke to had a sense of 'how things work round here' and 'what needs to be done'. Some had put considerable time and effort into understanding the areas they served. In principle, these understandings could be shared through the collaborative structures and could be refined as different perspectives and different sorts of evidence began to interact with one another. Out of such deepened understandings of local conditions, a coherent strategy to address fundamental issues could, in principle, have emerged.

Promoting district initiatives

Bearing the lessons of these earlier experiences in mind, the process of analysing the context of Greater Manchester led me to want to encourage those involved in the Challenge to develop area-based approaches. This led us to determine what we referred to as 'hot spots'; that is to say, neighbourhoods where there were high concentrations of families living in relative poverty.

These initiatives took a variety of forms. For example, in one district it was noted that many of the most vulnerable children and young people in one district attended five different schools. There were some advantages in this arrangement, not least in that it avoided the danger of one school becoming a 'sink' school. On the other hand, the heads of the schools remained concerned about the lack of coordinated support for the families of these students, many of whom came from homes where there was evidence of conditions that were hardly supportive of educational development. Working with one of our Challenge Advisers, the heads developed the idea of a 'virtual school'. This involved them in pooling some of their own resources, alongside additional funding provided through the Challenge, in order to create a family support team that worked across the five schools.

In another district, a well-established partnership of 20 schools decided that more support was needed for vulnerable families well before their children enrolled in school. This led them to develop a team of parent support workers who worked with families that were deemed to be most vulnerable, providing advice and assistance in matters of childcare.

In these and other similar initiatives I witnessed the benefits of groups of schools within an area getting together to address mutual challenges within their communities. It is significant, too, that many of these partnerships have continued well after the money that was provided through the Challenge has dried up. In some instances, they have developed into area trusts or local academy chains that have formalized what were originally voluntary cooperatives. My sense is that these developments are, in part at least, of the social capital that was strengthened through City Challenge.

To take another illuminating example, some time after the end of the Challenge I attended a breakfast meeting attended by some 50 or so parents (all women) from three primary schools that have developed a longer-term partnership. All the schools serve areas of social disadvantage, two on a public housing estate where most families are white, and the other serving an inner city district where many families have recently arrived from other countries. The groups of parents from each school took it in turns to tell their experiences of acting as champions who foster parental involvement. One group presented posters summarizing changes in their school over the previous four years. Together they explained how a school that had been largely excluding of parents had been turned into a warm and welcoming context. All the groups talked about particular strategies they had developed. For example, the inner city school uses what they call 'walking buses'. These involve volunteer parents picking up children each morning who have previously had records of poor attendance and/or punctuality.

Many of the women wanted to speak, offering personal testimonies as to how their involvement had influenced them. One talked about how it had 'changed her life', in that her own schooling had been disastrous in ways that meant that she had little confidence about supporting her own children's learning. A woman who had recently arrived from Brazil talked emotionally about what it was like arriving at the school with no knowledge of English. Accounts such as these led to occasional tears, and much hugging amongst the participants.

Some of the parents explained how their involvement had encouraged them to return to education in order to gain formal qualifications. As a result, some are now employed in their child's school in support roles. One woman explained how she had started as a cleaner, then became a lunchtime supervisor, and is now a teaching assistant. She went on to talk warmly about how senior staff in their schools had encouraged their active involvement, using first names to refer to particular school leaders. Significantly, it was reported that each of the schools has designated a senior member of staff to support these activities.

Drawing on wider resources

Our concern to look beyond the school gate also led to a series of strategies that attempted to use cross-border collaboration to inject further innovation and pace into the system. Referred to as 'Work strands', these sometimes proved to be effective in facilitating the exchange of expertise, resources and lessons from innovations across the city region to raise aspirations and open up pathways for groups of students from disadvantaged backgrounds. Most importantly, these strategies proved to be helpful in drawing on wider community resources to support school improvement. Each of the initiatives was led by one of the local authority partners and focused on educational issues facing all local authorities, linking improvement efforts to broader social and economic agendas.

The work strands proved to be reasonably effective in facilitating the exchange of expertise, resources and lessons from innovations across the city region in relation to issues such as: raising aspirations, strengthening the contributions of governors, and closing the gap between high and low achieving groups of students. Importantly, this led to the involvement of local businesses, professional sports clubs, universities and media organizations. For example, the four universities in Greater Manchester worked together on a project known as 'Higher Futures for You'. The overall aim was to raise self-belief and aspirations amongst primary school children from disadvantaged backgrounds. Through carefully orchestrated visits to local places of employment, including a university, TV station and hotel, pupils were helped to understand the career opportunities that are available to them. During a final workshop, the children shared their knowledge with their parents. This initiative, which worked with some 200 primary schools, was originally developed by the headteacher of one school. Through the Challenge, this creative project now reaches many more children and families.

Another of the work strands set out to explore the use of learner voice as a strategy for rethinking what schools offer to their students. In carrying out this initiative a partnership was developed with an independent charity that promotes democratic citizenship and citizenship life skills. This led to an additional focus on the experience of young people outside of school. As a result, schools across Greater

Manchester collaborated in addressing the question: *In developing children as participative citizens in designing the way things are in school, can we achieve greater civic participation beyond school?* One specific outcome was the involvement of some of the students in a BBC television programme, *Question Time,* which was broadcast nationally from Salford. The schools involved in these activities were enthused by the opportunities provided, and in some instances became committed to widen and deepen the involvement of students.

In another experimental initiative known as 'Better Futures', 16 students from disadvantaged backgrounds shared jobs in three major companies. Each student attended their internship one day per week throughout the year and caught up with missed schoolwork during the rest of the week. The evidence suggests that parents were very positive once they saw the impact on children's social skills in their home environment. Meanwhile, within school, aspirations regarding future destinations were seen to change. So to, the students' attitudes to catching up on missed school work changed as they students made links between a good career and attaining targets at school. For example, there was evidence of shifts in young people's aspirations, such as, from mechanic to engineer, childcare to business, and 'don't knows' to IT and law. The approach was subsequently developed in many more schools, involving other local business organizations.

Using the media

As I carried out my role as the public face of the Challenge I found increasing evidence that there were many other groups and organizations in the wider community that wanted to support schools in their efforts to educate children, particularly those from economically disadvantaged backgrounds. Often the comments of those I spoke to were rather similar. So, for example, people I met in organizations such as the Halle Orchestra, the two Manchester football clubs and local radio stations, told me that they already had initiatives going on with schools and community groups to support the development of children and young people. However, they wanted to do more and found it difficult to establish relationships that would enable them to have a wider involvement. The implication for me was that efforts have to be made to create better pathways through which such resources can be mobilized.

With this in mind, we set up arrangements for using the media in order to promote the Challenge and encourage the involvement of community stakeholders. During the launch period, the Minister and I were each interviewed on various radio and TV channels. Then, in 2009 we negotiated with the city's evening newspaper and its local partner papers across the city region to have an 8-page colour supplement. Through its print, digital and TV media, the paper claimed to connect with over 88 per cent of the region's adults every week.

The aim of the supplement was to celebrate Greater Manchester schools' achievements, include a number of calls to action, and provide and point to useful materials for parents to support their children's learning. At the same time, the

Minister agreed to appear on the local TV breakfast show to promote progress in the city region and schools' and pupils' achievements.

One year into the Challenge we saw this as a timely opportunity to:

- celebrate progressive educational improvements across the region;
- heighten the aspirations of schools, parents and children;
- raise awareness of the Challenge and provide a platform for new plans as we moved into the second year;
- call a number of different stakeholder groups to action – in particular, parents, schools and businesses – encouraging the take-up of activities and the sharing of best practice.

The supplement included items on the following:

- the 'first birthday' – outlining the objectives of the Challenge, news and updates;
- case studies – highlighting schools' successes and pupils' achievements;
- calls to action – invitations to get involved in the parent engagement and learners' entitlement work strands (focused on encouraging parent and pupil voice respectively);
- celebrity case studies – to highlight successes and show the real picture of improvements across the city region;
- top tips for exam preparation – for both parents and pupils, as well as pointers to where more resources can be accessed;
- competitions – aimed at different age groups, to engage both parents and pupils.

In order to reach as many different stakeholders as possible, arrangements were made for additional copies of the supplement to be distributed through schools and local authorities. In addition, electronic copies of the supplement to the entire Challenge Newsletter distribution list (including all schools and local authority colleagues), encouraging stakeholders and partners to pass it on.

Moving forward

Over the last 15 years or so, successive governments have committed themselves to promoting equity in the education system. In particular, they have focused on raising standards of attainment for all, narrowing the gap between more and less advantaged students, and ensuring that everyone has access to high-quality educational experiences in childhood and beyond. This commitment is laudable, but there is little evidence that government has been able to deliver on it. Despite these repeated policy interventions, the most disadvantaged children and young people continue to be at greatest risk of impoverished educational experiences, low achievements and limited life chances. A major reason for this is that policy has focused on 'improving' schools and other education settings and making them more 'effective', despite the fact that the source of inequities lies largely beyond the school, in social disadvantage. Somehow, efforts at educational improvement have to be linked into a coherent strategy to address wider social and economic issues.

Previously my colleagues and I have argued that this can be done at the local level by locking schools and settings into area strategies to tackle disadvantage (Ainscow et al., 2009). As explained earlier in this chapter, we have also reported that multiple coordinating mechanisms already exist, in the form of local strategic partnerships, neighbourhood management initiatives, integrated children's service networks, extended services clusters and the like. In practice, however, these have to a large extent failed to deliver coordinated strategies that might address educational inequity. As I have explained, these mechanisms usually have little effective involvement from schools and wider community stakeholders. Even where they do, their ability to generate strategy is hamstrung by the perverse consequences of the government's target-setting regime. Participants are accountable for separate sets of targets, and have to achieve these within short timescales. As a result, target chasing takes precedence over any more searching attempt to understand and respond to local issues.

Through the Challenge we saw some examples of moves towards more genuine forms of area-based collaboration. These were characterized by a *contextual analysis* leading to a *local strategy*. In this way, participants probed beneath the surface of headline performance indicators to understand how local dynamics shape particular outcomes. As a result, they sought out the key underlying factors at work in local areas, and identified those which policy can influence. They then formulated a long-term shared strategy for tackling these factors.

Consistent with the Fourth Way thinking of Hargreaves and Shirley (2009) – particularly its emphasis on 'an equal and interactive partnership between the people, the profession, and their government' – these experiences suggest that for such approaches to flourish, action is needed at three levels. First of all, school leaders need to:

- be proactive in joining and forming partnerships with other key actors in the areas they serve;
- work with their partners to understand 'how things work round here' and to formulate a long-term area strategy to tackle inequities;
- harmonize work within their schools and settings with this wider strategy.

Secondly, local authorities need to:

- promote the development of partnerships at the area level;
- offer support to partnerships for contextual analysis and strategy formulation;
- develop their own contextual analyses and strategies as a framework within which area partnerships can operate;
- bring a democratic voice to bear on the work of area partnerships.

And thirdly, this requires central governments to:

- create spaces in which local partnerships can flourish;
- encourage these partnerships to undertake contextual analyses and formulate long-term strategies;
- counter the perverse consequences of the target-setting regime by locating accountability at the level of the partnership, entering into dialogue about local goals, and extending the timescale over which achievements are measured and the range of evidence this involves;
- develop its own contextual analyses and strategies as a framework within which local authorities and area partnerships can operate.

Conclusion

The experiences described in this chapter lead me to argue that, in order to achieve greater equity within education systems, **school focused strategies have to be complemented with efforts to engage the wider community.** Furthermore, these are likely to have a much greater impact if they are carried out on an area basis and involve partnerships between the many individuals, groups, services and organizations that have a potential to have a bearing on the future life chances of young people.

All of this is based on the idea that closing the gap in outcomes between those from more and less advantaged backgrounds will only happen when what happens to children *outside* as well as *inside* the school changes. This means changing how families and communities work, and enriching what they offer to children.

The chapter has explained that, despite good intentions, efforts over recent years to create 'joined-up' initiatives within the English policy context have experienced considerable difficulties. Activities that were encouraged through the Greater Manchester Challenge were promising in this respect, although much more could and should have been done. In particular, these experiences suggest the need for some form of framework that enables external partners to get involved. All of this has major implications for those who take on leadership roles.

6

LEADING SELF-IMPROVING SCHOOL SYSTEMS

As with other large-scale improvement initiatives, a big concern within the Greater Manchester Challenge was with sustainability. Put simply, how could we ensure that improvements would continue after the money runs out? With this in mind, head-teachers were seen as having wider roles beyond their duties within their own organizations. The experience suggests that many successful headteachers were motivated by the idea of taking on such roles.

This chapter describes how new approaches to school leadership were developed, focusing in particular on the work of some 170 or so outstanding headteachers who were designated as system leaders. Known as National (NLEs) or Local Leaders of Education (LLEs), increasingly they drove forward improvement efforts across the city region. Furthermore, this has continued beyond the period of the project through the creation of a headteacher-led agency, 'By Schools For Schools', that continues to coordinate processes of school-to-school collaboration across the city region.

Before describing these developments, however, I begin by summarizing our earlier research on leadership, management and governance that influenced my thinking as we developed a leadership strategy within the Challenge.

Earlier research

Over the ten years prior to City Challenge, with colleagues, I had taken a particular interest in developments in the field with respect to school management and leadership (see various chapters in Ainscow and West, 2006). A particularly relevant study was one carried out in 2007–8. In it, my colleagues and I examined the extent to which alternative patterns of practice were emerging in response to the different school governance arrangements that were being introduced in England during that period, i.e. trusts, federations, academies and all-through schools. In carrying out this work we were guided by a set of questions designed to interrogate newly emerging leadership, management and governance practices across a group of schools embracing a variety of these new structural arrangements (Chapman *et al.*, 2008).

Many of the school leaders we interviewed for the study recognized that they faced increased challenge and complexity as result of the policy changes that were occurring. Some argued that this was enabling them to think more strategically about their school's organization in relation to these demands. Often this meant widening the participation of other members of staff in management and leadership duties. This was, they argued, creating new opportunities for professional growth and experience. It was also providing school leadership teams with different perspectives on the workings of their schools.

If authority was becoming increasingly common in the roles of staff, many stakeholders recognized a parallel shift in the headteacher's role. It was particularly noticeable that many were increasingly liaising and working beyond the school, collaborating with other schools and agencies to an unprecedented degree. Often this was driven by the need to provide strategic direction for multiple national policy agendas within their own school. However, in some settings it was part of a more ambitious attempt to provide a coherent integrated service across phases, communities and localities. For example, the senior team in one federation of schools had expanded to incorporate collaborative work with their primary feeder schools. Eleven assistant headteachers each took on a specific leadership role for an issue or theme across all schools in the group.

While it had not been uncommon for headteachers to be connected into local authority policy-making procedures, many of them now appeared to be developing greater expertise in strategic analysis, and, as a result, exhibiting some of those characteristics that are associated with system leadership roles. So, for example, some had worked as consultants to senior staff in other schools, while others had direct contacts with government agencies and served on steering or policy groups. All of these activities suggested that school leaders were increasingly finding themselves operating outside of traditional school hierarchies and, therefore, needing to draw on a wider range of social skills, including those of negotiation, brokerage, facilitation and disturbance-handling, often within highly politicized environments where agendas and the balance of power and influence are unclear.

The findings of the study suggested that these new leadership practices were emerging in relation to particular local circumstances. These seemed to be encouraged by one or more of the following factors:

- **Local dissatisfaction with current arrangements.** For example, this occurred in one school where radical change was deemed necessary to tackle a prolonged record of failure. In this case the director of education approached the headteacher of a very successful school and asked whether the school would consider forming a federation with another school that had a history of difficulties. After a period of consultation and negotiation, the federation was launched in September 2006. Early signs were encouraging, and the ethos and branding of the successful school seemed to have permeated into the struggling school.

- **Individual enterprise.** Increased choice and diversity within the system had presented some successful school leaders with an unprecedented range of opportunities. These tended to involve broadening their sphere of influence by taking on new challenges and pursuing alternative career pathways beyond the traditional routes of moving on to lead a larger school or working in a local authority. Many had begun to see themselves as system leaders and were developing a portfolio of activity working as consultants with government and private agencies.

- **Community action.** This third factor was exemplified by the case of a housing trust becoming involved in the creation of a new academy within the locality. Under the slogan 'improving the life chances of our tenants', the trust was seeking to extend the positive impact it had had within the community by amalgamating two of the most difficult and lowest performing schools in the authority. Representatives of the trust were under no illusions regarding how difficult this challenge would be, but were willing to invest considerable time and resources, as it was felt that their business was not simply the supply of housing, but contributing to the wellbeing of the community.

We noted that these factors acted independently or in combination, in different proportions in different localities. Importantly, this meant that they were context specific.

It was evident that many of the schools in the study had adopted, or were developing, innovative structural arrangements in order to cope with these new ways of working. On the other hand, the findings suggested that innovative approaches to leadership did not necessarily emerge in these settings. Rather, the leaders tended to adopt what might be described as more traditional approaches. As a result, they were often regarded as being 'strong', 'committed' and 'directive' by their colleagues, and usually had a reputation in the local community or media for having led a school(s) through particularly turbulent times. Many demonstrated a particularly high capacity for managing change. Often working with levels of commitment beyond the norm, they held high expectations and were perceived to 'get things done'.

It was noticeable, too, that many of these leaders seemed to be very active networkers and entrepreneurs. Sometimes, these traits were coupled with rather conservative leadership and management practices, relying on traditional hierarchies and involving high levels of monitoring aimed at promoting consistency across all areas of school life, from student (and sometimes staff) dress codes, to strict requirements for lesson planning and pedagogical approaches. Leadership of this type had often associated with schools in challenging circumstances during early phases of their development.

It struck us that the restructuring of schools was altering external accountability patterns, with some relocation of decision-making 'upwards' to newly created bodies (e.g. federation managers, academy chains and trusts). This sometimes provided interesting career opportunities, particularly for those headteachers who have an appetite for leading collaboratives of schools and other agencies, and engaging with a wider range of agencies at local and national levels than they have previously experienced. However, there were also cases where headteachers felt disempowered and even demoralized by the development of new structural arrangements.

In some contexts, the increased external demands on headteachers had created a shift in the roles of other senior members of staff, who had often tended to be focused more on lower level, day-to-day concerns in the past. Frequently, deputy heads were taking on more strategic roles and felt comfortable with being the most senior person on site for days and, on occasions, weeks at a time. This, in turn, had a knock-on effect on the role of assistant heads, many of whom were now engaged in significant managerial tasks, including timetabling, curriculum arrangements, or the management of substantial subject staff groups, activities which were previously the preserve of deputy heads.

In a number of instances it was evident that new structures brought with them high expectations from a wide range of stakeholders of improved educational standards within the locality. These expectations permeated through the school, since staff were aware of the implications of not delivering improved performance scores. Here, the danger is that short-term actions could create barriers to more sustainable change programmes. One example of how such actions can play out on the ground was provided in an academy where some of the staff talked about being placed under enormous pressure to improve test and examination scores. Echoing the comments of a number of her colleagues, one young teacher said that, in this school 'everything is for the children'. The implication, she added, was that little or no time was given to supporting staff. Another teacher explained that if you called for help over a disciplinary matter from members of the senior team, they were likely to ask to see your lesson plan.

Clearly, some increase in attention and expectations is inevitable in times of substantial, even radical, change to the organization of schools. However, it struck us as important that senior leaders are aware of the impact such expectations may have on classroom teachers. They must also have positive strategies to ensure that these do not turn into unreasonable pressures – not least because they have a responsibility to ensure that the changes taking place are not adversely affecting the work-life balance of their more junior colleagues.

Making sense of the changes

The findings of this earlier study suggested that school leaders in England were increasingly recognizing the limitations of existing patterns of management and governance. This was leading some to explore how new structural arrangements could provide opportunities to develop different practices. As a result, there was evidence of an increased level of naturally occurring experimentation within the system. Significant to the argument developed in this book, much of this experimentation involved collaboration between schools and with a range of other stakeholders at unprecedented levels.

These developments provided encouraging signs of a movement towards a more coordinated and systematic approach to educational provision. Schools were increasingly collaborating with a range of partners to a greater degree than we had previously seen. The reader will not be surprised to hear that I saw this move towards increased collaboration as a positive shift, which, under the right conditions, might well play a major role in strengthening the capacity of the education system to enhance equity.

Figure 6.1 is framework we designed for explaining the pattern behind these changes in school leadership, management and governance. It highlights what seems to be a significant change in headteacher roles and responsibilities. Specifically, it illustrates how they had been drawn into significant cross-boundary leadership activity, connecting at a strategic level with governors, other services, the wider community and local and national agencies (represented by arrow 1). Unlike in the past – where the majority of the headteacher's life was spent 'in school', leading and managing within clearly defined structures and relationships – these emerging activities operated outside of traditional line management hierarchies. They involved relationships that were quite different and required a complex set of skills, where those involved needed to be skillful in analyzing the wider contexts in which their schools operated. They also had to develop skills as negotiators, facilitators and brokers within often diffuse relationships, with minimal history and competing agendas.

These trends had major implications for other senior staff within schools (represented by arrow 2). Increasingly, they were taking on tasks previously carried out by headteachers. This provided new opportunities for such colleagues to take on responsibility and, in so doing, have greater possibilities to develop their leadership

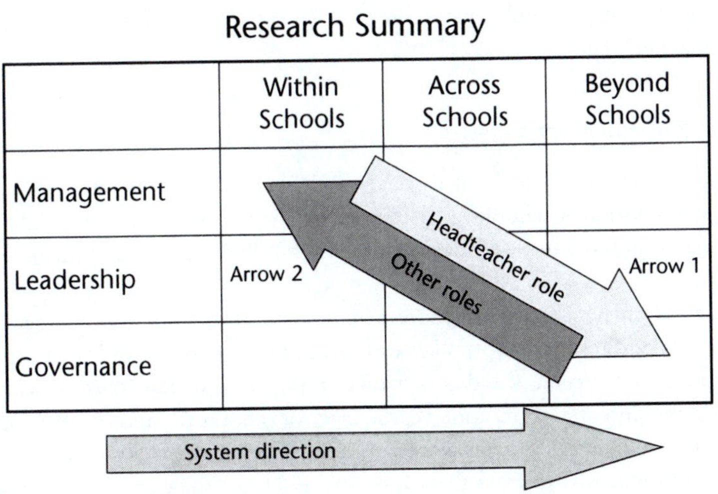

FIGURE 6.1   A framework for exploring emerging forms of school leadership

and management skills, particularly within their own school. All of this can be seen as an overall change in the ways in which schools position themselves in their local communities, represented by the 'direction of system travel' arrow. Such a repositioning was demanded by the national policy agenda. It also makes sense in terms of international research, which indicates school improvement, particularly in socio-economically disadvantaged contexts, will only be sustainable if it is connected to effective programmes of community regeneration (e.g. Anyon, 1997; Crowther et al., 2003; Lipman, 2004; Levin, 2005).

In terms of developing capacity for innovation within the system, such arrangements can be seen as a means of resolving what Hargreaves and Hopkins (1991) describe as the 'maintenance-development dilemma'. This arises from the tensions that occur when established organizations are faced with the need to change. Put simply, they have to continue carrying out existing requirements (maintenance) whilst, at the same time, inventing responses to new requirements (development). This is experienced as a dilemma in that however an organization responds there are associated risks: too much emphasis on maintenance means that it gets left behind; whilst an overemphasis on development may damage the quality of what is already in place.

The separation of roles of the sort seen in some of the schools seemed, on the surface at least, a promising way of dealing with all of this. For example, the executive head of a successful federation of two schools concentrated mostly on further innovations, leaving his two deputies to each manage one of the two sites. Governors continued to take responsibility for all day-to-day policy issues, leaving the trustees to focus on next steps. In this case the head was the only person attending meetings of both groups, so confirming his overall strategic role.

Interesting though such arrangements are, they are not without tensions. So, for example, in another trust that seemed to have created a remarkable capacity for development, some staff complained that the headteacher had taken his eye off routine matters. As a result, they argued, some aspects of the school's work had, they felt, deteriorated.

Possible implications

This study was carried out during 2007 and 2008 as we began our attempts to develop new forms of school leadership within the Greater Manchester Challenge. The findings pointed to three ideas that seemed to me to be of potential relevance:

1. They confirmed that there were a range of interesting developments taking place regarding the conceptualization and implementation of leadership practices, and management and governance arrangements. Many of these seemed to have the potential to increase the capacity of schools to innovate. It seemed to me that such developments would be vital if we were to find ways of improving overall standards while, at the same time, reducing the gap between high and low achieving groups of learners. But it was also clear that these examples were

closely tied into the local contexts in which they had developed. Consequently, they did not indicate 'solutions' that would transfer easily across boundaries. Rather, engagement with these cases helped to generate understandings about particular approaches that could enable a more informed development of ways forward in other contexts. In this sense, they represented starting points for the design of specific responses that would suit specific contexts, rather than models to be replicated.

2.   Though all of these developments had been driven by the desire to improve educational outcomes – and in some there were early indications of progress – the production of knowledge related to the impact of such developments on student outcomes was very limited at this stage. Therefore, further research investigating the impact of new models of leadership on student outcomes was needed. Furthermore, the study had highlighted the need to deepen understandings of the relationship between leadership and school development.

3.   It was clear that, across the accounts of practice compiled for the study, there were certain noticeable patterns. Specifically, we saw evidence that many headteachers were rethinking their priorities, looking much more outside the school, leaving their senior colleagues to manage day-to-day arrangements. We also saw that collaboration between schools – and between schools and other agencies – was increasingly a process that involved staff from a variety of levels in the school directly in discussions and decision-making.

It is worth adding that the study pointed towards something else that became apparent during the period of the Greater Manchester Challenge. As new stakeholders became more actively involved in supporting processes of educational improvement, this sometimes led to periods of turbulence as the status and assumptions of traditional partners were subject to challenge.

Creating system leaders

The development of the leadership strategy for the Challenge was a complex and, at times, irritating process as competing views of what were the best ways forward were debated. As with other aspects of the initiative, there were particular tensions that resulted from the centralizing instincts of many who were close to government. These included some colleagues from the National College for School Leadership, the government agency that acted as a partner to the three City Challenges.

As noted in Chapter 2, during the period prior to the formal start of the Challenge and, indeed, over the first year of the initiative, National College staff organized a small number of events for headteachers in Greater Manchester, where highly regarded national experts on school leadership offered their advice as to what actions were needed. Whilst not doubting the good intentions of these colleagues, the events ran the risk of offering a different theory of change to the one that was central to our emerging strategy. Specifically, they seemed to imply that external expertise of a sort that was not available locally was needed to bring about improvements in Greater Manchester schools. And, of course, the approach we were seeking to foster was based on a strong belief that the expertise that was needed was there within the schools themselves.

My concern about all of this grew at a working dinner for representatives of the three Challenges in 2009, when the then Director of the National College announced with great enthusiasm his decision to appoint a national director for their City Challenge activities. By that time, there was growing clarity amongst senior colleagues in the DFES, and within the Black Country, London and Greater Manchester, that our approach was to be largely driven by local players. This being the case, the three Chief Advisers shared little enthusiasm for the appointment of somebody who would carry a national responsibility for leadership development.

As far as I could tell, tensions between the National College and colleagues in the Black Country and in London continued in various forms. In our case, however, these were much less evident because one of our Challenge Advisers was appointed by the College to coordinate the development of our leadership strategy. Consequently, as far as we were concerned, for all practical purposes this individual was 'the College'. This led to the setting up of a local office where a team of staff worked with a group of headteachers to coordinate the development of our leadership strategy in a highly effective manner.

Towards a leadership strategy

By April 2009 a strategy for strengthening leadership had been developed, agreed with the Steering Group and approved by the Minister. The overall budget for the strategy for 2009–2010 was £7.74m. In explaining what this would involve it was noted that the priority for the first year had been focused mainly on developing tailored packages of support for Keys to Success schools. In years two and three of the Challenge, the leadership focus was to be placed on maintaining and enhancing support for Keys to Success schools in the Greater Manchester area, with additional programmes and initiatives being made available to further develop the capacity for improvement in these schools. In addition, work would be extended to give all schools in Greater Manchester access to a range of bespoke initiatives that would focus on developing the capacity of leaders at all levels within schools. These were to include:

- **The identification, training and deployment of Local Leaders of Education (LLEs).** Local Leaders would continue to be identified, developed and deployed into Keys to Success schools. These were all current serving headteachers with a minimum of three years' successful experience, a proven track record of excellent leadership – including their schools having been graded as being effective for leadership and management as a result of an Ofsted inspection – and also experience of supporting other schools in challenging contexts.
- **Supporting the national work on National Leaders of Education (NLEs).** National Leaders would continue to be identified and deployed across

the region. Following a rigorous process of selection, they were to provide additional leadership to schools in the most challenging circumstances.

- **Support for Keys to Success schools.** Tailored intervention programmes to strengthen leadership practices would continue to be made available for Keys to Success Schools. Building on what had happened during the first year, these would include school-to-school support packages, involving the schools of the LLE or NLEs.

In addition, the plan was to create a menu of leadership development programmes, including:

- induction opportunities for new headteachers;
- leading a challenging school for the first time;
- high level coaching skills for senior leaders;
- support for school business managers.

It was also decided to create Middle Leaders of Education. Identified through a rigorous quality assurance process, they were to work with heads of department or subject leaders in Keys to Success schools, with a particular focus on core subjects.

Beyond this basic offer, the decision was made to create various types of 'hub'. That is to say, centres of relatively strong practice that would have the task of encouraging further sharing of expertise across the system. In particular, building on work in London, it was decided to continue developing 'teaching schools'. Recognized as being outstanding in their context, these schools were to be encouraged to provide support and additional capacity for other schools, especially for those in the most challenging of circumstances. During the period of the Challenge a total of 19 teaching schools were created. One of their most important roles was to provide a suite of teaching and learning professional development programmes, initially for teachers in the Keys to Success schools, but subsequently across many other schools in Greater Manchester. These included:

- **The Improving Teacher Programme.** This was aimed at enabling teachers to provide (using the language of Ofsted) 'satisfactory to good' lessons.
- **The Outstanding Teacher Programme.** The aim of this was to develop teaching practices that were 'good to outstanding'.
- **The Teaching and Learning Immersion Programme.** For heads of department or curriculum leaders, the aim was to develop the skills to observe and mentor colleagues.

In addition, 'secondary lead departments' were to be identified. These would be available to work alongside departments in Keys to Success schools to help support and address the challenges they face in leading what were sometimes large 'turbulent' departments.

System leaders

During the first year, the participation of headteachers and other senior school staff in Challenge activities was largely on an ad hoc basis, as individuals agreed to take part in the Families of Schools and Keys to Success activities described in earlier chapters. Inevitably, their participation was largely based on a desire for their own schools to gain advantages, not least from the financial resources that were known to be available. As things developed, however, it became increasingly evident that some headteachers were enjoying the professional opportunities that were opening up through their involvement. At the same time, the Challenge Advisers developed a growing awareness of where the strengths within the system lay in this respect and so gradually encouraged more headteachers to take on more substantive roles.

The developing national policy regarding the appointment of National and Local Leaders of Education gave further momentum to this process.[1] The designation of these individuals created an opportunity to bring them together in order to encourage them to share responsibility for the coordination and further development of the leadership strategy in particular, as well as in the overall programme of the Challenge. Our assumption was that the strengthening of this cadre of strong headteachers would evolve into a structure that would seek to maintain the momentum for improvement beyond the formal period of the initiative.

With this in mind, termly gatherings were organized of the group of National and Local Leaders of Education from across the city region. Initially these events were rather formal affairs, as colleagues with no knowledge of one another took part in structured discussions, during which some were seen to see opportunities for self-promotion. Indeed, on one occasion I joked with the group that we were thinking of having the entrance widened in order to get all the egos into the room.

Gradually, however, all of this changed such that the meetings became a source of inspiration for many of us who were involved. In general terms there were two main agenda items: How can we learn from one another about becoming system leaders? And, what else might we do collectively to strengthen leadership across all of our schools? In this way, the meetings became a means of sharing ideas and a stimulus for mutual learning. At the same time, they led to an increasing sense of shared responsibility.

Many of these headteachers came to be seen as having a central role as what Hopkins (2007) refers to as 'system leaders'. The good news is that our experience suggests that many successful headteachers are motivated by the idea of taking on such roles, particularly that of supporting developments in schools experiencing difficulties. Reflecting on his experience of working in this way, one head commented:

> I have a strong conviction that impact is maximized through a willingness to learn oneself when giving support and to ensure that, at all times, the client school is at the centre. In other words, no matter how experienced or skilled you might believe yourself to be, it is important to be flexible and meet the

school where it is at – rather than to go in with a template of answers. To do this, strong professional and objective relationships have to be established with all key players you are working with and supporting.

Another headteacher explained that, for her, the key to successful partnership working across schools is mutual trust and an understanding that there are opportunities for the development for both schools. She explained,

> It's just about working together to try to support each other and making sure we are doing something really useful, not just reinventing the same thing.

Using the image of an orchestra, she added,

> The school's own staff are the principal instruments, the external partners are just helping with the conducting.

By the end of the Challenge, there were some 170 or so outstanding headteachers designated as system leaders in Greater Manchester. Increasingly, over the three years, they drove forward improvement efforts across the city region. In addition to their involvement in the Families of Schools and the partnerships set up to support Keys to Success schools, they explored other mechanisms for making better use of the expertise that exists within the schools.

Hub schools

One important strategy developed by headteachers to facilitate the movement of expertise was provided through the creation of the various types of 'hub schools', referred to earlier. So, for example, hub schools were created which provided specialist support for students with English as an additional language. These schools engaged enthusiastically in the process of sharing practice through workshops attended by practitioners from across the region. Similarly, the teaching schools[2] providing professional development programmes focused on bringing about improvements in classroom practice. Over 1,000 teachers from across the city region took part in these programmes that involved powerful adult learning strategies, such as the modelling of effective classroom techniques, practice and feedback, and peer coaching. Once again, here, there was strong evidence of mutual benefit in this approach – it often had a positive impact on the quality of classroom practice and student learning in both the schools receiving support and within the teaching schools themselves.

Other hub schools offered support in relation to particular subject areas, and in responding to groups of potentially vulnerable groups, such as those categorized as having special educational needs. In this latter context, a further significant development involved new roles for special schools in supporting developments in the mainstream.

A particular powerful development focused on providing support for schools in working with learners for whom English is an additional language (EAL). Supported by a Challenge Adviser with specialist expertise, this provided advice and professional development for teachers and support staff through the creation of a series of hub schools. In addition, conferences were held where practitioners shared their ideas and resources. This led to the development of a directory of resources.

In proposing this initiative the Challenge Adviser argued that a significant proportion of Greater Manchester schools (and particularly Keys to Success schools) had large numbers of students with English as an additional language. She went on to suggest that once more than 25 per cent of students in a school have English as an additional language, it becomes increasingly difficult for schools to meet their needs effectively without integrated provision. An analysis of 2008 data had shown that in 112 primary schools and 30 secondary schools in the region such pupils make up more than 25 per cent of students on roll. Across Greater Manchester as a whole, approximately 15.7 per cent of pupils had a first language other than English, compared to 9.5 per cent nationally. Furthermore, data produced by a government analyst had suggested that as the percentage of pupils with EAL in a school increases, the average percentage of pupils with 5 GCSEs A* to C including English and maths decreases.

In developing a strategy it was felt that well focused support for both new arrivals and advanced bilingual learners would enable students to fulfil their academic potential, and help schools to raise their achievement levels significantly. We had been providing some EAL support to Keys to Success schools since the beginning of the Challenge through our specialist Adviser. She had assessed needs and brokered in additional support in a number of the secondary Keys to Success schools. This support was typically focused on identifying a member of staff to be the lead on EAL, providing training and development of key members of staff, and funding the release of staff from various hub schools with good EAL provision to support others.

Looking to the future

During the final year of the Challenge many meetings were held with representatives of the group of leading headteachers in order to plan a strategy for maintaining the impetus beyond the formal period of the Challenge. Eventually a group of some 25 headteachers volunteered to put more time into thinking about what form this would take. No doubt they were encouraged, in part at least, by knowing that the DfE had allocated some funding to support their activities. As a result, the negotiations led to periods of tension as certain heads appeared to jockey for position in relation to who would lead the initiative. Indeed, at one point I had to act as referee between two 'big hitting' heads who were clearly competing for the status that they perceived to be at stake.

Fortunately, a consensus was gradually achieved and what emerged was a decision to create an independent agency that would take on this role after City

Challenge ended. Eventually, after much debate, the decision was made to call this organization 'By Schools For Schools'. Over three years later it is pleasing to report that this initiative is continuing, albeit within a context of increased competition, not least from the many private companies that now offer support for school improvement. This being the case, By Schools for Schools has to demonstrate it offers value for money with regard to the services it provides.

In terms of the current English policy context, there are other new challenges to be addressed in taking this thinking forward, most notably the increasing diversity of governance arrangement, with many more schools choosing to become independent of their local authorities. This leads me to feel that recent efforts to encourage collaboration between schools of the sort that was so powerful in City Challenge remain something of a disappointment in respect to their capacity to foster equity within the education system. Other features of the new national policy are creating barriers to progress. At the same time, this new context is creating much uncertainly within the field, all of which opens up opportunities for those who are committed to a more collaborative approach to have a greater influence.

During such periods of uncertainty, the search is on for what Fullan (1991) describes as 'order and correctness'. Those searching for correctness in a complex education system that is involved in substantial change will inevitably experience ambiguity and a lack of understanding of the direction and purposes of the change. Thus the search for order is a search to determine what actions to take when faced with ambiguous situations. However, whilst schools are at the centre of these changes they do not exist in isolation. They are influenced by forces which exercise significant power upon the climate of the school in both predictable and unpredictable ways. It is in this climate that school staffs construct the realities of their working lives.

Weick (1985) characterizes schools as 'underorganised systems' in that, although they tend to be ambiguous and disorderly, there is, nevertheless, some order. Furthermore, he argues, anyone who can help to create more order within an underorganized system can bring about change. This may in part, at least, throw some light on what occurred through the Greater Manchester Challenge. Unusual and disturbing circumstances, emanating as they did from both outside and inside schools, created a sense of ambiguity across the system. Collaborative arrangements helped to resolve this, and, as a result, drew stakeholders together behind broadly similar principles.

As Weick explains, because ambiguity in organizations increases the extent to which action is guided by values and ideology, the beliefs of 'powerful people' (i.e. those who can reduce ambiguity) affect what the organization is and what it can become. Thus, according to Weick, those who resolve ambiguity for themselves and others can implant a new set values in an organization, which creates a new set of relevancies and competencies, and, in so doing, introduces a source of innovation. In this way ambiguity sets the scene for organizations to learn about themselves and their environments, allowing them to emerge from their struggles with uncertainty in a different form than when they started the confrontation.

All of this leads me to argue that the perspective and skills of committed school leaders is central to efforts to use collaboration as a strategy for creating self-improving school systems. Their visions of schools and the extent to which they believe that it is possible to foster the learning of all children and young people will be key influences. All of this means, of course, that replication of these processes in other contexts will be difficult if those in senior positions are unwilling or unable to make fundamental changes in working patterns.

Conclusion

The overall recommendation that emerges from the evidence presented in this chapter is that **in order for education systems to become self-improving leadership has to come from within schools**. Within the Greater Manchester Challenge, many successful headteachers were motivated to take on system leadership roles. Indeed, the role of senior staff within schools became an increasing factor in the success of the initiative and in ensuring that progress continued beyond the period of the funding that was provided. In this way, through the collective efforts of many successful practitioners, the emphasis on creative action increased, providing a springboard for many new initiatives that had not been included in the initial project design.

This emphasis on leadership from within schools is also a promising strategy in respect to the challenge of sustainability. The evidence from many other large-scale system change initiatives is that progress often fades once the additional resources have disappeared. Three years after the end of the Greater Manchester Challenge it is clear that progress has been maintained, not least because of the strengthening of relationships that occurred across the city region. Local leadership seems to have been a key factor in this respect.

As I argue in the next chapter, all of this has significant implications for policy makers at the national and district levels. In order to make use of the power of locally-led collaboration, they need to foster greater flexibility so that practitioners have the space to analyze their particular circumstances and determine priorities accordingly. This means that policy makers must recognize that the details of policy implementation are not amenable to central regulation. Rather, these have to be dealt with by those who are close to and, therefore, in a better position to understand local contexts. They should be trusted to act in the best interests of the children and young people they serve, and encouraged to work together, pooling their knowledge and experience, for the benefit of students and teachers alike.

Notes

1   This is now part of a national scheme where outstanding headteachers are designated as National Leaders of Education. As such, they are expected to provide support to other schools.
2   Teaching schools are seen as having a similar role as teaching hospitals. On the basis of the excellent practice that exists, they offer professional development to staff from other schools. This approach, which was developed within City Challenge, is now a central feature of national policy.

7

ADDRESSING THE POLITICS

By now it will have become apparent to readers that developing a consistent strategy throughout the three-year period of the Greater Manchester Challenge was always the major concern as far as I was concerned. What quickly became clear was that there were a variety of views as to what should happen as a result of the different priorities that existed amongst the many stakeholders, both at the local and national levels. My sense was that these competing views reflected a variety of theories of change.

In this chapter I bring to the surface some of the struggles that took place in order to get people pulling in the same direction. These included my own ideas as I attempted to build on the research evidence that I have summarized in the preceding chapters. In addressing this agenda, I try to make sense of the political pressures that occur when trying to bring together many stakeholders within a common strategy. Talking of this in relation to a large scale improvement initiative in Ontario, Levin (2008) comments:

> The literature on educational change tends to ignore politics or treat it as an exogenous force, yet political factors have a huge impact on which changes get considered, adopted, supported and maintained.
>
> *(p. 6)*

Rather depressingly, this leads him to conclude:

> Political pressures are one reason that worthwhile changes in education do not last.
>
> *(p. 7)*

Bearing this in mind, in what follows I draw on my archive of notes and documents from over the three years to explain how my colleagues and I attempted to overcome these sorts of difficulty. In reflecting on what this involved, I was frequently reminded of Robert Bales' theory of group systems that we had used in earlier research (see Ainscow, Hargreaves and Hopkins, 1995). As Bales predicts, the attempts to get different stakeholders to pull together led to tensions between the need to establish cohesion amongst groups, whilst, at the same time, taking actions to achieve our goals. Put simply, it was relatively easy to maintain cooperation until the moments when hard decisions had to be made, most particularly regarding the setting of priorities and the allocation of resources.

A partnership?

City Challenge emerged during an unprecedented period of centralization of decision making regarding education policy in England. Alongside the changes that had followed on from the Education Reform Act of 1988, such as the introduction of the national curriculum, assessment systems and inspections, the Labour government had introduced National Strategies that were intended to improve classroom practices. Initially focused on raising standards in literacy and numeracy in primary schools, this widened to focus on many other aspects of practice in all state schools. The approach involved prescriptive strategies set out in centrally determined templates for 'high quality' teaching, which teachers were required to follow (Kerr and West, 2010).

As I explained in Chapter 1, the implementation of the National Strategies was rather unusual – a series of system-wide improvement approaches commissioned from a private organization and supported by teams of consultants employed nationally, regionally and within each local authority. Within this centrally-driven policy context, City Challenge stood out in the sense that those involved were given considerable space to explore different ways of working. Recognition of this factor was indicated by the appointment of particular Ministers for each of the Challenge areas. Nevertheless, there was a constant struggle to maintain this space within an overall emphasis on one-size-fits-all policies. Much of my own work involved attempts to deal with the contradictions this created.

At the outset of the initiative much use was made of the term 'partnership' in describing the Challenge. I sensed that for some within the ten local authorities this was a source of irritation in that the decision to have the initiative was imposed by national government in what was clearly seen as an intervention. One of the factors that was behind these tensions was that there were different views as to what needed to happen in order to improve education systems. One view was starkly expressed in an email note sent to colleagues within the DfES which stated that, as far as improving attainment amongst disadvantaged pupils was concerned, 'the strategy must be exactly the same whether it is in Plymouth (*in the south west of England*), or in Sunderland (*in the far north east*)'.

This instinct to direct from the centre kept popping up at our fortnightly meetings of the Advisers, when our civil servant colleagues took opportunities to brief the group on the latest proposals from central government. In general the team found these inputs helpful in the sense that they made them feel ahead of the game regarding policy decisions. My own concern was that, too often, they gave the wrong message in respect to the theory of change we had adopted. A striking example of this that created a significant distraction was the publication in 2009 of the White Paper, 'Building a 21st Century Schools System'. The civil servant who led on this initiative as far as primary schools was concerned became particularly dogged in her efforts to impose the strategy on the schools. With this in mind, for some months she guided the agenda of the team of primary advisers in a direction that, for me, represented a significant deviation from the rationale we had developed together.

The role of the middle tier

Writing in the introduction to her novel *South Riding*, Winifred Holtby, whose mother had been the first woman Alderman in the city of Hull, describes local government as 'the first-line defence thrown up by the community against our common enemies – poverty, sickness, ignorance, isolation, mental derangement and social maladjustment' (p. ix). This is worth remembering as we consider the future role of local authorities in relation to the development of self-improving school systems.

The creation of a system for improvement that is driven by schools themselves, and that involves cooperation between schools and other community organizations, begs questions regarding the roles of local authorities. Indeed, it raises the possibility that the involvement of a middle level administrative structure may not even be necessary.

The authors of the influential McKinsey report, having analyzed 'how the world's most improved school systems keep getting better', express their surprise at the critical role that what they call the 'mediating layer' plays between school delivery and central government (Mourshed, Chijioke and Barber, 2010). This leads them to conclude that sustaining system improvement in the longer term requires 'integration and intermediation' across each level of the system, 'from the classroom to the superintendent or minister's office'. They explain:

> The operating system of the mediating layer acts as the integrator and mediator between the classrooms and the centre. This is not to suggest that school reforms should begin here. In every system we looked at, the first focus of school reforms was on the schools and the centre. Efforts to strengthen the mediating layer usually came later, as the need for an active intermediary in delivering the system improvements became clearer.
>
> *(Mourshed, Chijioke and Barber, 2010, p. 82)*

The authors of the report go on to suggest that the specific functions the mediating layer plays are: providing targeted support to schools; acting as a buffer between the centre and the schools, while interpreting and communicating the improvement objectives in order to manage any resistance to change; and enhancing the collaborative exchange between schools, by facilitating the sharing of best practices, helping them to support each other, share learning, and standardize practices.

All of this points to questions regarding the roles of what is sometimes referred to as the 'middle tier' – in England, local authorities – particularly as a self-improving system matures. The experience of Greater Manchester suggests that local authority staff can have an important role as 'the first-line defence against our common enemies', acting as the conscience of the system, and making sure that all children and young people are getting a fair deal within an increasingly diverse system of education. In order to do this, however, they must have the big picture about what is happening in their communities, in order to identify priorities for action and broker collaboration. This requires significant structural and cultural changes, with local authorities moving away from a command and control perspective, solely focused within their own boundaries, towards one of enabling and facilitating collaborative action across the city region. Borrowing a phrase from former US Secretary of State, Dean Acheson, I suggested in a discussion paper for local authority officers that this would involve them in 'losing an empire and finding a role'.

In what follows I explain how local authority colleagues found these changes challenging, particularly during a time of reducing budgets and frequent changes in national policy. I go on to illustrate how the strengthening of cross-border cooperation, at many levels, provided contexts within which mutual support could be provided in addressing these concerns. I also provide an explanation of the arrangements that were put in place to build on the success of the Greater Manchester Challenge, including the creation of an area school improvement partnership board and the development of the headteacher-led agency known as 'By Schools for Schools'.

Rethinking the roles of local authorities

As we studied efforts to foster more attempts to build greater equity during the years prior to the City Challenge, my colleagues and I had taken interest in the changing roles of English local authorities (e.g. Ainscow, Farrell and Tweddle, 2000; Ainscow 2005). The lessons of these earlier experiences were in my mind as we developed our strategy within the Greater Manchester Challenge. On the positive side, I recalled the value of having local authority colleagues who were close to the schools, developing deep knowledge of the challenges they faced, as well as the areas of expertise within the system that could be mobilized. On the negative side, I was conscious that national policy had encouraged these colleagues to view schools through the narrow and, at times, perverse lens created by the so-called standards agenda.

During the early part of the Challenge it became evident that officers in some of our partner authorities did not know the schools in their areas well. As I had anticipated, they tended to only rate their schools in relation to crude levels of performance. The limitations of this were most obvious when, as sometimes happened, schools were placed in an Ofsted category following an inspection despite the fact that local authority staff had expressed no concerns.

It became increasingly obvious, therefore, that the Challenge strategy had to help local authority staff to rethink their roles in relation to the development of a self-improving system. With this in mind, a number of arrangements were gradually put in place. Many of these involved structures that encouraged authority representatives at different levels of the system to work together. Given my previous experience in other parts of the country, where regional cooperation was more advanced, I found it surprising that this was not already occurring.

The first of these arrangements was the Steering Group, set up at the start of the Challenge. As I explained in Chapter 2, I chaired the meetings of the group, the members of which were: a chief executive, four directors of children's services and an assortment of civil servants, who, as I sometimes joked, 'wrote everything down'. Occasionally, too, the Minister would attend.

The early meetings were formal but cordial, as the 'two sides' – representatives of local and national governments – exchanged their ideas. The atmosphere tended to change, however, when we came up against questions regarding how financial resources were to be used, as predicted by Robert Bale's theory of the tensions that are likely to occur within working groups. It was obvious at this stage that local authority colleagues had little or no power in this respect. Handling this was difficult for me and after one early meeting I brought the civil servants together to suggest that it did not help if they kept saying things like, 'we have decided', or 'it has been decided'.

Fortunately, these difficulties gradually faded as relationships between the participants warmed and agreements were reached as to the priority areas for developments. Evidence of impact was also a factor in this respect – somehow it becomes easier to cooperate when things are going well. At the risk of sounding immodest, I also think my own contributions were important here, not least because I tried to maintain a degree of independence from the two groups.

In addition, there were matters of organizational detail that we changed that appeared to help in the process of building bridges between the two sides. For example, the early meetings of the Steering Group were held in the offices of one of the local authorities. Recognizing that this might be a factor in creating the sense of formality, during the second year of the project I suggested we relocate the meetings to my University's conference centre. At the time of this move, I also decided to seat the participants in sub-groups around smaller tables, with members of the two sides mixed, rather than the earlier boardroom format we had previously used, where they tended to sit across from one another in a way that was reminiscent of meetings between American and Chinese politicians.

The second structure to foster cross-authority cooperation was the forum I suggested, where the ten directors of children's services could meet on a regular basis. They were, of course, the most senior officers as far as education policy was concerned. However, as a result of national policy changes their responsibilities had been extended beyond education to include other services for children and young people, not least social care. As a result, an increasing number of the directors had no direct professional experience of working with schools. Indeed, it became apparent that some of them found schools, and particularly secondary headteachers, difficult to handle. The story was told, for example, of how one had been badly bruised by the challenges she faced at a meeting of headteachers soon after her appointment. It was noticed that she subsequently avoided these meetings and, in fact, rarely visited schools. It was notable, too, that during the three years of the Challenge, seven new directors were appointed across the ten authorities. In some authorities, directors were replaced more than once over that period, perhaps indicating the pressures these colleagues were under as they struggled to provide leadership across such a broad range of services.

The directors' meetings we instigated became an established pattern and it was evident that they led to a whole series of joint activities beyond the remit of the Challenge. My contribution was a standing item at each of these meetings and I used these to keep the directors informed and to maintain their support. Sometimes this involved me in discussions which added little to our strategy, as they chose to get involved in matters of detail about which they had little knowledge or, indeed, expertise. Nevertheless, I saw this as a good investment of my time in the sense of heading off possible blockages. It was evident, too, that some of my civil servant colleagues found some of the directors difficult to deal with. Indeed, one regularly asked me to act as the 'middle man' in her negotiations with a particular officer whom she found threatening.

Moving to the next level of the system, early on in the Challenge I instigated regular meetings of the senior school improvement officers from the ten local authorities. I designated this as a 'thinktank' in a way that was intended to signal that it should be a forum for reflecting on our Challenge strategy and making recommendations as to actions that needed to be taken. Members of this group explained that there had previously been a similar forum organized by staff of the National Strategies but that they tended to stay away because the agenda was imposed. Conscious of this, I avoided a tight agenda for the meetings, preferring to suggest more general themes for discussion.

Over the following months the meetings became a helpful context in which relatively senior colleagues who were clearly struggling within a changing policy context could share ideas and offer support to one another. One helpful idea that was generated was to develop a virtual school improvement service, which would coordinate the use of strengths in one authority to intervene in areas of concern in other parts of the city region.

Working together for school improvement

From the outset we had decided that the Challenge team would work with local authority staff in attempting to improve schools. Some of my civil servant colleagues were anxious about this approach in that they felt that it might slow down the improvement process. To some degree their thinking was, I suspect, informed by earlier experiences in the London Challenge, where the strategy had tended to bypass the local authorities. As things developed, their concerns were further heightened as a result of what they saw happening in the Black Country Challenge, where, I was told, the presence of local authority staff and elected members on most of the planning groups was seen to delay progress.

Whilst recognizing these concerns I could see no option but to work with local authority colleagues, particularly if the changes we wanted to make were to be sustainable. This being the case, we developed strategies for cooperating on school improvement efforts that were meant to be both supportive and yet challenging. This led us to designate small teams of Challenge Advisers – typically one for primary schools and one for secondary – for each authority.

Each term, these teams of Advisers, plus a civil servant, met with local authority colleagues to review the progress of schools, particularly those involved in the Keys to Success programme. In this way, where necessary, the involvement of schools would change, with some being taken out of the programme as a result of the rapid progress made, whilst others were introduced. I attended as many of these meetings as possible. Sometimes the discussions became heated, as local authority staff and Challenge Advisers attempted to impose their own views. Tensions also surfaced when it was implied that local authority colleagues did not know their schools well enough and that, as a result, were not acting effectively.

Of course, practices varied in different authorities in this respect. During our fortnightly meeting of Challenge Advisers these differences were frequently debated. As a result of these discussions, during 2009 the decision was made to adopt a more strategic approach to the strengthening of school improvement arrangements in each authority. With this in mind, I wrote a discussion paper for the Advisers and civil servant team.

In the introduction to the paper I argued that we needed to alter the emphasis of our work in order to strengthen the capacity of local authorities to foster school improvement in the changing policy context. In so doing, it was important that we stayed consistent with our overall rationale, which I summarized as follows:

- The long term aim is to strengthen the capacity of the education system to improve the achievement and life chances of all children and young people.
- This requires experimentation in order to develop more effective ways of working in all schools and colleges.
- Much of the expertise that is needed in order to make this happen exists within the city region.
- There is a need for a sharp local analysis in order to locate and make better use of available expertise.
- Effective networking is needed in order to 'move knowledge around'.
- Headteachers and other school leaders are the key agents for improving educational achievement and attainment.

I argued that all of this had very significant implications for the roles of local authority staff. It meant that they had to adjust their priorities and ways of working in response to the development of improvement efforts that are led from within schools. For some this would involve a major change in the way they carry out their duties.

In the discussion paper I proposed the following strategy:

> The question is, **how can we help local authorities to develop effective school improvement systems?** In what follows I outline for discussion an approach that attempts to respond to the varied stages of development within each of the ten authorities. It involves a two-phase approach, where, in some cases, it may not be necessary to move on to the second phase. Put simply, for some it may mean increasing efficiency (i.e. Are we doing things right?), whereas for others it may mean a more fundamental rethink in relation to effectiveness (i.e. Are we doing the right things?).
>
> I should stress here that I am not suggesting that all the LAs should work in the same way. Given the varied contexts and circumstances, different approaches may well be needed. However, whatever the style of working that is adopted, we need to ensure that these are effective in improving the quality of educational provision across the whole LA.

I went on to suggest the two-phase strategy, as follows:

> **Phase 1: Strengthening school improvement arrangements.** Over the next two or three months we will hold a review meeting in each LA, using as a starting point our observations of the effectiveness and efficiency of current ways of working as a stimulus for discussion. With this in mind, prior to the meeting, we will prepare a short written commentary in relation to the following strategic questions:
>
> - Is there a common understanding within the LA of the rationale of its school improvement strategy?
> - Are officers and school leaders committed to this rationale?
> - Do school improvement staff have appropriate working relationships with their schools in respect to support and challenge?
> - How effective is the work of the school improvement partners?
> - Are sound systems in place for checking the way staff are working and providing necessary support for individuals?
>
> The meeting, which will be chaired by the Chief Adviser, will usually involve the Director of Children's Services and the senior officer(s) responsible for school improvement, the Challenge Advisers who work with schools in the LA, and a member of the DCSF team. The intended outcomes will be an agreement as to what actions are needed in order to further strengthen school improvement arrangements and a timeline as to when progress will next be reviewed. Where it is felt that there is a need to think in more detail about the authority's overall approach to school improvement, a decision will be

made to instigate a more fundamental review process, using a 'health check' framework.

Phase 2: Rethinking school improvement arrangements. Where it is felt to be appropriate, there will be a more detailed review of current ways of working in order to rethink the local authority's improvement strategy. This will involve a facilitated process, involving local authority school improvement staff, representative headteachers, relevant Challenge advisers and a member of the DCSF team. It will lead to an agreement as to the actions needed in order to define: the approach to be taken, areas for development, strategies for encouraging new ways of working, and a timeline as to when progress will next be reviewed. At this stage, one option will be to link with another GM authority that has strengths in the areas that have been pinpointed for development through the proposed 'virtual school improvement service'.

I suggested that a practical implication of the outcomes of both these review processes was that Challenge Advisers would increasingly work more closely in their Keys to Success schools *alongside* their counterparts in the local authority. This would involve advisers in:

- modeling effective ways of working;
- coaching their LA colleagues;
- encouraging collaborative problem-solving;
- creating a professional dialogue about the sorts of working practices that are needed in the light of the local authority's developing approach to school improvement.

Reviewing local authority arrangements

The discussion provoked by this paper led us to arrange a series of termly meetings in each authority to review arrangements for supporting school improvement. Prior to the meetings, I worked with the relevant Advisers in writing an evaluative commentary on current practices. These reports were then circulated before the meeting took place. The writing of the reports was in itself a challenge, in that we wanted to maintain levels of cooperation whilst at the same time offering a frank assessment of the situation. An example will provide a flavour of what this looked like.

In one particular local authority we were concerned about the poor quality of support provided for its primary schools. Our pre-meeting report, presented to the local authority in January 2010, read as follows:

Strengthening school improvement arrangements in (*Authority*): some observations and thoughts

The Authority is currently reviewing its arrangements for improving the performance of its schools. It is likely that new ways of working will emerge that will require different relationships with schools and, indeed, with other services working with children and young people. All of this is set within a rapidly changing policy context that places additional responsibilities on those involved.

As Advisers working on the Greater Manchester Challenge, we have been pleased to get involved in these developments. We have been grateful too for the way senior staff within the Local Authority have welcomed our contributions and gone out of their way to collaborate with us.

In the spirit of this collaborative relationship, in these notes we offer some observations and tentative thoughts on what is happening on the ground. Inevitably our picture of what is happening is partial, based in the main on our work in the Keys to Success schools, and supplemented with more superficial impressions gathered through our involvement with other schools in the Authority.

Agenda for discussion. Our intention is to stimulate detailed discussions with our Local Authority partners regarding the various contributions we should all be making in respect to next steps. We would like to do this in relation to the following broad questions:

- Is there a common understanding within the LA of the rationale of its school improvement strategy?
- Are officers and school leaders committed to this rationale?
- Do school improvement staff have appropriate working relationships with their schools in respect to support and challenge?
- How effective is the work of the School Improvement Partners?
- Are sound systems in place for checking the way staff are working and providing necessary support for individuals?
- Are there any other matters that need to be considered?

Some impressions and thoughts. Our partnership with the Authority got off to a very good start, with productive meetings with senior colleagues to share the aims and discuss the processes of the Challenge. In the early days, however, the outcomes did not always reach LA colleagues on the ground. Subsequently, changes in personnel within the LA and, indeed, amongst the GMC team have led to occasional difficulties in communication.

Within the **primary** sector, the Authority's arrangements for school improvement have been and are going through a period of change. In this respect, we hope that the discussion stimulated by these notes will help in deciding how these arrangements can be restructured in a way that will be fit for purpose. And, of course, all of this will need to be addressed in relation to the new directions set out in the White Paper on the development of 21st Century school systems.

The Authority has a worrying proportion of its schools that have gone into Ofsted categories. In addition, others have been noted as a cause for concern during the second year of the Challenge. Our work has been mainly concentrated in these schools. At the same time, we are conscious that there are some very strong primary schools that can be used as a resource for supporting improvement efforts.

In carrying out our work, we have noted the impact of uncertainties regarding procedures, communication, roles and responsibilities. As a result, there is, we feel, a sense of fragmentation within the improvement arrangements made for some primary schools. Inevitably, this has also led to some difficulties in respect to the roles and contributions of the GMC team. We have recently started to hold regular joint reviews with the LA and this has led to an improvement in communication and shared understanding around Keys to Success Schools.

At an individual school level we have had some very positive experiences with LA school improvement officers and have developed close working relationships which have benefited schools. Some LA officers have welcomed the Challenge and have seen this as an extra resource to support their own work in the school.

Many of the School Improvement Officers (SIOs) are former primary headteachers from within the Authority. Our impression is that they are focused, know the schools well and set out to offer challenge to the schools. This being the case, we are left reflecting on why, at the end of the first year of the Challenge, the list of schools that were to be Keys to Success did not include some of the most challenging?

This leads us to raise questions regarding the robustness of the analysis carried out by the School Improvement Partners (SIPs) and the overall accuracy of the LA's procedures for identifying schools causing concern. Clearly there are instances where these procedures have proved to be effective, where the SIO has been focused, the SIP reports challenging, and effective support has been provided so that Governors are in a position to challenge leadership. However, the evidence of those schools that have 'surprised' the LA indicates that this is not always the case. In a minority of cases the LA has been aware of historical issues regarding leadership but has not been able to tackle them until changes of headteacher.

We have also been concerned that there appears to be a lack of intensive challenge for some primary schools. This leads us to ask about the consistency of the quality and effectiveness of the School Improvement Service. We have a sense that perhaps it relies too heavily on a small number of individuals who do know the schools well and are used in many guises.

At the same time, there are uncertainties about the multiple roles played by some LA staff. SIOs are also SIPs and we are not convinced that the two roles work well together. This arrangement will, of course, need to be rethought in relation to national policy changes.

Another area for concern is the number of primary schools that have large deficit budgets and what appear to be poor arrangements for addressing these situations. For example, one Keys to Success school, with a one-form entry, has a budget deficit of around £300,000. The relatively new headteacher did not receive support and advice from financial management in order to help with future planning. We understand, however, that the LA has very recently held a meeting for primary headteachers to support them in addressing budget issues. This is a very welcome step forward.

There are positive signs that the Authority is developing a longer term strategy; for example, we are aware that currently some schools are being closed and some amalgamated. In addition, we understand that the LA is keen to move on federations and we believe that this could be a significant move forward, particularly given the number of small primary schools. Support will be available for these moves.

We conclude, then, that there is an urgent need to develop a strategic plan for the improvement of standards across the primary education sector.

Moving to the **secondary** sector, recent years have seen significant overall improvements in the performance of many of the Authority's high schools. In general, working relationships between heads and LA officers seem to be strong, and Challenge Advisers have worked alongside LA staff in supporting the designated Keys to Success schools, including the pupil referral unit.[1]

Our overall impression is that members of the school improvement team know the secondary schools well, and offer effective support and intervention within the confines of that which they can directly influence. However, the absence of an overall strategic plan – understood by and communicated to all stakeholders – is, we believe, a source of frustration. This means that, whilst the school improvement team knows what needs to be done around specific schools, they cannot always act, since they are unclear of how such actions fit into any larger plan. Our work in the pupil referral unit is a good example of this: the main problem there is not so much the unit (although it is still very weak) but the fact that there is no overall strategic plan for alternative provision.

Part of the frustration we hear expressed by some headteachers and officers is that it is difficult to get behind something they are unclear about. There is also growing frustration around a number of what are seen to be mixed messages; for example, around proposals to establish one school as a trust. We sense that this has created an unnecessary sense of uncertainty in a school that is already far from stable.

We feel that the LA needs to explore the possibility of using more creative responses of the sort that we see being developed in other GM authorities. For example, there seems to be very little collaboration between schools, outside of that brokered through the Challenge. Yet, where we have encouraged such an approach, it seems to be welcomed and successful.

Similarly, we think there is a need to think further about the Authority's approach to SIPs in the secondary sector, not least because of changes in national policy in this area. Many SIPs seem to be LA officers or former officers. Of course, this has some potential benefits and the ones we have worked with have an excellent understanding of their schools. On the other hand, it occurs to us that a different approach might be more effective in some contexts, not least to ensure an appropriate level of challenge.

As in the primary sector, then, we feel that it is now time for the Authority to carry out a thorough review of its arrangements for supporting secondary school improvement in order to formulate an appropriate strategy for moving forward.

Moving forward. On a more general level, it is evident that the LA has embraced with enthusiasm the opportunities provided by GMC, recognizing the possibilities it provides to use cross-border collaboration as a means of sharing expertise and addressing areas of concern. In this respect, it is pleasing to see the leadership provided by senior staff within the LA in a variety of contexts. Similarly, schools are more and more taking up the opportunities provided by the various work strands and the leadership strategy, and through the activities of the Families of Schools, where a significant number of heads are taking on key roles.

We hope that the discussions stimulated by these notes will lead to a set of joint actions to build capacity for strategic interventions to raise standards across the system. With this in place, we would aim to continue working closely in a challenging and supportive role to enable the Authority to further refine its school improvement efforts.

The meeting to discuss this report took place in the university at the end of a working day. It involved the newly appointed Director of Children's Services and three of his senior staff, two Challenge Advisers, a civil servant and myself. Despite our efforts to provide a balanced assessment of the situation, most of the discussion focused on the concerns we had raised with regard to the primary sector.

At times the meeting became heated, as Authority staff attempted to challenge our analysis or defend the status quo. The senior officer for primary schools was clearly distressed at times. Indeed, at one point he explained that he had never felt so personally humiliated during his long professional career. In an understandable effort to support his colleague, the Director also attacked some of the statements in our report. Unfortunately, his lack of local knowledge meant that many times his remarks were, at best, unconvincing.

This particular meeting did not lead to an immediate outcome that could be described as being positive. And, of course, it was disturbing to see colleagues getting distressed. Nevertheless, I still think it was necessary for us to intervene in a context where thinking and practices were limiting opportunities for children.

Subsequently, a series of further meetings did lead to agreement as to necessary actions to strengthen the work of this particular local authority in supporting its schools. This included the appointment of a new member of staff with a strong track record of supporting school improvements and the creation of a link with another local authority that could provide professional advice. In addition, there was a private meeting with the Director, at which he was confronted about the impact of his own approach during the initial meeting. As a result, he agreed to the idea of having a personal mentor who would meet with him occasionally to help think through his approach in a context where he was likely to face continuing challenges, not least in respect to the attitudes and actions of elected members.

Rethinking the roles of local authorities

As the Challenge strategy started to have an impact, the need to rethink the roles of local authority staff became increasingly urgent, as the sense of a maturing school-led improvement strategy became more apparent. By that time, the overall strategy was increasingly being led by headteachers, some of whom now attended our fortnightly Adviser meetings. I set out to provoke widespread discussion of this theme at various meetings, through a series of discussion papers. In one of these, written in June 2009, I wrote:

> Developments stimulated by the Greater Manchester Challenge are suggesting new possibilities for strengthening educational provision across the city region. In particular, the emphasis on school-led improvements, collaboration between schools, and the presence of headteachers who are increasingly seeing themselves as systems leaders, is pointing to more effective ways of raising standards for all children and young people.
>
> All of this raises challenging questions as to what needs to happen in order to build on these developments. This, in turn, points to questions regarding the future roles of local authorities in relation to the improvement of education.
>
> In this paper I explore these trends in order to provoke discussion. In so doing, I suggest a possible direction of travel, recognising that local authorities will have a central role in sustaining progress made during the period of the Challenge. At the same time, I argue that there is a need for significant changes in relationships and patterns of work, both within and between local authorities, and with other services. These changes are likely to be deeply challenging to many of those involved.

Using some of the arguments I have presented earlier in this book, I went on to propose the following:

> All of this has very significant implications for the roles of local authority staff. It means that they have to adjust their priorities and ways of working in response to the development of collaborative arrangements that are led from within schools. And, at a time when local authorities too are under increasing pressure to deliver improvements in results, this can lead to misunderstandings and tensions between senior staff in schools and their local authority colleagues. It seems likely that these difficulties will intensify through the increasing school autonomy that will occur with the moves to academies, federations and trusts.

Despite such tensions, it is difficult to conceive of a way forward that does not involve some form of local co-ordination, particularly in relation to equity. Specifically, local authority staff can monitor and challenge schools in relation to the agreed goals of collaborative activities, whilst headteachers share responsibility for the overall management of improvement efforts within schools. We also know that careful facilitation of networks – a supportive, confirming but rigorous contribution from outside – can make an enormous difference to their chances of early survival and eventual success. This means that local authorities can position themselves as guardians of improved out-comes for young people and their families, and protectors of the collegiate approach, but not as custodians of day-to-day activities.

This distinction sharpens understanding of the sorts of roles that I think local authority staffs will need to take on: not managing and leading change, but rather working in partnership with senior people in schools to strengthen collaborative ways of working. In such contexts they can ensure that specific challenges which derive from their knowledge of the bigger picture across the authority are addressed. In this context they must act as the conscience of the system in making sure that every child and young person is being treated fairly. At the same time, they can help to broker the sharing of resources and expertise, within and across local authority boundaries.

I concluded the paper by suggesting an agenda for debate:

> Given these arguments, then, what should be the key roles of local authority staff in relation to educational development? How can they ensure continuing improvements beyond the period of the Greater Manchester Challenge? And, in what ways can cross-authority cooperation contribute?

Over the following months considerable discussion took place within and across the local authorities in response to this paper. The most important of these took place in the Directors' group and at the meetings of the thinktank of senior school improvement staff. There was what for me seemed like a defining moment at a meeting of the latter group when one of the officers – obviously frustrated by the nature of the conversation – made the following statement:

> Look, this is simple. The job of schools is to improve themselves. Our job is to make sure it happens.

By the formal close of the Challenge, at the end of March 2011, I was able to sum-marize the developing situation in each of the ten authorities, noting that these arrangements should be seen as 'work in progress'. I argued that these developments would need to continue within what was a period of further uncertainties as the policies of the new government were implemented.

My summary was written for the partnership board that was being created at that point in order to coordinate the continuation of the cross-border cooperation that had been created through the Challenge. In summary, it described the situation as follows:

> **Local authority 1** has embraced the cross-border collaboration arrangements set up as part of the Challenge. It intends to retain a small core team of officers. Their role will involve risk management, i.e. monitoring the stage of development in each school. Support for school self-evaluation will be offered by a group of associates, as a traded service. The LA is creating what it calls 'The Educational Exchange'. This web-based framework will provide a means by which local schools can develop quality assurance arrangements (a form of 'TripAdvisor') regarding providers of school improvement support.
>
> **Local authority 2** is working with heads to introduce a new head-teacher-led approach to school improvement. The LA will retain a small number of officers. In the primary sector there will be six area clusters, each of which has at least one National or Local Leader of Education. The aim is to use internal strengths within the cluster to improve the performance of the member schools. The schools have themselves employed a facilitator to support the development of school-to-school support activities. It is intended that a best practice register will be developed to encourage cross-cluster cooperation. Representatives of each of the primary clusters will meet together as a collaborative board. One role of the board will be to plan professional development activities. In the secondary sector it is anticipated that there will be a single cluster of schools. Cross-phase collaboration will also be encouraged, including secondary schools and the local further education college.
>
> **Local authority 3** is clear that its role is that of commissioning support, as and where it is necessary. This being the case, the intention is to have a 'lean' directorate that will take responsibility for quality assurance and act as the 'conscience of the system'. There will also be a trading arm, offering services within and beyond the Authority from September. The LA has embraced the idea of cross-border cooperation and this will continue to be a strong feature of the overall approach. Schools are grouping into neighbourhood clusters of 6–8 schools each (so the aim is for 30 or so eventually), underpinned by a memorandum of agreement with the LA. Each will have one school improvement officer attached, with the aim of building capacity for schools and clusters to commission services directly. In addition there are six districts that provide a mechanism for multi-agency cooperation.
>
> **Local authority 4** has been working with a group of headteachers to formulate a new approach. In the meantime, it is intending to retain a core team of school improvement officers. It is anticipated that some schools may choose to continue commissioning school improvement partners. Meanwhile, the LA is providing funding to each school in exchange for agreement on

regular data reporting. The approach has to be seen in the context of the authority's view of itself as a 'championing council'.

Local authority 5 sees itself as being in a period of transition regarding school improvement arrangements, not least because of forthcoming changes in key staff. In due course, the intention is to work with heads to design a new approach. It is anticipated that the local professional development 'trust' could be a vehicle for this development. In the meantime, the central group of officers will continue to work in its current way.

Local authority 6 is working with a core group of headteachers to develop a new approach. Central to this will be the 'Provider Arm' (PA). Set up as a cooperative, it is currently supported by a senior school improvement officer. By April, the PA will have its own budget. These arrangements are well advanced in the secondary sector. Work is currently going on to develop similar arrangements in the primary and early years sectors. The work of the PA will be closely aligned to the school-to-school support arrangements being developed across GM. The LA's role will be to commission school-to-school support, through the PA.

Local authority 7 has put in place interim arrangements, whilst officers work with a group of ten headteachers to design a new approach. Traded services have been ruled out for now; instead it is anticipated that this will emphasize 'practice transfer' within the LA but also linked to wider GM collaborative arrangement. There will continue to be a team of school improvement advisers who will take over the SIP role and facilitate quality assurance of support including externally sourced. Their work will be partly funded through a service-level agreement with schools. A website already exists to provide information about within-LA support and will help facilitate and broker school-to-school support. It can also be used to cover wider GM support too.

Local authority 8 is expecting to move to what they call 'traded services' but is actually more about brokering school-to-school support, i.e. not expecting schools to 'buy back' LA direct provision. Teaching schools, National and Local Leaders of Education and other outstanding schools will be key to this. The overall approach is out to consultation with schools at present but implementation is likely to start in April. The LA will then focus on quality assurance and support/challenge around closing the gap and the use of the pupil premium[2] – as well as getting the overall model to work effectively. They will also have a role in identifying emerging problems – and are looking at how they can use information from wider LA services (e.g. human resources, finance, legal, parental complaints) to assist with this. The former School Improvement Board will become a wider, strategic stakeholder forum, including academies – and potentially with some input from the developing GM 'agency'. They expect the school-to-school support to be offered across LA boundaries.

Local authority 9 sees itself as having more of a co-ordinating role, to help to build capacity and not direct provision. They have a good body of outstanding schools and academies to support this, and are aware of the need for good relationships and information flows to help spot emerging problems promptly. They have completed a phase of restructuring and are currently considering what further needs to be done and on what timescale. Two specific concerns are: (i) school budgets appear to be down, even with pupil premium, so will they have resources to invest in school improvement? And (ii) quality assurance of what's available 'on the market' – LA has had a key role here in the past.

Local authority 10 is moving towards a devolved model of school improvement, which will be led by 8 'consortia' of schools: 5 primary consortia (consisting of 16–24 schools each), and 3 secondary consortia (7 schools each). Each consortium will be chaired by a National or Local Leader of Education. The consortia will have key priorities in supporting and improving vulnerable schools, and also providing school-to-school support to help good schools become outstanding. The chairs of the consortia will meet on a School Improvement Board. This Board will challenge the work of the consortia, and will be accountable for the work of the consortia. LA officers will categorise schools using an agreed annual benchmarking process, to identify schools low performing/under-performing or likely to be graded as inadequate by Ofsted – 'soft intelligence' from the consortia will also feed into this. Each consortium will receive funding from the LA, in addition to any funding from DfE, to support vulnerable schools, based on the number of schools identified as vulnerable. The LA will co-ordinate the communication across all consortia and maintain an updated Good Practice Directory. It is expected that the consortia will market their school-improvement services beyond the authority.

Clearly, the overall direction of travel in the ten summaries was towards the development of new roles within the local authorities, with a greater emphasis on them supporting school-led improvement strategies. In this sense it was encouraging to see that cooperation between the senior officers across the ten authorities had stimulated considerable rethinking. However, my informed rereading of the plans indicates considerable variations as to how this was viewed at that time. So, for example, authorities 1, 2, 3, 6, 8 and 10 seemed to have each made definite decisions to redefine their roles and responsibilities in ways that appear to indicate they recognize that they had 'lost their empire'. Others, such as 4 and 7, seemed to be attempting to carry on largely as before, whilst at the same time adopting the language of the new thinking. Similarly, the extent to which the plans build in assumptions about continuing cross-border cooperation varied considerably.

This reminds us, in case we forget, that bringing about significant change in large, complex organizations remains a continuing challenge. It means that even when we think that change has occurred as a result of our plans, previous thinking, alongside vested interests and, possibly, fear of the unknown, will continue to surface in ways that tend to hold back progress. As the boxer Mike Tyson noted, 'Everyone has a plan 'till they get punched in the mouth'. All of which brings us to the concern my colleagues and I had right from the outset of the Greater Manchester Challenge: how do we ensure sustainable progress?

Legacy and sustainability

Throughout the three years, the issue of sustainability was frequently raised in the many planning and review meetings that took place. Certain of the civil servants, in particular, were preoccupied with this matter when it came to the use of resources. As a result of their efforts, plans for funding developments, at both the school and system levels, always had to include an explanation of how progress would be maintained once the additional resources were gone.

As we moved towards the end of second year of the Challenge this agenda became paramount, with much debate taking place of what was referred to as 'the legacy'. An important context for these discussions was the Steering Group, which by this time had matured into a context in which frank discussion could take place and differing positions could be aired. Its membership had also been strengthened by the involvement of headteacher and Challenge Adviser representation.

Through their various contacts across the system, members of the group helped to orchestrate a wide debate about what should happen next. This included a very successful workshop attended by representatives of local business, sports and arts organizations, faith groups and the media, all of which reminded me again of the resources that exist within communities that can and should be mobilized to support educational improvement.

As a stimulus to these discussions, in February 2010, the Steering Group produced a strategic statement entitled, 'Great Education, Greater Manchester'. Its stated aims were as follows:

> As we move towards the final phase of the Greater Manchester Challenge, the Steering Group is keen to ensure maximum impact on children and young people. This must be driven by a commitment to make sure that our education system no longer lets down any of our children and young people. At the same time, our aim is to put in place systems and working relationships that will ensure that progress continues in subsequent years. With this in mind, this statement sets out our agenda for developing a world-class education system.

The statement went on to summarize what had been achieved up to that point:

> Since its launch in April 2008, the Challenge has brought together schools and colleges, local authorities, community organisations and government in a collective effort to improve educational outcomes for all children and young people, and narrow the gap in achievement between learners from disadvantaged backgrounds and their peers.

Driven by our commitment to the '3As' (Access, Aspiration and Achievement), and focused on a series of pledges agreed at the outset, the partnership has progressed a great deal in a very short time. In particular:

- **Families of Schools** have been created that are enabling schools from different local authorities to move knowledge around in ways that are helping to make best practice available to more and more learners
- Intensive support coordinated through the **Keys to Success** programme has led to striking improvements in the performance of some 130 schools facing the most challenging circumstances
- The **Leadership Strategy** has fostered powerful school-to-school partnerships, led by a growing team of outstanding headteachers who are increasingly taking on system level leadership roles
- Through a series of **Work strands** – involving a wide range of partners, including local universities, businesses, sports and arts organisations – innovation and pace has been injected into the ten education systems
- **Local authorities** are working together to respond to the opportunities provided by a system of educational change that is increasingly being driven by school practitioners

Looking to next steps, the statement explained:

Our strategy now is to focus everybody's efforts by concentrating on three specific priorities. These are:

- In terms of **Access,** our priority is to address underperformance so that all children and young people attend great schools
- In terms of **Aspirations,** our priority is to give all children and young people a sense of the positive opportunities open to them, by raising expectations about how good education across Greater Manchester can and should be
- In terms of **Achievement,** our priority is to make sure that all children and young people are able to achieve their potential, by breaking the link between the home backgrounds of learners and educational outcomes and life chances

The Steering Group believes that a collective effort to push forward in relation to this ambitious agenda will help to develop an education system designed to meet the challenges of the 21st Century.

The statement concluded as follows:

Using our three priorities as signposts, we will allocate resources in order to develop schools that are excellent, not least in their capacity to close the gap between low and high achieving groups of learners. At the same time, we will make sure that each of our ten local authorities has strong arrangements for supporting school improvement and encouraging innovation. Finally, we will establish sustainable mechanisms for sharing expertise and human resources across the City Region. In these ways, we will ensure a great education for all children and young people in Greater Manchester.

The endgame

In the summer of 2010 a new government was elected, involving a coalition between the Conservative and Liberal Democrat parties. As I explained in Chapter 1, its arrival signalled a new round of education reforms, much informed by the idea of using market forces to inject energy into the state education system.

It was clear that the new government wanted to draw a line with regard to what had previously happened. For example, instructions were issued requiring those involved in policy developments (including me) to avoid making reference to past policy documents and agendas, such as Every Child Matters and the Children's Plan. At the same time, much of the terminology used under the previous government was to be changed. So, for example, 'personalized learning' was to be avoided – 'We are now using teaching and learning instead'; and 'narrowing the gap' was to be replaced with 'closing the gap'.

For those of us involved in City Challenge, including some of my civil servant colleagues, this was a worrying period. Indeed, there seemed to be a strong chance that the programme would simply be pulled, with almost ten months still to go. During this period I was frequently told to continue with what we were doing, whilst 'staying below the radar'.

Much to our relief it gradually became apparent that members of the government had realized that City Challenge had been an effective improvement strategy. My strong impression was that this decision was made as a result of the Secretary of State, Michael Gove, and his colleagues meeting with headteachers in the Challenge areas, who made the case for the initiative to continue. Indeed, I accompanied Mr Gove on a visit to one of the Greater Manchester schools where a forceful headteacher made her position very clear on this issue.

Later, in a much quoted speech in June 2011, the Secretary of State talked about the importance of 'embedding a culture of collaboration' in the national education system. He then went on to mention, by way of example, Wigan's plans to commission groups of schools to run improvement activity across the authority. This, he explained, underlined how 'schools across Manchester are working together to embed the success of the Greater Manchester Challenge'.

All of this gave us an opportunity to regroup in planning arrangements to continue the progress that had been achieved. With this as the purpose, during the final year of the Challenge, the two local authority directors on the Steering Group argued that a sustainable plan for the future needed high-level political support. Consequently, they joined me in attending a series of meetings of the ten Chief

Executives, the officers who have overall responsibility for the public services provided by local authorities.

At the first meeting we presented an analysis of what had happened over the previous period and suggested the following 'agenda for change':

- What are the issues that most lend themselves to the sorts of cross-border cooperation that have been established through the Greater Manchester Challenge?
- What arrangements need to be established in order to coordinate, further develop and sustain such cooperative actions?
- And, above all, what needs to be done in order to foster and maintain a sense of shared responsibility amongst all the relevant stakeholders?

Whilst the views around the table were generally positive and optimistic in relation to this agenda, there were some doubting voices. Reference was made to the concern that this was simply another fad, 'bolted on with funny money'. One of the directors who represented her colleagues at the meeting suggested that we must not 'replace old dogma with new dogma'.

By July 2010 a series of interconnected proposals had emerged from the various discussions that had taken place with the Chief Executives. These related to five areas:

1. **Intelligence – establish a pan-GM data management system, building on the existing collaboration between local authority specialists and the expertise within the authorities.** This would monitor trends across the city region, pinpointing areas of policy and practice that need collaborative responses, and monitor the impact of these responses. It would also assist in identifying effective practices. Greater awareness of these could be achieved through the creation of some form of directory.
2. **Strategic management – strengthen the role of the existing Heads of School Improvement group in order to coordinate cross-border collaboration in relation to areas of need.** Given the emphasis on schools supporting one another, it would be important to invite representative head-teachers to join this group. It will be important, too, to build on the lessons of recent collaborative experiences, such as the successful efforts that have been made in respect to areas such as 16 to 19 provision, governor development, closing the gap and support for bilingual learners.
3. **Operational support – commission the setting up of an agency for coordinating various forms of cross-border school-to-school partnerships.** Its task would be to raise standards in all schools and reduce the gap between high and low performing groups of learners, through, for example, the further development of the Families of Schools and various forms of hub schools. The agency would be led by a group of outstanding headteachers (i.e. National and Local Leaders of Education), supported by senior local authority staff.

4. **Joint delivery – develop joint delivery of some local authority func-
    tions, either across GM or within smaller clusters** (some developments
    are already being discussed in various parts of the region). These would set
    out to tackle educational issues that cut across local authority boundaries,
    such as support for children with low incidence disabilities and other vulner-
    able groups, and the development of personalized 14–19 learning pathways.
    It would also make sense to establish a small team of highly experienced
    professionals who could be commissioned to intervene in low performing
    schools.

5. **Wider partnerships – establish a mechanism for coordinating the
    involvement of community partners, such as governors, local busi-
    nesses, universities, media and other organizations.** Given the increas-
    ing diversity of providers within the education system, as a result of the
    anticipated expansion of academies and free schools, this will be particularly
    important. At the same time, the aim must be to link educational improvement
    to broader social and economic agendas (such as, population mobility, employ-
    ment, transport, housing, community safety, health), none of which respect
    local authority boundaries.

These proposals led the Chief Executives to set up a working party that worked
with me to determine practical arrangements for ensuring that the progress made
continued beyond the period of the additional funding.

In the summer of 2011 the Greater Manchester School Improvement Partnership
Board was formed. Its agreed 'statement of purpose' was as follows:

> After reviewing the impact of the Greater Manchester Challenge, the Chief
> Executives group decided to set up a pan-city region Partnership Board to
> help coordinate collaborative school improvement activities. Chaired by a
> Director of Children's Services, the Board members are representative
> officers, headteachers and from the DfE.
>
> Given its overall purpose, the Partnership Board is taking on a big picture
> strategic role, using various forms of intelligence to pinpoint areas of concern
> that might lend themselves to pan-GM collaborative actions. It will not itself
> commission actions in response to this analysis.
>
> On this basis, high level **objectives** for the Board are to:
>
> *   provide mutual, collective accountability and challenge to the overall
>   GM school improvement system;
> *   ensure interface and coordination between LAs and the developing
>   GM 'By Schools for Schools' body; and
> *   identify and discuss areas of common/shared challenges, approaches and
>   practices, including opportunities for closer collaborative working or
>   moves towards shared services.

In terms of specific **tasks**, the Board will:

- receive and scrutinise reports, including from the GM data management group;
- publish commentaries based on its consideration of these data and other forms of intelligence;
- determine and recommend issues that might lend themselves to cross-border collaborative action of some kind; and
- monitor the progress of collaborative actions that are taken.

The Board will report regularly to the DCS group. Its commentaries and recommendations will also be made available to appropriate officers in each of the ten LAs and to those headteachers taking on system leadership roles.

Alongside this process, as explained in the previous chapter, discussions amongst the various national and local leaders of education had led to the creation of 'By Schools for Schools', the headteacher-led agency that has the role of coordinating and continuing collaboration across the city region. As policies have subsequently developed, its duties have come to include the coordination of the work of system leaders, national leaders of governance and the various teaching school alliances that have been developed. In carrying out these tasks it liaises with the Partnership Board.

Conclusion

This chapter has described and illustrated the social and political challenges involved in trying to develop collaborative improvement efforts across a complex urban education system, which, in practice, consists of ten interconnected systems. In particular, it has revealed how cooperation becomes much more difficult when decisions have to be made about priorities for action and the use of financial resources. There were, therefore, inevitable periods of 'turbulence' of the sort my colleagues and I had described earlier, as those involved worked together in making sense of the process of change (Hopkins, Ainscow and West, 1994)

In relation to these challenges the account of what happened in Greater Manchester indicates how, with sensitive and persistent leadership, such difficulties can eventually be overcome, to some extent at least. We have also seen how being involved in such struggles can help working groups to mature, such that heated debates can take place in ways that encourage joint problem solving, leading to a shared commitment to move forward.

Returning to the central theme of this book, all of this underlines the extent of the untapped potential within education systems that can be used for self-improvement. The lesson is that **national governments have to create the conditions within which local action can be taken and that local authorities have to take responsibility for making sure this happens.** As I have illustrated, this requires new thinking, practices and relationships. Drawing on the ideas of Fielding and Moss (2011), it means that the role of the local authority should be as:

> a leader and facilitator of the development of a local educational project, a shared and democratic exploration of the meaning and practice of education and the potential of the school.
>
> *(p. 125)*

The plan for such a project should, I suggest, be formulated in partnership with practitioners, as well as with community representatives. In this way, it takes on the thinking of the Fourth Way, suggested by Hargreaves and Shirley (2009):

> Community organisation in education goes far beyond parent involvement and its traditional one-on-one deals between individual parents and the educators who serve their children. It is about mobilising entire communities and public networks to agitate for significant reform. When fully realised, it is about changing the power dynamics of an entire city by creating new civic capacity for previously disenfranchised populations.
>
> *(p. 59)*

All of which takes me back to the Yorkshire novelist, Winifred Holtby, whom I quoted earlier in this chapter. She reminds us that 'we are not only single individuals, each face to face with eternity and our separate spirits; we are members one of another' (p.ix).

Notes

1   This is an off-site provision for students excluded from school, usually because of behaviour difficulties.
2   The pupil premium is additional funding given to publicly funded schools in England to raise the attainment of disadvantaged pupils, and close the gap between them and their peers.

8

A DIFFERENT WAY OF THINKING

In this final chapter I pull together the lessons drawn in the earlier parts of this book in the form of a strategic framework. This allows me to present what I argue is a different way of thinking about the improvement of school systems, one that places a particular emphasis on equity. The experience of working with colleagues in using this approach in a number of other contexts leads me to argue that it has wider relevance, such that it can be adapted for use in different parts of the world. With this in mind, I consider the implications for the growing number of national systems where there is an increasing emphasis on school autonomy, competition and choice.

The chapter further illustrates the role of politics when attempts are made to develop self-improving systems. This reinforces the key role of national governments. In particular, I argue that central governments need to act as enablers: encouraging developments, disseminating good practice and holding local leaders to account for outcomes. There are also major implications for the work of those who coordinate developments at the local district level.

A strategic framework

Building on lessons from London Challenge, the strategies developed in Greater Manchester helped to foster new, more fruitful working relationships: between national and local government; between administrators and practitioners; within and between schools; and between schools and their local communities. As I explained in Chapter 1, a useful theoretical interpretation that can be made of these strategies is that, together, they helped to strengthen social capital within the city region. In other words, they facilitated relationships across different levels of the system and established many new pathways through which energy, expertise and lessons from innovations could spread. At the same time, the greater awareness of what was happening elsewhere often challenged expectations as to what is possible, particularly amongst students from economically disadvantaged backgrounds.

Brought together, the recommendations that emerged in the earlier chapters led me to refine the ideas I had presented to the interview panel that appointed me as Chief Adviser in 2007. Together, these ideas provide a strategic framework that can be used to think about how school systems can address the issue of equity by becoming self-improving. In summary, the framework focuses on the following interconnected propositions:

1. **Education systems have untapped potential to improve themselves** – therefore, on-going contextual analysis is needed in order to identify areas of concern and the human resources that can be used to support improvement efforts in relation to these issues.

2. **School partnerships are the most powerful means of fostering improvements, particularly in challenging circumstances** – however, such partnerships have to be carefully orchestrated, using evidence as the catalyst that focuses attention on overlooked possibilities for moving practice forward.

3. **Networking is a means of sharing expertise and stimulating experimentation with new ways of working** – this means that pathways have to be created that cross the multiple social boundaries that prevent the movement of ideas within a system.

4. **School focused strategies have to be complemented with efforts to engage the wider community** – therefore, a framework is needed that enables external partners to get involved.

5. **In order for education systems to become self-improving, leadership has to come from within schools** – my experience suggests that many successful headteachers are motivated to take on systems leadership roles.

6. **National governments have to create the conditions within which local action can be taken and local authorities have to be responsible for making sure this happens** – this requires new thinking, attitudes and relationships across education systems.

What connects these six propositions in a way that makes them coherent are processes of collaborative inquiry that focus attention on various forms of evidence. This helps to make the familiar unfamiliar in ways that challenge expectations as to what is possible, whilst, at the same time, drawing attention to examples of different practices that can be moved from place to place. Where this works effectively it also stimulates collective efforts to explore new possibilities for addressing old problems.

As I have illustrated through my account of the Greater Manchester Challenge, this framework has implications for the various key stakeholders within education systems. In particular, it requires teachers, especially those in senior positions, to see themselves as having a wider responsibility for all children and young people, not just those who attend their own schools; it means that those who administer district school systems have to adjust their priorities and ways of working in response to improvement efforts that are led from within schools; and it requires that what schools do must be aligned in a coherent strategy with the efforts of other local players – employers, community groups, universities, public services and so on.

Making it happen

As we have seen, none of this happens by chance. Strategic leadership and effective facilitation are vital in order to get things moving. In the case of the Greater Manchester Challenge, our team of Advisers proved to be crucial in this respect. In summary, the vital tasks they carried out were as follows:

- **Knowing the schools** – Whilst this started with a thorough scrutiny of statistical data, it had to go much deeper. Specifically, it required the Challenge Advisers to work with headteachers in reviewing their schools, through the observation of practice, scrutiny of pupils' work, and by listening to the views of different stakeholders. We found it helpful to develop a variety of frameworks to guide such school review processes. In addition, the Advisers found it useful to involve practitioners from other schools in reviewing practices, in particular, successful headteachers and heads of departments. However, the most important thing is that the headteacher of the school should take responsibility for leading the review, using external colleagues to bring different perspectives to the process. Through these internal review processes, heads developed a better understanding of their schools' relative strengths and weaknesses. This was then used for strategic purposes to bring about improvements within the school.
- **Brokering partnerships** – These same review processes enabled the Challenge Advisers to develop a deeper knowledge of the schools. In this way, they could pinpoint areas of concern, as well as human resources that might be drawn on to address these challenges. Their task was then to help broker appropriate partnerships between schools, such that the best practices were made available to a wider number of learners. These partnerships took many forms. In some cases, they involved two schools, where the strength of one was used to provide support in addressing concerns in another. In other instances, trios of schools were formed. Within the primary sector, where schools are sometimes small, trios were found to be a particularly effective strategy.
- **Monitoring the impact** – As such partnerships developed, Challenge Advisers had to continue monitoring what happened, since, too often, a proliferation of meetings could result in no actions being taken. As part of this process of monitoring developments in the schools, Advisers sometimes had to make decisions as to whether an individual school had, in fact, got the leadership capacity to move their organization forward, even with the support they were receiving from other schools. Where leadership capacity was not sufficient,

Advisers were expected to require the local authority to use its powers of intervention. In making such decisions, individual Advisers needed to draw on the support of their colleagues. With this in mind, we held fortnightly team meetings where concerns about particular schools were discussed. This allowed individuals to think aloud about their concerns in a mutually supportive context, whilst, at the same time, encouraging the sharing of ideas and knowledge of expertise available across the system in order to develop further responses. Where serious concerns continued, it was also found helpful for pairs of Advisers to do joint visits to a school.

In telling the story of what happened in Greater Manchester I have also drawn attention to the difficulties involved in drawing stakeholders together around a common purpose, particularly when this requires the development of new practices and relationships in ways that may challenge the status quo. In addition, I have signalled some potential pitfalls in using this way of thinking. In summary, these are:

- It can lead to lots of nonproductive time, as members of staff spend periods out of school.
- It might simply be a fad that goes well when led by skilled and enthusiastic advocates but then fades when spread more widely.
- Schools involved in working collaboratively may collude with one another to reinforce mediocrity and low expectations.
- Those schools that most need help may choose not to get involved.
- Some headteachers may become 'empire builders', who deter others from getting involved.

Bearing these concerns in mind, in what follows I describe three experiences of using this 'way of thinking' in very different policy contexts since the conclusion of the initiative in Greater Manchester. These stories illustrate the importance of taking account of contextual factors related to history, geography, language, cultures and, of course, policies.

The first example is set in the local authority that serves the small island of Anglesey, off the northern coast of Wales; the second takes the form of a collaborative research project in the massive state of Queensland, Australia; and the third took place in the context of the new national policy that emerged in England during the period after the City Challenge programme ended.

An island in crisis

It is important to recognize that the Welsh education system operates independently of national policy in England. Formulated by the Welsh National Assembly, which meets in the capital city, Cardiff, the policy is administered through 22 local authorities, some of which are extremely small. Some aspects of the policy are similar to those in England but the Welsh government remains fiercely independent and, indeed, recent years have seen considerable tensions between Ministers from the two countries, not least in relation to arrangements regarding national tests and examinations. So far, too, there have been no moves to encourage schools to become independent of local authorities.

Recent years have seen increasing concern about the performance of Welsh schools, as reflected in their relatively poor record in comparison with schools in other countries, including the other three that make up the United Kingdom (OECD, 2014). There is a national inspection system, Estyn, which operates in a similar way to Ofsted in England. One significant difference, however, is that Estyn regularly inspects the performance of local authorities, as well as schools. In the last few years, six local authorities have been placed in special measures as a result of inspection and most of the others have been designated as needing improvement.

In November 2012 I was asked by the then Minister for Education and Skills to chair the unfortunately named 'Recovery Board', set up to help bring about improvements in Anglesey, one of the authorities placed in special measures. Estyn had concluded that its 'education services for children and young people are unsatisfactory'. It had also set out seven areas that required urgent attention. The Recovery Board consisted of a small number of experienced professionals from elsewhere in Wales, including two successful headteachers.

Anglesey is an island off the north-west coast, where farming and tourism are the main sources of income. It has 54 schools (48 primary, 1 special and 5 secondary), many of which are small, serving rural communities. Most use Welsh as the language of instruction. The priority during the first few months of the Recovery Board's existence was to ensure that arrangements were in place to respond quickly to the concerns raised by the inspectors. In this sense, it was relatively easy to make progress.

Looking to the longer term, we used the strategic framework outlined at the beginning of this chapter to support the Authority in making significant organizational changes. My assumption was that these were needed in order to develop an education system that is fit for purpose. This required major structural reforms, as well as rethinking attitudes, roles and responsibilities. There was also a need to challenge expectations as to what was possible in relation to levels of achievement and attendance.

Developing a strategy

As had been the case in Greater Manchester, there was a record of relatively poor overall standards across the Anglesey system. Similarly, too, our analysis of the context convinced us that that good practices existed within the schools. In line with the thinking developed in this book, we encouraged a restructuring that would enable these practices to be made available to more pupils. This was to be achieved through the strengthening of various forms of cooperation between schools.

This required new roles for headteachers, some of whom volunteered to take on the task of leading these developments. With this in mind, we consulted with all the heads within the Authority. As a result, a new momentum for change quickly emerged in the primary sector, where a group of five relatively successful head-teachers took the initiative in moving things forward. Initially they needed considerable support in bringing about the changes they had in mind. An important moment in this respect was a visit they made together to schools in Greater Manchester that had taken on key roles in the City Challenge.

It was evident that this visit stimulated considerable rethinking, particularly in terms of what was possible. The two schools they visited served extremely disadvantaged communities. Nevertheless, pupil attendance was well above the national average, performance on national tests was high, and both schools had been designated as 'outstanding' as a result of recent inspections. Subsequently, the visitors explained to me that the most important part of the day was the debate they had in the mini-bus on their return journey as they reflected on the 'surprises' they had experienced. Over the following 18 months this was to stimulate them to work with others in rethinking the way that the Anglesey system does its business.

In discussing this work the heads commented on the social complexities they faced in getting colleagues to cooperate. In particular, they explained the implications of the fact that amongst schools in a small island community, 'everybody knows one another'. They explained that relationships were usually warm and cordial, something that I certainly experienced. However, it was also apparent that this closeness between colleagues had the potential to create barriers to genuine collaboration between schools. One headteacher summed this up when she said, 'we don't bare our souls around here'.

Somehow the group of heads was able to overcome these difficulties. Influenced by the Families of Schools approach used in Greater Manchester, they formed their own seven 'families', each made up of primary schools from different parts of the island. In forming these groups efforts were made to ensure that each had schools of varied size and at different stages of development.

Having encouraged these groups to get together and consider the profiles of each school, the heads group decided to organize a 'day of sharing'. Teachers and support staff in various schools volunteered to lead workshops that were attended by colleagues from across Anglesey. It struck me that the quiet country lanes must have been unusually busy that morning as almost every primary school teacher went off to take part. Then, in the afternoon, staff members returned to their own school to share what they had learnt during the morning. Following the day, further collaborative activities have been organized within the families of schools.

The secondary sector presented different challenges, not least the fact that there are only five schools. As in the primary sector, relationships were generally cordial even though the schools were effectively in competition with one another. There was, however, a recognition that none of the schools was achieving satisfactory results, even though there was considerable variation between them. It was perhaps significant, also, that three of the new schools had a change of headteacher. This in itself seemed to open up new opportunities for mutual support.

The five heads made a commitment with one another to share responsibility for improving levels of achievement in all of the schools. With this goal in mind, they formed professional learning networks across different levels of the system, with all teachers and school leaders being encouraged to take part in collaborative inquiry activities. These included learning walks carried out by senior and middle leaders in one another's schools, and lesson study groups in which teachers from different schools worked together to make their lessons effective for all students in their classes.

These activities are still going on and only time will tell what their full impact will be. Certainly it was encouraging to see that in the analysis of the examination results of all Welsh secondary schools, carried out by the government in the summer of 2013, all five of the secondary schools had moved into the top two bands nationally. And in June 2014, following a further inspection of the local authority it was announced that it was no longer in special measures.

Reflecting on what happened in Anglesey, it has to be noted that part of the reason that the education system had got into difficulties related to a political crisis, whereby a succession of council administrations had failed to establish a consistent policy for development over a period of years. This had led the Welsh government to suspend the powers of the council and to impose a team of commissioners to manage its services. This, plus the introduction of the education Recovery Board, helped to create a political atmosphere within which staying the same was no longer an option. This, in turn, opened up spaces for those at the school level to take more responsibility for system reform. At the same time, the newly appointed Director of Education provided effective leadership in relation to the redesign of the local authority support services in response to the emergence of a school-led improvement strategy.

Rethinking support for school improvement

As I argued in Chapter 7, moves towards a self-improving system imply very different roles for local authority staff. In this sense, the arrangements that we found in Anglesey had been far from satisfactory, despite the fact that they were generally well regarded within the system. In particular, these arrangements tended to imply that it is 'outsiders' who will drive school improvement efforts. The new thinking that we promoted demanded that those within schools take responsibility for improving themselves.

As the new strategy developed, local authority staff were assisted in rethinking their roles, acting as what I have referred to as the conscience of the system – making sure that all children and young people are getting a fair deal. In order to do this, they needed to know the big picture about what is happening in the schools and their communities, identifying priorities for action and brokering collaboration. As in Greater Manchester, this required significant structural and cultural changes, with local authority staff moving away from a command and control perspective, towards one of enabling and facilitating collaborative action.

We also emphasized the important role of local authority staff in monitoring developments in the schools. This means that they sometimes have to make decisions as to whether an individual school has, in fact, got the leadership capacity to move their organizations forward, even with the support they are receiving from other schools. Where this is not the case, local authority staff must be prepared to use their powers of intervention, which could include asking a head-teacher or chair of governors to stand down, something that had not occurred previously on the island.

In bringing about these changes we were fortunate in that our initial analysis of the context had led us to believe that the Director of Education was a person who had the necessary skills to provide leadership for the change process. As things developed, this assessment proved to be correct. At the same time we encouraged the energetic support of elected members, not least in taking decisions about changes in provision and working practices that might sometimes be opposed by some sections of the local community. We argued for a new consensus around an agreed long-term strategy to ensure that all children and young people in Anglesey experience an excellent education.

In summary, then, there are encouraging signs that the use of the strategic framework, developed as a result of experiences in the dense urban context of Greater Manchester, is making a difference in a relatively isolated part of rural Wales. In particular, it has stimulated new thinking and the formulation of strategies to put this into action. At times, however, the pace of change remained frustratingly slow. This reminds us that what we are promoting is a process of cultural change that challenges deeply-held beliefs and well-established patterns of working across different levels of an education system. On the other hand, there was evidence of a widespread recognition that carrying on as before was not an option, and a desire to collaborate in addressing an agenda for change. In this sense, the political crisis created as a result of the inspection provided an opportunity to bring stakeholders together around a common purpose. It also provided leverage in relation to local political processes, such that those involved felt that they had little option but to get behind those in schools who were trying to bring about significant organizational change.

The progress achieved in Anglesey has subsequently influenced developments in other parts of the country, particularly the design of the Central South Wales Challenge, which involves over 400 schools in five local authorities, and Schools Challenge Cymru, the Welsh government's multi-million pound flagship programme to accelerate the rate of improvement across the country (Claeys, Kempton and Paterson, 2014). I am privileged to have a role in both of these initiatives.

A divided system

There is considerable concern in a growing number of countries that high stakes testing regimes, set within policy contexts that encourage competition between schools, are further marginalizing groups of learners who have traditionally done badly in schools. In what follows I describe the first phase of an ongoing research study that draws on the thinking in this book in order to find ways of overcoming these challenges. Carried out with a splendid team of colleagues at Queensland University of Technology,[1] it builds on the thinking developed in this book, plus evidence from our earlier research, which suggests that processes of collaborative inquiry, involving partnerships between teams of teachers and university researchers, are a promising way forward (Ainscow et al., 2012).

The study is set in the state of Queensland, Australia, where equity is a long-standing and seemingly intractable challenge. This relates, in part at least, to the way that the education system has developed into three parallel sectors – independent, Catholic and government – all of which receive some state funding. The evidence is that this has led to the privileging of the independent and Catholic sectors, leaving government schools to deal with the majority of students from the more disadvantaged sections of the community (Kenway, 2013). This being the case, it is hardly surprising that the performance of these schools on the high-stakes national testing regime tends to draw attention to them as a source of concern.

The study focuses on a network of six government schools and their efforts to use collaborative inquiry in order to become self-improving within this perverse policy context. In general, the schools are not exceptional in any way. Having said that, as might be expected, they each have a significant proportion of students from relatively poor backgrounds. In addition, within the so-called 'education market-place', their efforts to do their best for all of their students are influenced by the impact of other schools in their areas.

All the schools have been involved in broadly the same process of collaborative inquiry within which groups of teachers investigate challenges that exist within their communities. Given the emphasis this places on contextual analysis and decision-making within each organization, it is inevitable that the form of the intervention varies from school to school. However, what is striking is the way that local circumstances have influenced what happens.

Stepping closer to the action

Each of the six project schools had a different starting point and moved at its own pace to formulate a clear agenda and undertake its inquiries. As a result, the range of inquiries has been diverse and included investigations of various literacy strategies, pedagogic approaches, issues of student engagement and motivation, and relationships within the school and with the broader community. More recently, each of the schools has formed a partnership with a 'buddy school' with the aim of networking to foster the sharing of local problem-solving and responsibility for equity outcomes beyond the individual institution.

In order to explore the factors that impact on the ways schools engage with the collaborative inquiry process, in what follows I provide vignettes of two schools developed by our research team. On paper these schools appear to be rather similar yet have engaged with the project in different ways.

Bromsgrove and Sunnydale are both regional high schools that serve similar student bodies, in terms of both size and demographics. The two schools also share similar challenges in recruiting and graduating students, and offering an appropriate set of learning opportunities. Furthermore, their regional locations pose a range of challenges for their students. Located between 100 and 150 kilometres away from the closest major city, students who graduate from these schools face the choice of whether to stay in their local areas, which each offer a local university and limited employment options, or pursue opportunities for tertiary education and employment elsewhere.

In addition to sharing a range of demographic features, the two schools are structurally similar. That is to say, both have become 'independent public schools' during their involvement in this research, a governance arrangement similar to charter schools in the USA and academies in England. Their inclusion in this new category ostensibly provides them with greater autonomy with regard to budgeting and staffing, and opportunities to enhance local governance.

Bromsgrove State High School

The long-serving principal of this school was eager to engage his staff in the collaborative inquiry aspects of the project. In an interview, he reported his goal to develop a culture where it is 'commonplace' for teachers to use data to improve student learning. As a leader, he is engaged with research himself, and provides staff 'with as much data as possible', encouraging them to use this information to identify strategies for improvement.

The leadership team's openness and willingness to engage in conversations around data were evident in their response to the situational analysis provided by a member of our research team. This revealed a relatively low level of attainment in the school but evidence of some recent improvement. Responding to this, the principal indicated that these results 'could be attributed to a number of changed approaches' that had been implemented during the previous year.

When discussing student performance data, members of the leadership team outlined their concerns, plans and priorities for the school. As a result, three areas of focus were identified, namely: timetabling and developing effective pathways for senior secondary students; exploring issues related to student motivation; and developing and embedding improved strategies for literacy teaching and learning across the curriculum. For the purpose of this chapter, I focus on the latter.

In mid-2013, the principal called for volunteer teachers to engage in action research around literacy and received responses from a number of departments, including English, maths, science, visual arts and social science. These responses sent an important message about literacy being a responsibility of all subject areas. The school's literacy coordinator arranged for volunteer teachers to meet with university researchers to develop their understanding of action research, and explore possibilities in their own classrooms. The principal provided teachers with flexibility and time to work with university researchers and as a team. He occasionally dropped by to listen in on how the conversations were unfolding. The literacy coordinator acted as the informal leader of the research team and developed an action research project around this role, which included video-taping aspects of teacher practice in classrooms that could later be shared with a wider group of colleagues.

Teachers collected a range of data, including student work-samples, in-class assessments and student performance data, as well as surveying students to ascertain their views. A number of teachers adapted a survey tool, developed by the university researchers with teachers from another school, for their own needs. These surveys gave the teachers access to the opinions, attitudes and beliefs of all their students around these issues.

A teacher of English undertaking a project to improve student spelling in Year 9 reported that she also spent time with each student in her class discussing how they felt about spelling, and was surprised that students reported being very interested in improving their ability to spell correctly. She was also surprised to learn that some students had better spelling than she had expected, but was concerned to discover that a small number of girls had significantly worse spelling knowledge than she had assumed. The teacher was thus able to challenge some of her former beliefs and identify areas where additional help was required. This is the kind of productive and critical interruption to assumptions that action research can produce.

Although it is too early to report findings in terms of student academic gains, it is worth noting that the teachers have already begun to consider possibilities beyond their own projects. For example, they have discussed the importance of collecting evidence to demonstrate the effectiveness of their projects, and documenting what worked (and what didn't). By way of example, the teachers have discussed their concerns about the current approach to spelling in the school (a spelling workbook) and are excited about the possibility of collecting evidence for an improved approach based on the spelling action research project. They also plan to share video recordings of particular teaching episodes with their colleagues.

Sunnydale State High School

This second school faced significant organizational changes during the planning and establishment period of the project. A new principal started at the school mid-way through 2012, followed by a new deputy principal in early 2013. In addition, school staff voted to become an independent public school in 2013. The new principal and deputy principal inherited our project from the previous school leaders during this period of significant change. As such, the discussions, negotiations and preparatory work that the research team had engaged in with the other project schools started afresh with this new leadership team.

The principal demonstrated what struck us as a critical perspective regarding the use of data. During an interview he stated that 'often data can be interpreted in lots of different ways and there's all sorts of ifs and buts and maybes around it'. He suggested that his role is to 'filter what are the trends and patterns, and the useful things that we should consider and can do something about'. These trends and patterns are then shared back to 'the deputy level and the head of department level with the expectation that they also share that with their faculty teachers'.

The principal further indicated that the school is challenging teachers 'to use the data to better know their client group with the ultimate aim, I guess, of improving relationships and hence hopefully learning outcomes'. However, he expressed concerns about the potential for the 'naïve use and misinterpretation' of external student performance data, particularly the use of the national data system for measuring school performance.

These concerns were reflected in Sunnydale's response to the situational analysis provided by a member of the university research team. In this case, the process of presenting an analysis of external data did not function as an 'engine for change', nor did it appear to assist the school in identifying areas for action research. Consequently, a significant period of discussion around issues of data and school priorities was required to identify two potential areas for further examination. These were: improving the use of data within the school; and evaluating the impact of new structures in the junior section of the school, the focus of this vignette.

A new approach for the organization of classes in the junior section had been introduced mid-way through 2012 by the former school leadership team. This new structure, referred to as 'theming', was based on the concept that classes could be structured to support teachers to 'differentiate learning to suit the learner's style'. Parents of students entering the school were asked to select the class that they believed best suited their child's learning style and students were allocated according to these nominations and their primary school results. So, for example, parents could nominate classes for more self-directed students, those who enjoyed the performing arts, or those who required more direct instruction.

Working with the university research team, it was decided that an initial step for action research into understanding and evaluating these junior school structures would be to identify teacher, student and parent perceptions, and develop a shared understanding of what the programme involved at the classroom level. With this as the focus, the research team worked with the senior leadership group to develop a data collection strategy. Survey data were collected across each of the themed classes in four learning areas and in two learning support classes. Members of the university research team also carried out classroom observations, teacher surveys, and interviews with teachers and members of the leadership team. In addition, a parent survey was developed, although this received only a small number of responses.

The intention of collecting student and teacher perceptions of teaching and learning was to explore the school's aim of matching teaching styles with students' learning styles. The surveys asked teachers and students to rate, on a five-point scale, their opinions of various areas, including teacher knowledge (e.g., 'my teacher is knowledgeable in the subject area they teach'), pedagogy (e.g. 'my teachers give clear instructions and explanations in class'), feedback and assessment (e.g. 'my teachers give us clear guidelines for assignments'), as well as teacher, parent and student expectations (e.g. 'teachers in this school have high expectations of all students to do their best'). Students were also given space to provide answers to questions about what they liked about each class, as well as to identify areas for improvement ('what advice do you have for your teacher to make school better for you?').

The university research team presented analyses of these data to school leaders for further discussion that would inform future planning of action research. The principal commented that this challenged their perceptions of the meaning of the idea of themed classes. While the original purpose had been to match teaching styles to suit the learning styles of individual students, the data suggested that the strategy was viewed by many teachers and students as a process of allocating classes on the basis of student ability – in other words, a form of streaming. Furthermore, the analysis of student data revealed no significant differences in the students' perceptions of teaching and learning across the different themes.

Teacher interviews also revealed a number of issues about student equity. For example, one teacher claimed: 'The Academic classes definitely benefit the most out of the situation. The Directed Learning class [identified as providing more explicit instruction] I think it's disadvantaged, because … they move slower.' The challenges of working with streamed classes also impacted on teacher wellbeing: 'It certainly is so hard on the teacher. It was hell, it really was.'

The principal and deputy principal reported that all of this had provided them with new insights into their school, as well as generating a range of new ideas for them to think about. They also felt that this could lead on to possible action research projects that could address both the teachers' and students' concerns.

Making sense of difference

So, while Bromsgrove and Sunnydale appear to be quite similar schools, the ways they engaged with the project were significantly different. Much of this seems to be related to their approaches to the analysis, discussion and use of data.

On the one hand, the engagement of staff at Bromsgrove in the collaborative inquiry process suggests a preference for a bottom-up approach to data use. There, the principal encouraged staff to use all forms of school data for the purposes of better understanding their students. His encouragement was indicated by the school giving additional time and funding support to those teachers who volunteered to participate in the action research. The teachers' involvement in data collection, analysis and reflection was viewed as a way to build capacity across the school as they began to engage with data in ways that informed their practices and then began to discuss the implications with colleagues in their subject areas. Collaborative discussions provided volunteer teachers with opportunities to share their ideas and findings, which were then fed back to the school leadership team.

A possible rationale for this bottom-up approach to using data at Bromsgrove may be the principal's desire for teachers to develop a sense of ownership around the school's performance data. He reported that a number of teachers were 'quite comfy' with the school's performance before they commenced with their improvement agenda. As a result, the leadership team wanted to identify ways to engage all staff in improvement efforts. They were, he explained, working to 'continually get people to see that that [an effort to improve] was just one step along the process and we need to… try and kick on from there'. The engagement of teachers in the iterative process of action research thus represents a significant shift in the reported attitudes of staff.

On the other hand, the leadership team at Sunnydale seemed to advocate a more stratified approach to the sharing and analysis of data than that described in Bromsgrove. In an interview with the research team, the principal of Sunnydale reported that the leadership team works together in reviewing critically patterns and trends arising from performance data. This process, we were told, encourages the 'leadership levels, the head of department or deputy, to think along with me about what we can learn from what's happened', before 'reflecting it back' to the teachers.

The approaches to using and discussing data in this school reflect the principal's concerns about the potential for people 'to draw wrong conclusions through naïve interpretations of data', particularly externally reported data. He advocates a broad contextualized approach to data analysis, stating:

> Every piece of data has a story with it and I think the two need to go together. Just plonking data in front of someone without the story behind it can be quite a dangerous thing to do.

It was thus not unsurprising that ultimately it was data generated by students and teachers, offered in the context of the school's initiative to developing classes based on learning styles, and not data reported for external accountability purposes, that provided the Sunnydale leadership team with the 'space for reappraisal and re-thinking by interrupting existing discourses' (Ainscow, 2010).

Some reflections

In identifying these differences, my colleagues and I recognized their strengths and limitations. The bottom–up approach to data use advocated at Bromsgrove engages teachers in reflective processes through which they can explore, understand, and refine their professional practices. The limitations of this approach, however, include the time commitment required by teachers to engage in this practice. Furthermore, this approach encourages teachers to work with data from the classroom level and not with data used as part of the broader, external accountability agenda.

The more critical approach to examining data in context adopted by Sunnydale acknowledges and explores the limitations of externally reported school data. School leaders there interrogate data collaboratively within the broader context, leading them to question the 'story' behind each 'piece of data'. The 'filtering' of data trends and patterns from the leadership team throughout the school means that staff share an understanding of how the school can work with *between-school* and *beyond-school* contexts.

Wider influences

As my colleagues and I analyzed the experiences in all six schools in the study, we became increasingly aware of the way different factors in each case come together to influence what occurs. In making sense of the complexities involved we found it helpful to use the 'ecology of equity', developed previously by our Manchester research team, as a framework for analysis (Ainscow *et al.*, 2012). This draws attention to the following sets of factors that bear on what happens in schools:

1. *Within-school factors* – i.e. the respective histories of schools and the legacies these have left in relation to organizational cultures, attitudes and expectations.
2. *Between-school factors* – i.e. the impact of competition between schools in the local communities and the actions that are being taken in response to these circumstances.
3. *Beyond-school factors* – i.e. the influence of local economic circumstances, including possibilities for further training and higher education in the localities.

It struck us that the work of leaders in these schools can be characterized as a 'bricolage' (Koyama, 2014) that takes into account not only what is going on within their own schools but also factors related to the development of Queensland's so-called 'education marketplace' and the increasing federal involvement in Australian education. First and foremost, this context focuses principals' attention on ways of improving test scores and externally reported data. Inevitably, this leads to a tendency to narrow the curriculum and allocate teaching time to the areas of learning that are assessed.

Linked to this, schools often feel that it is necessary to stream students on the basis of their perceived abilities, despite considerable research evidence that doubts the effectiveness of such approaches (e.g. Ansalone, 2010). In general, schools report that they have taken this step in order to provide teaching that is geared to groups of learners that are deemed to be operating at particular levels. For example, the principal of one of the project schools indicated that they use a range of data to group students of similar ability levels in maths, English and science, so 'we can have less of a range in any teacher's class and make it easier to differentiate'. Other schools report using ability-based groupings as a way to extend students with high levels of academic ability.

A further pressure to stream appears to come from the marketized context that provides an incentive for schools to compete for students within their local area, particularly those currently in the Catholic and independent sectors. Principals refer to the fact that they are under pressure from their district administrators to achieve their 'market share' in this respect. This seems to generate a lack of trust between the sectors. For example, one principal reported that there is 'a private school a couple of hundred metres from our back fence…, which tends to take a lot of the good kids out of the feeder schools. So we get marginalized a bit'.

Furthermore, each of the secondary school principals reported increasing pressures to market their schools. For some, the pressure to improve school performance had resulted in suggestions to remove students whom they do not believe to be capable of achieving the required levels. The principal of Bromsgrove also indicated that he had felt pressured from within the education system to exclude particular students from national testing to improve the school's external data.

The push to lift test scores, together with the need to 'market' the school, is vividly illustrated in the 'themed classes' described in our account of Sunnydale. It will be recalled that senior staff regard these classes as a means of grouping learners on the basis of their preferred learning styles, to be matched with appropriate pedagogical styles. As reported, the data collected to evaluate perceptions of this approach indicate that many staff and students believe that this approach is, in practice, simply a streaming system based on test performance. Meanwhile, senior staff in the school remain convinced that their strategy is intended to achieve greater equity. At the same time, they work hard to market the benefits of the particular 'themed classes' to more aspirational parents who otherwise might enrol their children elsewhere.

These dynamics have to be understood in relation to other pressures from outside of the schools. So, for example, there are limited employment options in the districts where some of the schools are located and in some instances, we are told, this is damaging to motivation amongst some groups of students, particularly as their time in school draws to an end. Related to all of this, in a large and diverse state such as Queensland, access to university is influenced by a range of factors, including geographical location. Interestingly, the presence of a local university influences student decision-making about post-school options in a range of ways. So, for example, principals from different locations suggested that their senior students often display a reticence to move away from the regional areas to attend university in a major city, which is understandable given the associated costs, and the social and personal consequences of relocating. Reticence to leave regional areas, however, can limit students' choices. There have been reports from principals in our project schools that the lower entry requirements to courses in regional universities may also reduce students' motivation to achieve at high levels in their final examinations.

The accountability context and the unrelenting pressures on schools to market themselves can lead to unintended consequences. Staff involved in the study report that, for a number of schools, the competing pressures of marketization and improving performance have led to practices that impact on equity. However, by engaging in this collaborative research, each of the six project schools is demonstrating their commitment and attempts to improve outcomes for all students within the complex educational context of Queensland.

Implications

At this stage, it is important to emphasize that I am *not* suggesting that the introduction of the collaborative inquiry approach I have described will overcome the overall circumstances that disadvantage certain schools, and the students they serve, within the Queensland education 'marketplace'. Nevertheless, there is evidence that it can make a significant difference, for some students at least. This being the case, our research has thrown further light on the organizational conditions that are needed in order to fulfil this promise on a wider scale. It suggests that such efforts have to focus on creating the circumstances within schools that enable teachers and school leaders to understand and work with data to better understand and respond to all learners.

In these contexts, our role as critical friends is a complex one and while offering us challenges there are opportunities too, such as in Sunnydale, where the engagement in this project has facilitated more open communication and understanding around the new structures the school had implemented. We also appreciate the role of critical inquiry in helping teachers and leaders to develop a discerning eye regarding current (in)equitable practices and to take appropriate action following further exploration and analysis.

Given the impact that schools have on one another within a local area, however, there is also a need to find ways of encouraging partnerships across schools, such that the success of one is not achieved at the expense of another. Drawing on the lessons from Greater Manchester, it would make sense for such partnerships to cross the 'borders' that separate the three sectors. The fact that schools in all of these sectors are part funded by government offers potential leverage, provided there is a political will to make it happen. Sadly, I have so far seen no indication of this happening.

A new policy context

My third example is set in the new English policy context that emerged as we moved into the third year of the Greater Manchester Challenge, following the General Election that led to a new coalition government made up of the Conservative and Liberal Democrat parties. The general thrust of their policy was to continue and accelerate the emphasis on seeking improvement through school autonomy, competition and choice that was pioneered by earlier Conservative and Labour governments (Whitty and Anders, 2012).

The basis of the approach was outlined in a White Paper, 'The Importance of Teaching' (DfE, 2010). This set out plans to improve the quality of teaching and school leadership through school-to-school support and peer-to-peer learning. As I noted in the previous chapter, speaking about these plans in June 2011, the Secretary of State for Education argued that, in order to address the issue of educational underperformance, particularly amongst disadvantaged groups of learners, there was a need to develop a 'culture of collaboration'. More specifically, he emphasized his intention to develop networks of schools in order to create a 'self-improving system' based on the thinking that had emerged from City Challenge.

Central to these plans is the setting up of a national network of 'teaching schools', an idea that – as I have explained – had been pioneered within City Challenge. Analogous to teaching hospitals, the intention is that these schools will have a key role to play in leading the training and professional development of teachers and headteachers. According to the website of the Department for Education, teaching schools are expected to work together within an alliance; that is, a group of schools and other partners that is supported by the leadership of the teaching school. Alliances, it is argued, may be cross-phase and cross-sector, work across local authorities, and can include different types of organizations, including universities.

As of July 2014 there were 500 or so designated teaching schools. They are defined as 'outstanding schools with consistently high levels of pupil performance and a history of working collaboratively with other schools'. Normally designated for a four-year period, a teaching school alliance receives core funding to cover the management and coordination of activities (£60,000 in the first year of designation; £50,000 in the second year; then decreasing to £40,000 a year). It is also noted that they will receive additional funding if they provide initial teacher training, continuing professional development, middle leadership development, support for the development of headteachers and specific school-to-school support.

Our earlier research led my colleagues and me to take a positive view of the thinking that guides these developments, particularly the emphasis they place on school-to-school collaboration. Indeed, they appeared to open up new opportunities for taking our own work forward in a way that has the potential to contribute to system-level improvements. However, as I will show, there are considerable difficulties facing its implementation. I will argue that these difficulties arise from policy contradictions, not least in relation to pressures created by the emphasis on competition, high stakes testing and accountability procedures. All of this throws further light on the challenges facing efforts to use processes of collaboration to foster equity in education within current policies.

The Coalition of Research Schools

In 2011, as the Greater Manchester Challenge ended, my colleagues and I created a new network in an attempt to take advantage of the changing context created by the policies outlined in the White Paper referred to earlier. In particular, we saw the emergence of teaching schools as opening up an opportunity to explore further what is involved in using the approach we had developed to widen the impact across the education system.

We called the network the 'University of Manchester Coalition of Research Schools' (see Ainscow, Dyson, Goldrick and West, 2012 for more details). In setting it up our intention was to work with a small number of carefully chosen schools that had the capacity to take forward a pioneering agenda within their organizations and with their partner schools. During the subsequent two years, eleven schools were involved (primary, special and secondary), all of which were recognized as being outstanding by Ofsted. Eight of these schools became formally designated as teaching schools, each with their own 'alliances'. And, of course, the schools all belonged to a range of other networks and groupings for a variety of purposes.

Our hope was that involvement in the Coalition would increase creativity within these schools through the use of the sorts of collaborative inquiry we had used in earlier projects (Ainscow, Booth and Dyson, 2006; Ainscow *et al.*, 2012). In this way, our aim was to challenge them to aspire to greatness by placing inquiry at the heart of everything that goes on. This means they would become schools that are on the move, always seeking new ways to reach out to all of their students, particularly those that miss out within existing ways of working. In other words, they would be concerned with finding effective ways of improving the achievement of *all* of their students, particularly those from disadvantaged backgrounds. This makes clear what we had in mind when talking about 'great schools'. And, we should add, this related strongly to the government's expressed concern to use teaching schools as part of their strategy for closing the gap between high and low performing groups.

As in the Queensland study, involvement in the Coalition required each school to nominate a staff team to act as research coordinators, empowered to lead developments in the school. University staff supported this team in identifying areas where inequities persisted, collecting and analysing contextual evidence, developing and implementing an improvement plan and evaluating its impact. As these developments occurred, the schools were assisted in making use of recommendations from research carried out elsewhere regarding what works and why.

These activities were reinforced by a series of events that were intended to stimulate whole-school development and research. Links across the network of schools were also developed, such that they could learn from one another's research. At the same time, this enabled our university team to develop evaluative accounts of practice and impact, and facilitate cross-school analyses of the collective findings.

Our analysis of these developments links to research carried out by Sebba *et al.* (2012), who looked at the work of five teaching school alliances in relation to what they refer to as 'joint practice development'. Drawing on the work of Michael Fielding and his colleagues, this is defined as 'learning new ways of working through mutual engagement that opens up and shares practices with others'. Joint practice development, they suggest, involves interaction and mutual development related to practice; recognizes that each partner in the interaction has something to offer; and is research-informed, often involving collaborative inquiry.

The argument developed in what follows connects to these ideas. It is based on a cross-site analysis of developments within the Coalition schools as they were trying to develop new roles and, in so doing, explore ways of responding to the challenge of equity. This led us to gather further evidence of the *opportunities* that emerge when those within a school adopt an inquiring stance to their work. At the same time, it threw light on the *barriers* that exist within a policy context that has, for many years, emphasized compliance and standardization – whilst at the same time encouraging schools to compete with one another.

Collaborative inquiry

As I have indicated, the approaches used within the Coalition of Research Schools involved teams of teachers – and sometimes, support staff and students – collecting and engaging with various forms of evidence, using the types of techniques I described in Chapter 4. As I explained, their use is intended to '*make the familiar unfamiliar*' in order to stimulate the sharing of practices and the generation of new ways of working.

In working with the schools in using these approaches we saw further evidence of the impact of the collaborative inquiry approach developed through our earlier work. This was helped along by the strong leadership practices that existed within the schools. As a result, they seemed to have a confidence within their organizations regarding how to get things done efficiently and a sense of certainty that their actions were likely to lead to positive outcomes.

Despite the presence of these positive features, the schools did occasionally experience forms of turbulence of the sort we had seen in our earlier projects. In particular, staff and senior leaders described how their involvement in collaborative inquiry often led them to feel confused and uncertain as to how they should proceed. In some instances this included a sense of doubt regarding the roles of our university team, who, it was assumed, were going to take a lead in deciding how best to proceed. At times, too, this led to tensions within the staff research groups, as they tried to determine an appropriate way forward.

Evocative images were used by various senior colleagues to explain what this felt like, for example: 'wood for trees', 'lost in the fog', 'muddy waters', and 'herding sheep'. One headteacher explained this in a way that was typical of what happened in most of the schools:

> I think we struggled at first because we'd not done anything like this before, and I think it was allowing ourselves to not know. I think what we've got to do is to think it's ok to not know the answer to something: that's the very reason that we're doing this. So what is it that's bothering us? What is it that we want to find out more about? And let's just open our minds to it, and find out the answer and see what it picks up along the way…

She went on to argue:

> So, we've learned something, definitely, and I think that it's given us that vehicle to go and find out. This has helped us to think let's go and talk to the children, let's go and talk to the staff, let's shadow pupils, let's do all those things that are involved in research and see what we can find out.

It seemed to us that such an approach opened up potentially important spaces for new professional thinking, as colleagues learnt how to learn from one another in new ways. The challenges this creates, however, have obvious implications for the way such initiatives are led, as another head explained:

> What we had to do was actually remind everybody that this was not going to be straightforward. It wasn't following a formula because you've got different personalities that like different things.

The involvement of us as 'outsiders' – seeing things in different ways, asking questions, and bringing ideas from elsewhere, including from formal research – seemed to add a further significant set of challenges into this process. As a result, the areas of focus for the inquiries frequently changed, as new evidence led to the rejection of what seemed like promising ways forwards, whilst also pointing to new possibilities that had to be considered. In these ways, well-established ways of working were sometimes reconsidered. For example, another headteacher commented:

> Well, I think if you've got a philosophy you've got to be able to back it up with the fact that it's been effective; and I think you have to question how effective it's being and look at alternatives, because otherwise you can become quite stagnant and not really look at what you're doing.

We related comments such as this to the idea of 'double-loop learning' (Argyris and Schön, 1996). This is based on the view that practice within an organization is guided by some more-or-less deep-seated sets of assumptions and values. For the most part, routine problems can be overcome within the framework provided by these assumptions and values. As a result, emphasis is placed on making existing techniques more efficient in a way that is referred to as single-loop learning. However, from time to time something, or someone, throws the underlying assumptions into doubt, leading to double-loop learning. What follows is not simply the improvement of existing practices, but new ways of thinking about practice – new sets of assumptions and newly configured sets of values – leading to greater creativity in respect to ways of moving forward.

Gradually, too, we also saw some of the schools making use of their new expertise in research within their partnerships with other schools. For example, two of the teaching school alliances combined forces in a project called 'Unlocking Potential', which set out to address the question: How can we improve our confidence in responding to all children? The twelve schools that joined this initiative are using 'action learning', a collaborative inquiry approach originally developed by Reg Revans, an English physicist (Bray *et al.*, 2000). He recommended the creation of action learning 'sets', i.e. groups that work on solving real problems through repeated cycles of action and reflection. The starting point for the process is the existing experience and knowledge of the group. This means that colleagues within the group are seen as sources of challenge and support, bringing their experiences and perspectives to the discussions that take place. In order to encourage the development of more reflective practices, those involved have been asked to keep learning diaries. By recording thoughts and feelings, group members are able to think about the changes they make in order to make their classrooms more inclusive.

Whilst this particular project is still at an early stage, it is anticipated that it will eventually lead to: an audit framework that can be used to review school practices; a staff development guide; and accounts of practice that illustrate the flexible use of the guide. It is also intended that, eventually, these materials will be used to introduce other schools to the approaches being developed.

Barriers

Despite these encouraging developments, our involvement in the Coalition schools left us with a sense of frustration that greater progress was not being made. Consequently, we chose to analyze why this was so. This led us to focus on five interconnected themes. In what follows, we consider these themes in order to formulate an interpretation of what is happening on the ground in relation to this potentially important effort to make the English education system self-improving, focusing in particularly on the challenge of equity. As I will explain, these themes point to a series of barriers that are limiting attempts to foster greater cooperation amongst networks of schools through the idea of teaching schools.

Centralized directives

The activities of teaching schools so far have been largely centrally directed by the National College for School Leadership (recently renamed the National College for Teaching and Leadership). This has occurred despite the constant reference to the idea of school autonomy within the national policy narrative.

During the first year of the programme a series of meetings was held for all the teaching school headteachers in the country, at which they were asked to agree one area of focus that they would all follow. Areas considered included teaching and learning, equity and student engagement. Subsequently, all of this seemed to fade, leaving schools to determine their own agendas, albeit in relation to a centrally-determined set of priorities. From our point of view, the fact that 'research and development' was one of the priorities was a source of encouragement.

PowerPoint slides used by National College staff to present the programme at such meetings drew a contrast between *'Clarity of principle on how'* and *'Lack of prescription on precisely what'*, implying, I assume, that teaching schools have discretion in respect to the details of their actions. On quality assurance, the schools were told that this would be based on 'local priorities' and national 'key performance indicators'. The latter were summarized as being about 'pupil attainment, Ofsted grades, number of trainees trained, headship vacancy levels, numbers of schools in alliances, and specialist leaders of education[2] designated, trained and deployed'. Significantly, a National College advisor commented, 'all of this leaves little time for research and development'.

Improving practice

Consistent with this emphasis on centralized direction, the teaching schools are, we sensed, expected to adopt a particular view of how knowledge is transferred between schools. Usually this involves small groups of teachers from different schools observing examples of what is seen as good practice and then working together in one another's classrooms, trialling new ways of working and coaching one another through the process. Clearly, there are opportunities here to build collaborative inquiry into the process in ways that could stimulate experimentation. However, whilst some of these approaches are being used, there is a noticeable emphasis on the provision of short courses and workshops, led by external consultants, bought in by the teaching schools because of their perceived expertise. Teachers attending these activities pay the teaching school for their participation. Significantly, the courses and workshops are described as 'delivering training', using a metaphor that implies a particular form of knowledge transfer.

It strikes me that what we are seeing here is a resurrection of the model of teachers' centres of the sort previously managed by local authorities. Indeed, some of the consultants are staff who previously worked in these contexts. Our interpretation of the motivation for adopting this approach comes from the emphasis placed by the National College on the importance of teaching schools having a successful business plan, such that they are able to achieve a profit that can be used to support the growth of their work. A National College advisor commented:

> The weakest issue from my perspective is business planning – planning to become self-sufficient and quality assurance. I think the DfE/College will have to continue giving the teaching schools some annual funding to keep them going.

Another possible explanation is that by running what is, in effect, a programme of in-service training that is largely separate to the school's core activities, this is much less disruptive in respect to the school's usual ways of working.

Whatever the explanation, the disappointment is that effective strategies based on practitioner inquiry are less evident within the programmes offered by the new teaching schools. The predominant model involves training activities that present practice as being mainly about the passing on of technical knowledge, rather than as an activity that involves 'joint practice development' of the sort that is now widely endorsed by research evidence (Hargeaves, D.H., 2012a)

Accountability measures

A related disappointment relates to the noticeable absence of innovation that is evident in much of the current teaching school activities. To some extent this is a product of the central directives, which I have already indicated. However, a more powerful set of pressures appears to come from the national accountability arrangements described earlier.

Teaching schools are, by definition, formally designated as being 'outstanding' as a result of their relatively high level of test scores and positive inspection reports. Our involvement in the schools suggested a clear pattern in this respect. As I have indicated, all these schools have what might be described as a 'can-do' atmosphere that seems to permeate everything they do. That is to say, they know how to get things done and they have confidence in the approaches they use. These include: systematic strategies for tracking the progress of every student; arrangements to step in with additional support when students appear to be struggling; regular monitoring of teachers' practices through classroom observations by senior managers; and a strong emphasis on students complying with rules, not least in respect to the wearing of school uniform.

There is much to applaud in all of this, particularly the way it creates a safe and purposeful atmosphere for students and staff members to get on with their tasks. Clearly, it also 'delivers' in the sense that the schools achieve relatively high levels of attainment, as measured by national tests, and receive positive reports following their inspections. The other side of the coin, however, is that all of this leads to a sense of standardization that seems to allow limited space for experimentation. Indeed, our efforts to work with staff in these schools to use collaborative inquiry to stimulate new thinking and practices sometimes hit against a series of more subtle barriers, many of which seemed to relate to an unwillingness to take risks, particularly amongst senior staff. In some cases, too, the management styles of these successful headteachers further endorsed this attitude. Indeed, a number of them privately described themselves to us as being 'control freaks'.

It is worth adding here that there is a darker side to the policy context that is undoubtedly in the minds of senior members of staff, particularly the headteachers. This was revealed most strikingly when one of the teaching schools in our Coalition received a negative inspection report. The headline statement in the report was: 'This is a school that requires improvement. It is not good enough'. Inevitably, news of this event passed around the system quickly. In so doing, we can assume that it reinforced in the minds of some colleagues, at least, the need to step cautiously and not take risks. Our concern, therefore, is that these developing 'hubs' of effective practice and research are, too often, places where those involved firmly believe they have a formula that works for them. This being the case, they tend to see their role as being one of passing on this standard way of working. Linked to the other pressures I have outlined, this acts as a barrier to the sort of experimentation that is surely needed if we are to transform a school system that works well for some into one that can work well for all.

Competing policies

Alongside the teaching school policy, the government has introduced a number of other radical policy changes, all of which are informed by the idea of using market forces to improve standards (O'Shaughnessy, 2012). As I explained in Chapter 1, an important element of these changes is the introduction of independent state schools, referred to as academies and, in addition, through the creation of so-called 'free schools' based on the Swedish model. This is leading to a variety of new govern-ance arrangements. So, for example, some academies are part of 'chains' that are led by sponsors, which may be faith based or voluntary groups, businesses, community organizations, or universities. In other cases, successful schools are themselves taking on the role of sponsors of other schools that are seen to be failing.

Inevitably, the successful schools in the Coalition have become involved in var-ious ways in these policy moves. Some have chosen to convert to academy status; a few are joining existing chains, or creating their own groups in the form of 'trusts'; and some are effectively 'taking over' other schools that are facing difficulties, usu-ally because of poor test scores and/or a negative inspection report. Meanwhile, most of the schools continue to belong to other well-established groupings, such as local neighbourhood clusters, or networks of schools that share a common religious faith. The implication of all of this is that staff in the schools – particularly those in leadership positions – are tending to spend lots of time attending meetings of these various groups.

Alongside these demands, their role as teaching schools involves a range of activ-ities beyond that of school improvement that also take up management time. Currently the most significant of these is the requirement that they become centres of initial teacher training. So, for example, in September 2013 each of the teaching school alliances we are working with enrolled a group of student teachers, typically between 15 and 20 in number, whom they are expected to support in gaining their teaching qualifications. Whilst these activities have support from a university, most of the actual training goes on within the alliance schools.

It is, therefore, understandable that senior staff in these designated successful schools are struggling with the competing demands on their time. On the positive side, there is some evidence that this is leading to new forms of organization that build greater leadership capacity amongst teams of senior colleagues. On the nega-tive side, however, it further adds to the sense that there is little time for reflection, leading to a feeling of limited space for creativity. Further to this, we have noted a strong sense of fragmentation within some schools, as senior staff deal with the demands of competing responsibilities by compartmentalizing their tasks, thus overlooking possibilities for connecting different strands of activity in more enter-prising ways.

Coordination

As I have explained, a significant outcome of the recent national policy reforms has been the demise of the influence of local authorities. As a result, my sense is that, in many parts of the country, no organization has the full picture of what is hap-pening amongst schools within a local area and nobody is able to step in when things start to deteriorate. It follows that there is no mechanism to coordinate the new arrangements, as the teaching schools alliances begin to develop the capacity to support improvement across the education system.

My worry in this respect is that as more teaching schools choose to become academies the absence of local coordination may mean that we will lose the benefits of collaborating in local efforts to address issues of equity. Furthermore, in the case of those academies that are part of sponsorship chains, there is a tendency for them to see this as their major organizational loyalty.

In the new English policy context my colleagues and I concluded that a way to address this would be for all schools within a district, including the academies, to agree a protocol that would seek to ensure coherence within their local area, such that educational provision provides effective support for all children and young people throughout their time in schools. The effectiveness of this would require shared responsibility in order that the success of one school is not achieved at the expense of others. However, this raises the question of how such a collaborative effort would be coordinated and monitored.

Here, there could be a new role for local authority staff. As I have argued elsewhere in this book, this would require them to adjust their ways of working in response to the development of improvement strategies that are led from within schools. And, at a time when local authorities are under increasing pressure to deliver improvements in results, this can lead to misunderstandings and tensions between senior staff in schools and their local authority colleagues. Such tensions are likely to intensify through the increasing school autonomy that is occurring with the move to academies and free schools.

Despite such difficulties, it is difficult to conceive of a way forward that does not involve some form of local coordination. Specifically, local authority staff could monitor and challenge schools in relation to the agreed goals of collaborative activities, whilst headteachers share responsibility for the overall management of improvement efforts within schools. We also know that careful facilitation of school partnerships – a supportive, confirming but challenging contribution from outside – can make an enormous difference to their chances of early survival and eventual success.

Some reflections

The three examples I have presented in this final chapter have illustrated how the way of thinking that emerged from the experiences of City Challenge has been used in different ways, in a variety of national contexts, and under different conditions. In the Welsh context, the initiative occurred in response to a crisis that resulted from a failed inspection. All of this was set in the context of what might be described as a rather traditional state system, with limited variety in terms of forms of school governance. It also took place in an overall context where there are strong political influences, mixed at the national and local levels, such that the potential within the system has previously been limited by controlling forces that created barriers to progress.

The Australian example takes the form of a collaborative research study and therefore carries no political mandate. Nevertheless, it shows how factors to do with divisions that are created in an increasingly unequal system are reflected in the shape of a country's education system. The three parallel sectors lead to a lack of trust and perverse incentives that tend to encourage divisions that work against some schools and, again, mean that resources are poorly used. Similar to the situation in Wales, power struggles between national, state and district levels administrations create further barriers to progress. An additional worry is the growth of independent public schools, within a context where there is no effective form of regulation.

Meanwhile, the recent example from England is set in the new, much more radical policy context that has been developing since 2010, where the work of the Coalition of Research Schools extended my understanding of the way evidence of various kinds can stimulate developments in thinking and practice. As I have explained, this experience has also thrown further light on the social and political complexities that exist when groups of schools attempt to become self-improving. In some ways this looks positive in the sense that David Hargreaves suggested when he referred to how increased decentralization might bring a new era in which the school system becomes 'the major agent of its own improvement', not least in the way it has opened up new space for experimentation. However, in reality, the mixing of what seem to be different theories of change – or, to use Andy Hargreaves's notion, different ways of thinking about educational change – creates further barriers to progress.

For me, these three experiences confirm Kurt Lewin's suggestion that the best way to understand an organization is by trying to change it (Schein, 2001). As I have shown, my involvement with schools in these various national contexts has put me in privileged positions that have enabled me to learn from their successes, as well as their frustrations, as they have attempted to work collaboratively in order to find more effective ways of educating all of their students within national policy contexts that, at times, seem perverse.

New challenges

It is increasingly evident that, around the world, national education policies are encouraging more schools to become autonomous; for example, in Australia, the independent public schools; the academies in England; charter schools in the USA; concertado schools in Spain; and free schools in Sweden. Such developments have the potential to open up possibilities to inject new energy into the improvement of education systems. On the other hand, they can lead to a dangerous fragmentation that will, I fear, further disadvantage learners from poorer backgrounds. Recent developments in England's second city, Birmingham, have also illustrated the potential dangers of so-called independent state schools being taken over by extremist elements within a community (Kershaw, 2014). All of which suggests that 'educational marketplaces' need some form of checks and balances.

The experiences described in this book suggest a way forward that policy makers could use to ensure that the impetus that comes from greater school autonomy will lead to improvements that will benefit all children and young people. This is based on an assumption that the education system still has further potential to improve itself, provided policy makers allow the space for practitioners to make use of the expertise and creativity that lies trapped within individual classrooms. The aim must be to move knowledge around and, as I have argued, the best way to do this is through strengthening collaboration within schools, between schools and beyond schools. I have also suggested that an engagement with evidence can act as a catalyst for such developments, as well as being a means of encouraging shared accountability.

As I have explained, there are important implications here for the future roles of local authority administrators and support staff. They have to adjust their ways of working in response to the development of improvement strategies that are led from within schools. Specifically, they must monitor and challenge schools in relation to the agreed goals of collaborative activities, whilst headteachers share responsibility for the overall management of improvement efforts within schools. In taking on such roles, local authority staff can position themselves as guardians of improved outcomes for all young people and their families − protectors of a more collegiate approach but not as custodians of day-to-day activities. Thinking specifically of England, this seems to echo the suggestions made by former Education Minister, Jim Knight, writing in the *Times Educational Supplement* on 24 February 2013:

> The days of councils delivering education through their schools are largely over. However, it is essential that councils retain a clear commissioning role. Here we can go back to [*Secretary of State*] Gove's inspiration − US charter schools. They are granted a charter for three to five years by the local school board and are judged on the basis of a contract to deliver their plans, including results. I propose that councils should be given the authority to contract the new governing body to deliver the education in schools in their area for five years. If the council chooses not to renew the contract they should run a school competition to decide who is best to take over. This returns local accountability to councils without going back to the days of them delivering education themselves.

Finally, of course, all of this has significant implications for national policy makers. In order to make use of the power of collaboration as a means of achieving both excellence and equity in our schools, they need to foster greater flexibility at the local level in order that practitioners have the space to analyze their particular circumstances and determine priorities accordingly. As I have argued, this means that policy makers must recognize that the details of policy implementation are not amenable to central regulation. Rather, these have to be dealt with by those who are close to and, therefore, in a better position to understand local contexts.

In this connection, having reviewed the way London Challenge has triggered off an increasing number of regional initiatives across the UK, Claeys, Kempton and Paterson (2014) emphasize the importance of having a political mandate for locally driven action. They state:

> One of the defining lessons from London is the importance of high-level sponsorship and support from politicians and policymakers. The learning from the emerging challenges, which are predominantly bottom-up initiatives, points to the difficulty of operating a challenge at a region-wide scale in today's educational landscape without the strong sense of cohesive mandate that only central government can provide. This would not require the same level of top-down involvement government had in London Challenge because greater capacity now exists across the system. What is required is to supplement this bottom-up drive with the necessary political will and impetus to draw things together at scale in a concerted attempt to transform outcomes for pupils right across the country.
>
> *(p. 5)*

For my own part, I continue to work with groups of schools in various parts of the world, exploring how an engagement with evidence can be used to stimulate collaboration and experimentation. Like Copland (2003), I believe that inquiry can be the 'engine' to enable the shared leadership that is needed in order to foster participation in such efforts and the 'glue' that can bind school communities together around a common purpose. My experience also suggests that, given more favourable national policy conditions, this can encourage the rethinking that is needed in order to reach those learners who are marginalized by current arrangements.

In moving forward, I take with me the spirit of enterprise and the sense of optimism that grew in Greater Manchester as a result of the emphasis placed on people working together to make things happen. In so doing I am reminded of a saying that was coined in the nineteenth century to describe the inventiveness that the most progressive city in the United Kingdom had to offer:

What Manchester does today, the rest of the world does tomorrow.

Notes

1 A paper authored by Suzanne Carrington, Barbara Comber, Lisa Ehrich, Jess Harris, Val Klenowski, Judy Smeed, Nerida Spina and myself, titled 'Promoting equity in the context of high stakes accountability: emerging lessons from a collaborative study in Queensland, Australia', is currently under review.
2 Specialist leaders of education are teachers who have a strong record of middle leadership within their schools. They are expected to help strengthen practice in other schools.

BIBLIOGRAPHY

Adonis, A. (2012) *Education, education, education: reforming England's schools*. London: Biteback.

Ainscow, M. (1999) *Understanding the development of inclusive schools*. London: Routledge.

Ainscow, M. (2005) Developing inclusive education systems: what are the levers for change? *Journal of Educational Change* 6, 109–24.

Ainscow, M. (2006) From special education to effective schools for all: a review of progress so far. In L. Florian (ed.) *The handbook of special education*. London: Sage.

Ainscow, M. (2008) Teaching for diversity. In M. Connelly, M.F. He and J. Phillion (eds) *The Sage handbook of curriculum and instruction*. London: Sage.

Ainscow, M. (2010) Achieving excellence and equity: reflections on the development of practices in one local district over 10 years. *School Effectiveness and School Improvement*, 21(1), 75–91.

Ainscow, M. (2012) Moving knowledge around: strategies for fostering equity within educational systems. *Journal of Educational Change*, 13(3), 289–310.

Ainscow, M. (2013) Developing more equitable education systems: reflections on a three-year improvement initiative. In V. Farnsworth and Y. Solomon (eds) *What works in education? Bridging theory and practice in research*. London: Routledge.

Ainscow, M. and Goldrick, S. (2010) Making sure every child matters: enhancing equity within education systems. In A. Hargreaves, A. Lieberman, M. Fullan and D. Hopkins (eds) *Second international handbook of educational change*. Dordrecht: Springer.

Ainscow, M. and Howes, A. (2007) Working together to improve urban secondary schools: a study of practice in one city. *School Leadership and Management* 27, 285–300.

Ainscow, M. and Kaplan, I. (2005) Using evidence to encourage inclusive school development: possibilities and challenges. *Australasian Journal of Special Education*, 29(2), 106–16.

Ainscow, M. and Tweddle, D. (2003) Understanding the changing role of English local education authorities in promoting inclusion. In J. Allan (ed.) *Inclusion, participation and democracy: what is the purpose?* Dordrecht: Kluwer Academic Publishers, pp.165–77.

Ainscow, M. and West, M. (eds) (2006) *Improving urban schools: leadership and collaboration*. Maidenhead: Open University Press.

Ainscow, M., Booth, T. and Dyson, A. (2004) Understanding and developing inclusive practices in schools: a collaborative action research network. *International Journal of Inclusive Education*, 8(2), 125–39.

Ainscow, M., Booth, T. and Dyson, A. (2006) Inclusion and the standards agenda: negotiating policy pressures in England. *International Journal of Inclusive Education*, 10(4–5), 295–308.

Ainscow, M., Booth, T., Dyson, A., with Farrell, P., Frankham, J., Gallannaugh, F., Howes, A. and Smith, R. (2006) *Improving schools, developing inclusion*. London: Routledge.

Ainscow, M., Crow, M., Dyson, A., Goldrick, S., Kerr, K., Lennie, C., Miles, S., Muijs, D. and Skyrme, J. (2007) *Equity in education: new directions. The second annual report of the Centre for Equity in Education, University of Manchester*. Manchester: Centre for Equity in Education.

Ainscow, M., Dyson, A. and Kerr, K. (2006) *Equity in education: mapping the territory. The first annual report of the Centre for Equity in Education, University of Manchester*. Manchester: Centre for Equity in Education.

Ainscow, M., Dyson, A., Goldrick, S. and Kerr, K. (2009) Using research to foster equity and inclusion within the context of New Labour educational reforms. In C. Chapman and H.M. Gunter (eds) *Radical reforms: perspectives on an era of educational change*. London: Routledge.

Ainscow, M., Dyson, A., Goldrick, S. and West, M. (2012) *Developing equitable education systems*. London: Routledge.

Ainscow, M., Dyson, A, Goldrick, S., Kerr, K. and Miles, S. (2008) *Equity in education: responding to context*. Manchester: Centre for Equity in Education.

Ainscow, M., Farrell, P. and Tweddle, D. (2000) Developing policies for inclusive education: a study of the role of local education authorities. *International Journal of Inclusive Education*, 4(3), 211–229.

Ainscow, M., Hargreaves, D.H. and Hopkins, D. (1995) Mapping the process of change in schools: the development of six new research techniques. *Evaluation and Research in Education*, 9(2), 75–89.

Ainscow, M., Howes, A. and Tweddle, D.A. (2006) Moving practice forward at the district level. In M. Ainscow and M. West (eds) *Improvement in urban schools: leadership and collaboration*. Maidenhead: Open University Press.

Ainscow, M., Howes, A.J., Farrell, P. and Frankham, J. (2003) Making sense of the development of inclusive practices. *European Journal of Special Needs Education*, 18(2), 227–42.

Ainscow, M., Muijs, D. and West, M. (2006) Collaboration as a strategy for improving schools in challenging circumstances. *Improving Schools*, 9(3), 192–202.

Ainscow, M., Nicolaidou, M. and West, M. (2003) Supporting schools in difficulties: the role of school-to-school cooperation. *NFER Topic* 30, 1–4.

Ainscow, M., West, M. and Nicolaidou, M. (2005) Putting our heads together: a study of headteacher collaboration as a strategy for school improvement. In C. Clarke (ed.) *Improving schools in difficult circumstances*. London: Continuum.

Allen, R. and Burgess, S. (2012) *How should we treat under-performing schools? A regression discontinuity analysis of school inspections in England*. Bristol: The Centre for Market and Public Organisation.

Ansalone, G. (2010) Tracking: educational differentiation or defective strategy. *Educational Research Quarterly*, 34(2), 3–17.

Anyon, J. (1997) *Ghetto schooling: A political economy of urban educational reform*. New York: Teachers College.

Argyris, C. and Schön, D. (1996) *Organisational learning II: theory, method and practice*. Reading, MA: Addision Wesley.

Ball, S. (2010) New class inequalities in education. *International Journal of Sociology and Social Policy*, 30(3/4), 155–66.

Barrs, S., Bernardes, E., Elwick, A., Malortie, A. McAleavy, T., McInerney, L., Menzies, L. and Rigall, A. (2014) *Lessons from London schools: investigating the success.* Reading: CfBT Trust.

Benn, M. (2012) *School wars: the battle for Britain's education.* London: Verso.

Benn, M. and Millar, F. (2006) *A comprehensive future: quality and equality for all our children.* London: Compass.

Bray, J.N., Lee, J., Smith, L.L. and Yorks, L. (2000) *Collaborative inquiry in action.* Thousand Oaks, CA: Sage.

Brighouse, T. (2007) The London Challenge – a personal view. In T. Brighouse and L. Fullick (eds) *Education in a global city.* London: Institute of Education, Bedford Way Papers.

Brighouse, T. (2013) The importance of collaboration: creating 'families of schools'. In J. Clifton (ed) *Excellence and equity: tackling educational disadvantage in English secondary schools.* London: Institute for Public Policy Research.

Chapman, C., Ainscow, M., Bragg, J., Gunter, H., Mongon, D., Muijs, D. and West, M. (2008) *New models of school leadership: emerging patterns of practice.* Nottingham: National College of School Leadership.

Chapman, C. and Hadfield, M. (2010) School-based networking for educational change. In A. Hargreaves, A. Lieberman, M. Fullan and D. Hopkins (eds) *Second handbook of educational change.* London: Springer.

Chenoweth, K. (2007) *It's being done: academic success in unexpected schools.* Cambridge, MA: Harvard Education Press.

Clark, C., Dyson, A., Millward, A. and Robson, S. (1999) Theories of inclusion, theories of schools: deconstructing and reconstructing the 'inclusive school'. *British Educational Research Journal,* 25(2), 157–77.

Clarke, P., Ainscow, M. and West, M. (2006) Learning from difference: some reflections on school improvement projects in three countries. In A. Harris and J.H. Crispeels (eds) *Improving schools and education systems.* London: Routledge, pp. 77–89.

Claeys, A., Kempton, J. and Paterson, C. (2014) *Regional challenges: a collaborative approach to improving education.* London: CentreForum.

Clifton, J. and Cook, W. (2013) The achievement gap in context. In J. Clifton (ed.) *Excellence and equity: tackling educational disadvantage in English secondary schools.* London: Institute for Public Policy Research.

Copland, M.A. (2003) Leadership of inquiry: building and sustaining capacity for school improvement. *Educational Evaluation and Policy Analysis,* 25(4), 375–95.

Crowther, D., Cummings, C., Dyson, A. and Millward, A. (2003) *Schools and area regeneration.* Bristol: The Policy Press.

Cummings, C., Dyson, A. and Todd, L. (2011) *Beyond the school gate: can full service and extended schools overcome disadvantage?* London: Routledge.

Department for Education (2010) *The importance of teaching (The schools white paper).* London: Department for Education.

Dobbie, W. and Fryer, R.G. (2009) *Are high-quality schools enough to close the achievement gap? Evidence from a bold social experiment in Harlem.* Cambridge, MA: Harvard University Press.

Duncan, G. and Murnane, J. (eds) (2011) *Wither opportunity? Rising inequality, schools and children's life chances.* New York: Russell Sage Foundation.

Dyson, A. and Kerr, K. (2013) *Developing children's zones for England: what's the evidence?* London: Save the Children.

Dyson, A. and Raffo, C. (2007) Education and disadvantage: the role of community-orientated schools. *Oxford Review of Education,* 33(3), 297–314.

Dyson, A., Kerr, K. and Wellings, C. (2013) Beyond the school gates: developing children's zones for England. In J. Clifton (ed.) *Excellence and equity: tackling educational disadvantage in English secondary schools*. London: Institute for Public Policy Research.

Dyson, A., Kerr, K., Raffo, C. and Wigelsworth, M. (2012) *Developing children's zones for England*. London: Save the Children.

Elmore, R.F. (2004) *School reform from the inside out*. Cambridge, MA: Harvard Education Press.

Fielding, M. (1999) Radical collegiality: affirming teaching as an inclusive professional practice. *Australian Educational Researcher*, 26(2), 1–34.

Fielding, M. and Moss, P. (2011) *Radical education and the common school*. London: Routledge.

Fielding, M., Bragg, S., Craig, J., Cunningham, I., Eraut, M., Gillinson, S., Horne, M., Robinson, C. and Thorp, J. (2005) *Factors influencing the transfer of good practice*. Nottingham: DfES Publications.

Fryer, R. and Levitt, S. (2004) Understanding the black–white test score gap in the first two years of school. *The Review of Economics and Statistics*, 86(2), 447–64.

Fullan, M. (1991) *The new meaning of educational change*. London: Cassell.

Gallimore, R., Ermeling, B.A., Saunders, W.M. and Goldenberg, C. (2009) Moving the learning of teaching closer to practice: teacher education implications of school-based inquiry teams. *Elementary School Journal*, 109(5), 537–53.

Giroux, H.A. and Schmidt, M. (2004) Closing the achievement gap: a metaphor for children left behind. *Journal of Educational Change* 5, 213–28.

Goodman, A. and Gregg P. (2010) *Poorer children's educational attainment: how important are attitudes and behaviour?* York: Joseph Rowntree Foundation.

Gray, J. (2010) Probing the limits of systemic reform: the English case. In A. Hargreaves, A. Lieberman, M. Fullan and D. Hopkins (eds) *Second international handbook of educational change*. Dordrecht: Springer.

Greaves, E., Macmillan, L. and Sibieta, L. (2014) *Lessons from London schools for attainment gaps and social mobility*. London: The Social Mobility and Child Poverty Commission.

Gunter, H. (2013) *The state and education policy: the academies programme*. London: Continuum.

Hargreaves. A. and Shirley, D. (2009) *The fourth way: the inspiring future for educational change*. Thousand Oaks, CA: Corwin.

Hargreaves. A. and Shirley, D. (2012) *The global fourth way: the quest for educational excellence*. Thousand Oaks, CA: Corwin.

Hargreaves, D.H. (2003) *Education epidemic: transforming secondary schools through innovation networks*. London: Demos.

Hargreaves, D. H. (2010) *Creating a self-improving school system*. Nottingham: National College for School Leadership.

Hargreaves, D. H. (2011) *Leading a self-improving school system*. Nottingham: National College for School Leadership.

Hargreaves, D.H. (2012a) *A self-improving school system in international context*. Nottingham: National College for School Leadership.

Hargreaves, D.H. (2012b) *A self-improving school system: towards maturity*. Nottingham: National College for School Leadership.

Hargreaves, D.H. and Hopkins, D. (1991) *The empowered school*. London: Continuum.

Harris, A. and Chapman, C. (2002) *Leadership in schools in challenging circumstances*. Nottingham: National College for School Leadership.

Hiebert, J., Gallimore, R. and Stigler, J.W. (2002) A knowledge base for the teaching profession: what would it look like and how can we get one? *Educational Researcher*, 31(5), 3–15.

Hill, R. (2008) *Achieving more together: adding value through partnership.* Leicester: ASCL.

Holtby, W. (1936/1988) *South Riding.* London: Virago.

Hopkins, D. (2007) *Every school a great school: realizing the potential of system leadership.* Maidenhead: Open University Press.

Hopkins, D., Ainscow, M. and West, M. (1994) *School improvement in an era of change.* London: Cassell.

Hopkins, D., Reynolds, D. and Gray, J. (2005) *School improvement lessons from research.* London: DfES

House of Commons Education Committee (2013) *School partnerships and cooperation.* London: The Stationery Office.

Howes, A. and Ainscow, M. (2006). Collaboration with a city-wide purpose: making paths for sustainable educational improvement. In M. Ainscow and M. West (eds.) *Improving urban schools: leadership and collaboration.* Maidenhead: Open University Press, pp. 104–16.

Howes, A., Booth, T., Dyson, A. and Frankham, J. (2005) Teacher learning and the development of inclusive practices and policies: framing and context. *Research Papers in Education,* 20(2), 133–48.

Hutchings, M. and Mansaray, A. (2013) *A review of the impact of the London Challenge (2003–08) and the City Challenge (2008–11).* London: Ofsted.

Hutchings, M., Hollingworth, S., Mansaray, A., Rose, R. and Greenwood, C. (2012) *Research report DFE-RR215: evaluation of the City Challenge Programme.* London: Department for Education.

Ingram, D., Louis, K.S. and Schroeder, R.G. (2004) Accountability policies and teacher decision making: barriers to the use of data to improve practice. *Teachers College Record,* 106(6), 1258–87.

Kenway, J. (2013) Challenging inequality in Australian schools: Gonski and beyond. *Discourse: Studies in the cultural politics of education,* 34(2), 286–308.

Kerr, K. and West, M. (eds) (2010) *Insight 2: Social inequality: can schools narrow the gap?* Macclesfield: British Education Research Association.

Kerr, K., Dyson, A. and Raffo, C. (2014) *Making the local matter: breaking the link between education, disadvantage and place?* Bristol: Policy Press.

Kershaw, I. (2014) *Investigation report: trojan horse letter (prepared for Birmingham City Council).* London: Eversheds.

Kidson, M. and Norris, E. (2014) *Implementing the London challenge.* London: Joseph Rowntree Foundation/Institute of Government.

Koyama, J. (2014) Principals as bricoleurs: making sense and making do in an era of accountability. *Educational Administration Quarterly,* 50(2), 279–304.

Levin, B. (2005) Thinking about improvements in schools in challenging circumstances. Paper presented at the American Educational Research Association, Montreal, April.

Levin, B. (2008) *How to change 5000 schools.* Cambridge, MA: Harvard Education Press.

Lipman, P. (2004) *High stakes education: inequality, globalisation and urban school reform.* New York: Routledge.

Lupton, R. (2003) *Neighbourhood effects: can we measure them and does it matter?* London: LSE.

Manchester City Council (2009) *Manchester independent economic review.* Manchester City Council.

Matthews, P. and Berwick, G. (2013) *Teaching schools: first among equals?* Nottingham: National College for Teaching and Leadership.

Meadows, S., Herrick, D., Feiler, A. and the ALSPAC Study Team (2007) Improvements in national test reading scores at Key Stage 1: grade inflation or better achievement? *British Educational Research Journal,* 33(1), 47–59.

Messiou, K. (2012) *Confronting marginalisation in education: a framework for promoting inclusion.* London: Routledge.

Messiou, K., Ainscow, M., Echeita, G., Goldrick, S., Hope, M., Paes, I., Sandoval, M., Simon, M. and Vitorino, T. (in press) Learning from differences: a strategy for teacher development in respect to student diversity. *School Effectiveness and School Improvement.*

Meyland-Smith, D. and Evans, N. (2009) *A guide to school choice reforms.* London: The Policy Exchange.

Miles, S. and Ainscow, M. (eds) (2011) *Responding to diversity in schools.* London: Routledge.

Mourshed, M., Chijioke, C. and Barber, M. (2010) *How the world's most improved school systems keep getting better.* London: McKinsey & Company.

Muijs, D., Ainscow, M., Chapman, C. and West, M. (2011) *Collaboration and networking in education.* London: Springer.

Muijs, D., West, M. and Ainscow, M. (2010) Why network? Theoretical perspectives on networking. *School Effectiveness and School Improvement,* 21(1), 5–26.

Mulford, B. (2007) Building social capital in professional learning communities: Importance, challenges and a way forward. In L. Stoll and K. Seashore Louis (eds) *Professional learning communities: divergence, depth and dilemmas.* Maidenhead: Open University Press.

Nicolaidou, M. and Ainscow, M. (2006) The experience of failure in urban primary schools. In M. Ainscow and M. West (eds) (2006) *Improving urban schools: leadership and collaboration.* Maidenhead: Open University Press.

OECD (2007) *No more failures: ten steps to equity in education.* Paris: OECD Publishing.

OECD (2010) *PISA 2009 Results: overcoming social background – equity in learning opportunities and outcomes (volume II).* Paris: OECD Publishing.

OECD (2012) *Equity and quality in education: supporting disadvantaged students and schools.* Paris: OECD Publishing.

OECD (2014) *Improving schools in Wales: an OECD perspective.* Paris: OECD Publishing.

Ofsted (2010) *London challenge.* London: Ofsted.

Ofsted (2013) *Unseen children: access and achievement 20 years on.* London: Ofsted.

O'Shaughnessy, J. (2012) *Competition meets collaboration: Helping school chains address England's long tail of educational failure.* London: Policy Exchange.

Payne, C.M. (2008) *So much reform, so little change: the persistence of failure in urban schools.* Cambridge, MA: Harvard Education Press.

Phillips, M., Crouse, J. and Ralph, J. (1998) Does the black–white test score gap widen after children enter school? In C. Jencks and M. Phillips (eds) *The black-white test score gap.* Washington, DC: The Brookings Institute.

Putnam, R.D. (2000) *Bowling alone.* New York: Simon & Schuster.

RSA (2013) *Unleashing greatness: getting the best from an academised system.* London: RSA.

Sammons, P. (2007) *School effectiveness and equity: making connections.* Reading: CfBT.

Sammons, P. (2008) Zero tolerance of failure and New Labour approaches to school improvement in England. *Oxford Review of Education,* 34(6), 651–64.

Sammons, P., Mujtaba, T., Earl, L. and Gu, Q. (2007) Participation in network learning communities and standards of pupil achievement: does it make a difference? *School Leadership and Management,* 27(3), 213–38.

Schein, E.H. (2001) Clinical inquiry/research. In P. Reason and H. Bradbury (eds) *Handbook of action research.* London: Sage.

Sebba, J., Kent, P. and Tregenza, J. (2012) *Improving outcomes through effective knowledge transfer in teaching school alliances: a research and development network project.* Nottingham: National College for School Leadership.

Schleicher, A. (2010) International comparisons of student learning outcomes. In A. Hargreaves, A. Lieberman, M. Fullan and D. Hopkins (eds) *Second handbook of educational change*. London: Springer.

Simon, H.A. (1987) Satisficing. In J. Eatwell, M. Millgate and P. Newman, (eds) *The new Palgrave dictionary of economics*, Vol. 4. New York: Stockton Press.

Stringfield, S. (1995) Attempting to improve students' learning through innovative programs – the case for schools evolving into high reliability organisations. *School Effectiveness and School Improvement*, 6(1), 67–96.

Talbert, J.E., Mileva, L., Chen, P., Cor, K. and McLaughlin, M. (2010) *Developing school capacity for inquiry-based improvement: progress, challenges, and resources*. Stanford, CA: Stanford University Center for Research on the Context of Teaching.

Tomlinson, S. (2005) *Education in a post welfare society*. London: McGraw-Hill.

Tymms, P. (2004) Are standards rising in English primary schools? *British Educational Research Journal*, 30(4), 477–94.

UNESCO (2010) *EFA global monitoring report: reaching the marginalized*. Paris: UNESCO/Oxford University Press.

Villegas-Reimers, E. (2003) *Teacher professional development: an international review of the literature*. UNESCO: Institute for Educational Planning.

Weick, K.E. (1985) Sources of order in underorganised systems: themes in recent organisational theory. In Y.S. Lincoln (ed.) *Organisational theory and inquiry*. Beverley Hills, CA: Sage.

West, M., Ainscow, M. and Stanford, J. (2005) Sustaining improvement in schools in challenging circumstances: a study of successful practice. *School Leadership and Management*, 25(1), 77–93.

Whitehurst, G.J. and Croft. M. (2010) *The Harlem children's zone, promise neighborhoods, and the broader, bolder approach to education*. Washington, DC: The Brookings Institution.

Whitty, G. (2010) *Marketization and post-marketization in education*. In A. Hargreaves, A. Lieberman, M. Fullan and D. Hopkins (eds) *Second international handbook of educational change*. Dordrecht: Springer, pp. 405–13.

Whitty, G. and Anders, J. (2012) *(How) did New Labour narrow the achievement and participation gap?* Paper presented at a seminar of the Centre for Learning and Life Chances in Knowledge Economies and Societies, Institute of Education, University of London, 5 December.

Wilkinson, R. and Pickett, K. (2009) *The spirit level*. London: Allen Lane.

Wohlstetter, P., Malloy, C.L., Chau, D and Polhemus, J.L. (2003) Improving schools through networks: a new approach to urban school reform. *Educational Policy*, 17(4), 399–430.

INDEX

Added to a page number 'n' denotes a note.